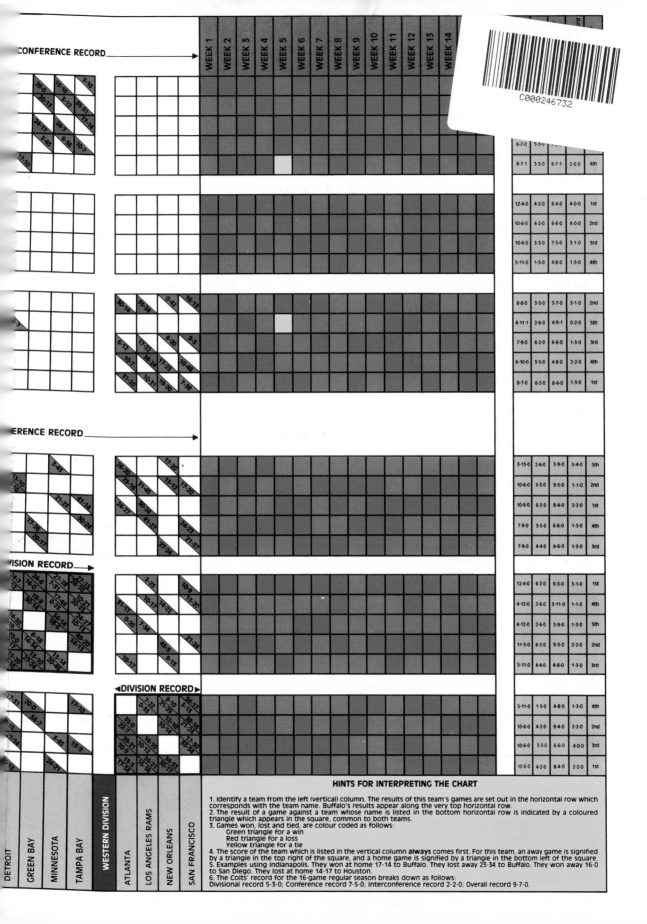

CONFERENCE RECORD →

| | WEEK 1 | WEEK 2 | WEEK 3 | WEEK 4 | WEEK 5 | WEEK 6 | WEEK 7 | WEEK 8 | WEEK 9 | WEEK 10 | WEEK 11 | WEEK 12 | WEEK 13 | WEEK 14 |

C000246732

9-7-0	5-3-0			
8-7-1	3-5-0	6-7-1	2-0-0	4th
12-4-0	4-2-0	8-4-0	4-0-0	1st
10-6-0	4-2-0	6-6-0	4-0-0	2nd
10-6-0	3-3-0	7-5-0	3-1-0	3rd
5-11-0	1-5-0	4-8-0	1-3-0	4th
8-8-0	3-5-0	5-7-0	3-1-0	2nd
4-11-1	2-6-0	4-9-1	0-2-0	5th
7-9-0	6-2-0	6-6-0	1-3-0	3rd
6-10-0	3-5-0	4-8-0	2-2-0	4th
9-7-0	6-2-0	8-4-0	1-3-0	1st

CONFERENCE RECORD →

3-13-0	2-6-0	3-9-0	0-4-0	5th
10-6-0	5-3-0	9-5-0	1-1-0	2nd
10-6-0	6-2-0	8-4-0	2-2-0	1st
7-9-0	3-5-0	6-6-0	1-3-0	4th
7-9-0	4-4-0	6-6-0	1-3-0	3rd

DIVISION RECORD →

12-4-0	6-2-0	9-3-0	3-1-0	1st
4-12-0	2-6-0	3-11-0	1-1-0	4th
4-12-0	2-6-0	3-9-0	1-3-0	5th
11-5-0	6-2-0	9-3-0	2-2-0	2nd
5-11-0	4-4-0	4-8-0	1-3-0	3rd

◄DIVISION RECORD►

5-11-0	1-5-0	4-8-0	1-3-0	4th
10-6-0	4-2-0	8-4-0	2-2-0	2nd
10-6-0	3-3-0	6-6-0	4-0-0	3rd
10-6-0	4-2-0	8-4-0	2-2-0	1st

DETROIT
GREEN BAY
MINNESOTA
TAMPA BAY
WESTERN DIVISION
ATLANTA
LOS ANGELES RAMS
NEW ORLEANS
SAN FRANCISCO

HINTS FOR INTERPRETING THE CHART

1. Identify a team from the left (vertical) column. The results of this team's games are set out in the horizontal row which corresponds with the team name. Buffalo's results appear along the very top horizontal row.
2. The result of a game against a team whose name is listed in the bottom horizontal row is indicated by a coloured triangle which appears in the square, common to both teams.
3. Games won, lost and tied, are colour coded as follows:
   Green triangle for a win
   Red triangle for a loss
   Yellow triangle for a tie
4. The score of the team which is listed in the vertical column **always** comes first. For this team, an away game is signified by a triangle in the top right of the square, and a home game is signified by a triangle in the bottom left of the square.
5. Examples using Indianapolis. They won at home 17-14 to Buffalo. They lost away 23-34 to Buffalo. They won away 16-0 to San Diego. They lost at home 14-17 to Houston.
6. The Colts' record for the 16-game regular season breaks down as follows:
Divisional record 5-3-0; Conference record 7-5-0; Interconference record 2-2-0; Overall record 9-7-0.

INTERPRETING THE ALL-TIME HEAD-TO-HEAD
CHART (See inside back cover)

1. Identify a team from the left (vertical) column. The
   status of this team's games is set out in the horizontal
   row which corresponds with the team name. Buffalo's
   results appear along the very top horizontal row.

2. The rectangles are colour coded to show a team's
   status in the all-time head-to-head series as follows:
   A green rectangle if the team is leading the series.
   A red rectangle if the team is trailing in the series.
   A yellow rectangle if the series is tied.

3. Examples using the Buffalo Bills:
   The Bills hold a 14-9-1 won-lost-tied advantage in all
   games against the Denver Broncos.
   The Bills are behind 11-34-1 in all games against the
   Miami Dolphins.
   The Bills are tied 18-18-1 in all games against the
   Indianapolis Colts.

AMERICAN FOOTBALL
BOOK 7

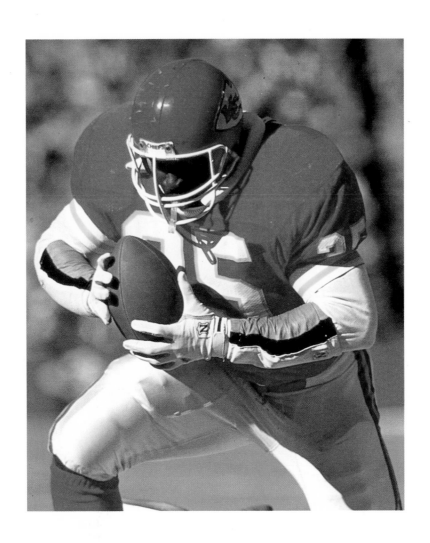

AMERICAN FOOTBALL

BOOK 7

KEN THOMAS

Macdonald   Queen Anne Press
In association with
Channel Four Television Company Limited

ACKNOWLEDGEMENTS

Each year, it seems, the list continues to grow. I refer of course to the many people on whom I call for assistance in writing this book. As always, my two good friends, Nick Wridgway and Roger Smith, have been unstinting in their efforts. Roger, who has the distinction of being the first British fan of the Dallas Cowboys, compiled many of the statistical tables, for which he has my gratitude. Nick's involvement has grown with the years. In the beginning he'd offer a few suggestions but now we both find it simpler if he just dictates while I type. Thanks a lot, Nick.

As usual I have drawn heavily on the goodwill and expertise of several Americans, beginning with Beau Riffenburgh, to whom I owe a special debt of appreciation, and on through Larry Eldridge, Jr., the Sports Information Director at the University of Pittsburgh, to Pete Abitante of the National Football League. Another name, that of John Herrera, who is the Senior Executive with responsibility for special projects with the Los Angeles Raiders, has been added to the help roster. Gentlemen all, I thank you.

Sharon Kuthe and Kevin Terrell of NFL Creative Services supplied the photographic material with their usual flawless efficiency. They, too, have my thanks.

On the home front, Celia Kent of Queen Anne Press has been most considerate with my unorthodox interpretation of the word 'deadline', while Susanna Yager of Channel Four Television has arranged the project with her usual efficiency and tact. To both ladies I extend my thanks.

Finally, Janie, my wife, has once again relinquished her authority over a substantial portion of our home so that a group of men can behave like a gang of kids. We'll try to improve but for the moment, thanks love.

K.T., June 1989

A *Queen Anne Press* BOOK

© Ken Thomas 1989

First published in Great Britain in 1989 by
Queen Anne Press, a division of
Macdonald & Co (Publishers) Ltd
66-73 Shoe Lane
London EC4P 4AB
A member of Maxwell Pergamon Publishing Corporation plc

The American Football Book is associated with Channel Four Television's coverage of the sport

(TM) NFL Properties (UK) Ltd

Cover photographs – Front: Roger Craig in Super Bowl XXIII
(Rick Stewart/All-Sport)
Back: Joe Robie Stadium, Miami,
Super Bowl XXIII
(Caryn Levy/All-Sport)

British Library Cataloguing in Publication Data

American football book. 7-
1. American football
796.332

ISBN 0-356-617923-0

Typeset by SX Composing Ltd

Printed and bound in Great Britain by
BPCC Paulton Books Ltd

PHOTOGRAPHS

All photographs have been supplied by courtesy of the NFL. The following photographers took the pictures on the pages indicated: The Allens 58; Charles AquaViva 92; John Betancourt 115; John Biever 145; Vernon Biever 9R; Peter Brouillet 15, 20, 80T; Rob Brown 48, 49B, 64; Bill Cummings 51T, 133, 137; Scott Cunningham 70; Jonathan Daniel 79; Bruce Dierdorff 19, 45L; Brian Drake 23, 119; Malcolm Emmons 56, 57, 103; James F. Flores 55; Richard Gentile 141; George Gojkovich 31R, 91, 117, 127; Pete J. Groh 13, 44, 72B, 95; Paul Jasienski 12, 121; Ali Jorge 82; Hein Kluftmeier 59L; Rick Kolodziej 43R; Al Kooistra 123; Don Larson 16, 27; Richard Mackson 45R, 45B, 51B; John McDonough 28, 36; Craig Melvin 17T; Al Messerschmidt 29, 32, 60, 63L, 72T, 83T, 101, 113; Vic Milton 83B, 128; Kevin W. Reece 22, 39L; Bob Rosato 6, 10, 25, 42, 87L, 89, 143; Dave Rose 9L; George Rose 17B, 26, 87R; Ron Ross 39R, 139; Chris Schwenk 24, 105; Robert Shaver 2-3, 11; Bill Smith 74; Herb Snitzer 107; Paul Spinelli 41L, 41R, 43L, 50, 109, 124-5, 131, 151; Rick Stewart 97, 111; Damian Strohmeyer 133, 84, 129; Daniel Strohmeyer 8, 18; Al Tielemans 21, 86, 136; Tony Tomsic 46, 59R, 62, 65, 94; Corky Trewin 14, 37, 49T; Jim Turner 35R, 93; Ron Vesley 5, 47, 85B, 99, 147; Herb Weitman 31L; Ron Wyatt 78; Michael Zagaris 35L; 61, 63R.
All-Sport 149.

CONTENTS

INTRODUCTION

1989 could well see the most exciting developments in what now is the nineteenth year that American Football has been telecast in Europe. The story began with Super Bowl V, when World Of Sport presented edited highlights of Baltimore's last-second defeat of Dallas. At the time of writing, early June, the prospects for NFL games televised live are better than ever. And that's not all, by any means, for the NFL is seriously considering the possibility of setting up a Spring-Summer league involving teams based in the United States and Europe, to be known appropriately as the Worldwide American Football League. As a measure of the NFL's commitment, in charge of developing the project will be none other than the highly respected Texas E. (Tex) Schramm, who directed the daily operations of the Dallas Cowboys from their entry into the NFL in 1960 until early in 1989.

This little project, the *American Football Book*, enters its seventh year and there have been some changes to the usual format. It has been the normal practice to present a history of the reigning Super Bowl Champion, but the 49ers, who became the first team to win the title twice in the lifetime of the book, brought an end to that sequence. However, it means that I am able to include pen-portraits of several individuals who have been voted the Super Bowl Most Valuable Player. Also, in researching the material for what would have been 'Stars of the 1988 Season', the similarities with previous volumes quickly became apparent. A consideration of young prospects who might come through in the 1989 season turned out to be a far more attractive topic. Otherwise, as far as possible, the flavour of previous volumes has been retained.

Perhaps I might close with a reaffirmation of the sheer pleasure I derive from being allowed the opportunity to share my enjoyment of American Football.

Left: Atlanta linebacker Marcus Cotton collars Rams running back Gaston Green.

Contents page: Helped by a great offensive line, Chicago running back, Neal Anderson continues to enhance his status.

CHAPTER ONE

A REVIEW OF THE 1988 SEASON

Prologue

As usual, the Super Bowl Championship had gone to an NFC club, making it four in a row and the sixth time in seven years. In the latest triumph, the beginning had been different, with the AFC's Denver opening up an early, ten-point lead. But the end had been the same, as, led by MVP Doug Williams, the Washington Redskins blew the game open with a record-shattering, 35-point second quarter. Entering the 1988 season, Washington looked even tougher, having invoked a little-used, player-trading system to acquire the Bears' Pro Bowl outside linebacker, Wilber Marshall, at the bargain price of two future first-round draft options. Nonetheless, no matter how invincible Joe Gibbs' men looked, the odds were against them, for not since the Pittsburgh Steelers of 1978 and 1979 had a club won back-to-back NFL Championships.

One team which was not expected to challenge for a title was the Atlanta Falcons, the NFL's weakest member in the 1987 season but which now had the privilege of using the most valuable wooden spoon in professional sports, namely, number-one spot in all but the fourth of the twelve rounds which made up the collegiate draft. The Falcons saw defense as their top priority and, some three weeks before the day of the draft, Auburn outside linebacker Aundray Bruce was signed up. Twice before, in 1966 and 1975, Atlanta had occupied the top slot and they'd selected linebacker Tommy Nobis and quarterback Steve Bartkowski respectively. Bruce was in good company.

The Detroit Lions put their position, second overall, to excellent use. Simply by agreeing to exchange places with third-placed Kansas City in the first round (the Chiefs coveted Nebraska defensive end Neil Smith), Detroit received the Chiefs' second-round option with which they selected Ohio State inside linebacker Chris Spielman. Even

Aundray Bruce (# 93) was expected to lend authority to the Falcons' defense.

though dropping a notch in the first round, they'd still been able to pick the man they wanted most of all, University of Miami defensive back Bennie Blades.

Looking elsewhere in the first round of the draft, shrewd trading had brought the Raiders two extra picks, which they used to acquire cornerback Terry McDaniel and defensive end Scott Davis to go with Tim Brown, the latter who, together with veteran running backs Marcus Allen and Bo Jackson, gave the 'Silver and Black' three Heisman Trophy winners. Out of what was widely accepted as the all-time best crop of senior wide receivers, following Brown there would be five more selected in the first round alone, and a total of 40 in the draft as a whole. But if sheer quantity was any measure of quality, then

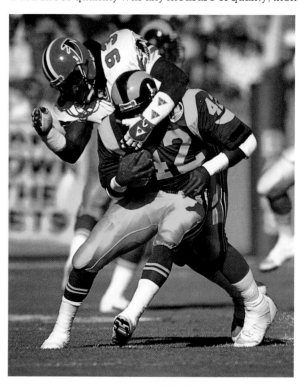

Mike Shanahan would be surrounded by some of the NFL's largest characters.

Lindy Infante became the tenth head coach in the Packers' 69-year history.

that honour went to the defensive backs, of which 63 were picked.

Unusually, there were only two new head coaches, and it had been a surprise appointment when the Raiders hired the former Denver offensive coordinator, Mike Shanahan. Aged 36 by opening day, Shanahan would be the NFL's youngest head coach. But the real interest centred around the way the Raiders, a club whose traditions lay in no-nonsense power-rushing and long-ball passing, would adjust to Shanahan's method, which had finesse as its cornerstone. Lindy Infante, who was hired by Green Bay, appeared to have the more demanding task with a club which had not logged a net-winning season since 1982. Like Shanahan, Infante's most recent position had been that of offensive coordinator, and over his two years in that role with Cleveland, 1986-87, the Browns had won more games, 22, than any other AFC club. Infante, too, found himself a top-class wide receiver – some said he was the best – in South Carolina's Sterling Sharpe.

As for individual goals entering the season, the way was clear for Seattle wide receiver Steve Largent, who already was the NFL all-time leader in pass receptions (752), to take the corresponding yardage record. He needed just 106 yards to go beyond Charlie Joiner's total of 12,146. Also, with 95 career touchdown receptions, he required just five more to surpass the remarkable total of 99 established by the finest receiver in NFL history, the much-revered Don Hutson. Former Dallas and now Denver running back Tony Dorsett was expected to rush for the 277 yards which would take him past Jim Brown's career total, 12,312, and into second place

in the all-time list. With 16,726 yards, the NFL leader in that category, Walter Payton, would not be challenged. But there was a chance that the Colts' Eric Dickerson would become the first man in league history to rush for a total of 10,000 yards over his first six seasons – he needed 1,744.

High amongst the individuals seeking to maintain strings of one kind or other, Dickerson had a sequence of five 1,000-yards-rushing campaigns and needed one more to equal the NFL record held jointly by Payton and Franco Harris. San Francisco's Jerry Rice was hoping to build on his existing NFL record, 13, for consecutive regular-season games in which he had caught at least one touchdown pass. Largent's record streak for consecutive regular-season games in which he had caught at least one pass (152) was still live and seemed certain to grow.

Looking at the prospects for the clubs, not very often had there been quite so many obvious contenders entering a season and yet, even with this quality, in the view of the pundits four teams stood out. The Cleveland Browns, who, in both 1986 and 1987, had lost narrowly in the conference title game to Denver, were almost unanimously fancied to rule the AFC. Turning to the NFC, the spread of opinion covered Chicago, Washington and San Francisco, with the Bears having a slight edge.

When it came to choosing which clubs should receive the annual kiss of death, in other words, selection by your writer, it was easy to stand in line with those who envisaged the 49ers and the Browns fighting out Super Bowl XXIII in Joe Robbie Stadium. And being an AFC man at heart, he had to go with Cleveland.

WEEK ONE

American Football Conference
Cleveland 6 at Kansas City 3
Houston 17 at Indianapolis 14 (OT)
New York Jets 3 at New England 28
San Diego 13 at Los Angeles Raiders 24
Seattle 21 at Denver 14

National Football Conference
Atlanta 17 at Detroit 31
Los Angeles Rams 34 at Green Bay 7
Philadelphia 41 at Tampa Bay 14
San Francisco 34 at New Orleans 33
Washington 20 at New York Giants 27

Interconference Games
Dallas 21 at Pittsburgh 24
Miami 7 at Chicago 34
Minnesota 10 at Buffalo 13
Phoenix 14 at Cincinnati 21

Interconference Play
AFC 3 – NFC 1

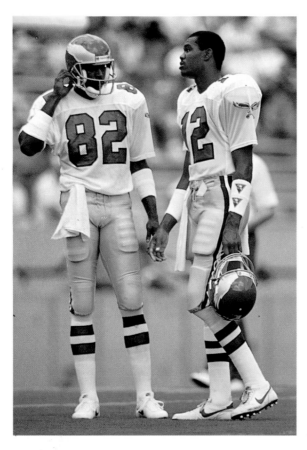

Philadelphia's Mike Quick (# 82) and Randall Cunningham reflect on a job well done.

The reigning Super Bowl Champion Redskins were given centre stage in more ways than one, for not only was their confrontation with the Giants selected as ABC's Monday Night Game but, also, it was the first ever regular-season game seen live on British television. Those who stayed up to watch saw the languid Redskins establish a first-half dominance without putting their opponents away. And wouldn't you just know it? In the second half, with a combination of opportunism and excellent special teams play, the Giants scored 24 unanswered points before surviving a late rally to win.

Of the NFC's other obvious contenders, Chicago beat Miami for the first time in their five-game series, but the Vikings were stifled by an outstanding Buffalo defense. The 49ers declared their intentions by knocking off New Orleans, the team which was expected to provide them with the toughest domestic competition. However, along with the victory came the worry that, after throwing three touchdown passes, 49ers quarterback Joe Montana left the field with an elbow injury. A former New Orleans player, Philadelphia free safety Terry Hoage, intercepted two passes and ran 38 yards for a touchdown on a fake punt as the Eagles opened with an impressive win at the expense of Tampa Bay.

In the AFC, there were wins for New England, Seattle and the Raiders and there was an early indication of things to come when all four Central division teams won. The Pittsburgh Steelers used a late interception by linebacker David Little to protect their lead over an old adversary, the Dallas Cowboys. Both Cleveland and Houston battled to three-point victories, and that coincidence was extended as each team lost its starting quarterback. For Cleveland, Gary Danielson came on after a first-minute injury to starter Bernie Kosar, but it was only in the closing stages that he gathered together all his veteran savvy to mount the 73-yard drive which set up Matt Bahr's 38-yard, match-winning field goal. The Oilers, for whom second-year quarterback Cody Carlson replaced injured starter Warren Moon, restricted Colts running back Eric Dickerson to 109 yards rushing and replied with 174 of their own. And after missing a chip-shot, 26-yard field goal with two minutes left in regulation time, Houston placekicker Tony Zendejas atoned from 35 yards out, 3:51 into overtime. Cincinnati beat Phoenix 21-14, but more interesting was the fact that they opened and closed the game by stopping the Cardinals on goal-line stands. Each time the Cardinals had been at first-and-goal from the Cincinnati one-yard line. Now there was a thought. Cincinnati, whose offensive powers were never questioned, might just have put together a defense!

STANDINGS

AFC East	W	L	T	PF	PA	NFC East	W	L	T	PF	PA
Buffalo	1	0	0	13	10	N.Y. Giants	1	0	0	27	20
New England	1	0	0	28	3	Philadelphia	1	0	0	41	14
Indianapolis	0	1	0	14	17	Dallas	0	1	0	21	24
Miami	0	1	0	7	34	Phoenix	0	1	0	14	21
N.Y. Jets	0	1	0	3	28	Washington	0	1	0	20	27
AFC Central						**NFC Central**					
Cincinnati	1	0	0	21	14	Chicago	1	0	0	34	7
Cleveland	1	0	0	6	3	Detroit	1	0	0	31	17
Houston	1	0	0	17	14	Green Bay	0	1	0	7	34
Pittsburgh	1	0	0	24	21	Minnesota	0	1	0	10	13
AFC West						Tampa Bay	0	1	0	14	41
L.A. Raiders	1	0	0	24	13	**NFC West**					
Seattle	1	0	0	21	14	L.A. Rams	1	0	0	34	7
Denver	0	1	0	14	21	San Francisco	1	0	0	34	33
Kansas City	0	1	0	3	6	Atlanta	0	1	0	17	31
San Diego	0	1	0	13	24	New Orleans	0	1	0	33	34

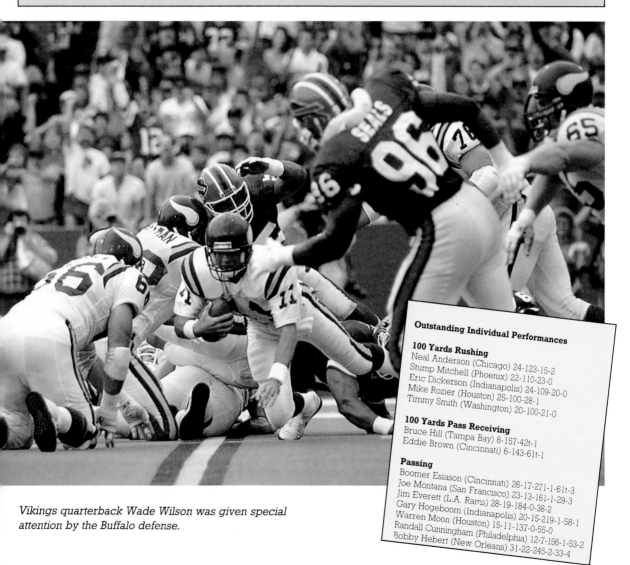

Vikings quarterback Wade Wilson was given special attention by the Buffalo defense.

Outstanding Individual Performances

100 Yards Rushing
Neal Anderson (Chicago) 24-123-15-2
Stump Mitchell (Phoenix) 22-110-23-0
Eric Dickerson (Indianapolis) 24-109-20-0
Mike Rozier (Houston) 25-100-28-1
Timmy Smith (Washington) 20-100-21-0

100 Yards Pass Receiving
Bruce Hill (Tampa Bay) 8-157-42t-1
Eddie Brown (Cincinnati) 6-143-61t-1

Passing
Boomer Esiason (Cincinnati) 26-17-271-1-61t-3
Joe Montana (San Francisco) 23-13-161-1-29-3
Jim Everett (L.A. Rams) 28-19-184-0-38-2
Gary Hogeboom (Indianapolis) 20-15-219-1-58-1
Warren Moon (Houston) 15-11-137-0-55-0
Randall Cunningham (Philadelphia) 12-7-156-1-53-2
Bobby Hebert (New Orleans) 31-22-245-2-33-4

WEEK TWO

American Football Conference
Kansas City 10 at Seattle 31
Los Angeles Raiders 35 at Houston 38
Miami 6 at Buffalo 9
New York Jets 23 at Cleveland 3
San Diego 3 at Denver 34

National Football Conference
Dallas 17 at Phoenix 14
Detroit 10 at Los Angeles Rams 17
New Orleans 29 at Atlanta 21
San Francisco 20 at New York Giants 17
Tampa Bay 13 at Green Bay 10

Interconference Games
Chicago 17 at Indianapolis 13
Cincinnati 28 at Philadelphia 24
New England 6 at Minnesota 36
Pittsburgh 29 at Washington 30

Interconference Play
AFC 4 – NFC 4

So the opposing quarterback has just thrown a touchdown pass to give his team a 17-13 lead with 81 seconds remaining. Then their defense comes on and has you in deep trouble at 3rd-and-12 on your own 22. As a backup to seeking the divine intervention of your god, just about the only terrestrial source of hope is the best passing combination in pro football. That duo is, of course, Joe Montana and Jerry Rice. And with time running out, Montana calmly dropped back and threw an inch-perfect pass to Rice, who ran for the balance of a 78-yard touchdown play which left the Giants in a state of disbelief. 'Just like we planned it,' said a poker-faced Montana. Cincinnati, too, remained at boiling point. Against Philadelphia, four times they came from behind before mounting a late defensive stand which held firm at their own 12-yard line. Houston remained unbeaten at the expense of the Raiders in

Former Dallas and now Denver running back Tony Dorsett swept into third place in the NFL's all-time rushing list.

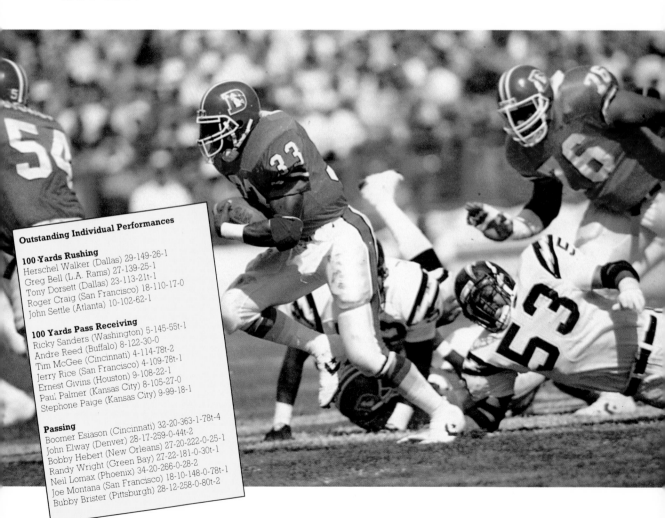

Outstanding Individual Performances

100-Yards Rushing
Herschel Walker (Dallas) 29-149-26-1
Greg Bell (L.A. Rams) 27-139-25-1
Tony Dorsett (Dallas) 23-113-21t-1
Roger Craig (San Francisco) 18-110-17-0
John Settle (Atlanta) 10-102-62-1

100 Yards Pass Receiving
Ricky Sanders (Washington) 5-145-55t-1
Andre Reed (Buffalo) 8-122-30-0
Tim McGee (Cincinnati) 4-114-78t-2
Jerry Rice (San Francisco) 4-109-78t-1
Ernest Givins (Houston) 9-108-22-1
Paul Palmer (Kansas City) 8-105-27-0
Stephone Paige (Kansas City) 9-99-18-1

Passing
Boomer Esiason (Cincinnati) 32-20-363-1-78t-4
John Elway (Denver) 28-17-259-0-44t-2
Bobby Hebert (New Orleans) 27-20-222-0-25-1
Randy Wright (Green Bay) 27-22-181-0-30t-1
Neil Lomax (Phoenix) 34-20-266-0-28-2
Joe Montana (San Francisco) 18-10-148-0-78t-1
Bubby Brister (Pittsburgh) 28-12-258-0-80t-2

STANDINGS

AFC East	W	L	T	PF	PA
Buffalo	2	0	0	22	16
New England	1	1	0	34	39
N.Y. Jets	1	1	0	26	31
Indianapolis	0	2	0	27	34
Miami	0	2	0	13	43
AFC Central					
Cincinnati	2	0	0	49	38
Houston	2	0	0	55	49
Cleveland	1	1	0	9	26
Pittsburgh	1	1	0	53	51
AFC West					
Seattle	2	0	0	52	24
Denver	1	1	0	48	24
L.A. Raiders	1	1	0	59	51
Kansas City	0	2	0	13	37
San Diego	0	2	0	16	58
NFC East	**W**	**L**	**T**	**PF**	**PA**
Dallas	1	1	0	38	38
N.Y. Giants	1	1	0	44	40
Philadelphia	1	1	0	65	42
Washington	1	1	0	50	56
Phoenix	0	2	0	28	38
NFC Central					
Chicago	2	0	0	51	20
Detroit	1	1	0	41	34
Minnesota	1	1	0	46	19
Tampa Bay	1	1	0	27	51
Green Bay	0	2	0	17	47
NFC West					
L.A. Rams	2	0	0	51	17
San Francisco	2	0	0	54	50
New Orleans	1	1	0	62	55
Atlanta	0	2	0	38	60

Cowboys favourite son, running back Tony Dorsett, had his first 100-yards rushing outing for Denver, sweeping past Franco Harris and into third place in the all-time rushing list, as the Broncos opened their account at the expense of San Diego. There was little to choose between Seattle and Kansas City but the Seahawks took their chances for the win which gave them ownership of top spot in the AFC West. Further down the Pacific coast the Rams moved quietly forward, as Greg Bell victimised the Lions with 139 yards rushing. Unthinkable it may seem, but neither Buffalo nor Miami could score a touchdown in a defensive struggle won by the Bills, 9-6, and which left Don Shula 0-2 for the first time in his 19 forays as the Dolphins' head coach. Already, the Colts were beginning to feel the pressures of their murderous schedule. An Eric Dickerson fumble on Week One had let the Oilers in for their overtime victory. And it was his fourth-quarter fumble at the Chicago 37-yard line which lingered in the memory, after the Bears had left the field with their 17-13 win.

Seattle defensive end Jacob Green registered three sacks, following one of which he recovered possession for a touchdown.

a 73-point shoot-out which saw the Oilers overcome Raider leads of 21-7, 28-14 and 35-31. Cleveland fared less well, losing second-string quarterback Gary Danielson to an injury and the game to the Jets. And the Steelers came away from Washington empty-handed after having led 19-10 and 29-20, only to go down to a Chip Lohmiller 19-yard field goal with 12 seconds remaining. Curiously, for quarterback Doug Williams, who passed for 430 yards and two touchdowns, it was the first regular-season win as a Washington starter. The Buccaneers, in whose colours Williams made his NFL debut in 1978, eased past Green Bay.

Elsewhere, there were initial wins for Minnesota, who took out their frustrations on the Patriots, New Orleans, who out-muscled a gritty Atlanta team, and Dallas, who spoiled the Cardinals' regular-season debut in their adopted city of Phoenix. A former

WEEK THREE

American Football Conference
Buffalo 16 at New England 14
Cincinnati 17 at Pittsburgh 12
Denver 13 at Kansas City 20
Houston 3 at New York Jets 45
Indianapolis 17 at Cleveland 23
Seattle 6 at San Diego 17

National Football Conference
Atlanta 34 at San Francisco 17
Minnesota 31 at Chicago 7
New Orleans 22 at Detroit 14
New York Giants 12 at Dallas 10
Philadelphia 10 at Washington 17
Phoenix 30 at Tampa Bay 24

Interconference Games
Green Bay 17 at Miami 24
Los Angeles Rams 22 at Los Angeles Raiders 17

Interconference Play
AFC 5 – NFC 5

Seattle's Steve Largent became the NFL's all-time career leader in reception yardage.

Sunday of Week Three was the day the little guys had their say, with the headline going to the Falcons who whipped San Francisco fair and square. 49ers quarterback Joe Montana completed 32 of 48 passes but the important ones bounced off and, of three that were intercepted, one was returned for a touchdown by Falcons safety Robert Moore. 'Somewhat unexpected' one felt was Denver's loss to the Chiefs, for whom the much-travelled quarterback, Steve DeBerg, out-performed John Elway, the man who'd unseated DeBerg with the Broncos in 1983. San Diego upset the Seahawks, who suffered the additional blow of losing starting quarterback Dave Krieg with a shoulder injury. On went the catalogue of shocks, with the Jets stunning the NFL's emerging 'meanies', Jerry Glanville's Houston Oilers, by the score of 45-3. For the Jets, quarterbacks Ken O'Brien and Pat Ryan each enjoyed the outing and veteran wide receiver Wesley Walker, as he occasionally does, decided that this was going to be one of his big days as he caught six passes for 129 yards and three touchdowns. Even the mighty Bears were not invincible, as was shown by the Vikings, who chose the finest possible way in which to reassert their title claim. Vikings quarterback Tommy Kramer was at his infuriating best while three Chicago quarter-

Gerald Riggs rushed for 115 yards and a touchdown in Atlanta's stunning upset of San Francisco.

Outstanding Individual Performances

100 Yards Rushing
Gary Anderson (San Diego) 19-120-25t-1
Eric Dickerson (Indianapolis) 22-117-41t-1
Gerald Riggs (Atlanta) 19-115-17-1
Stump Mitchell (Phoenix) 18-110-47-1
Greg Bell (L.A. Rams) 21-109-17-1
Joe Morris (N.Y. Giants) 28-107-12-0
Timmy Smith (Washington) 31-107-22-1

100 Yards Pass Receiving
Jerry Rice (San Francisco) 8-163-37-0
Lionel Manuel (N.Y. Giants) 9-142-35-1
James Lofton (L.A. Raiders) 4-130-57-0
Wesley Walker (N.Y. Jets) 6-129-50t-3
Mike Quick (Philadelphia) 4-105-55t-1
J.T. Smith (Phoenix) 6-103-26-0
Jay Novacek (Phoenix) 5-102-42t-1

Passing
Ken O'Brien (N.Y. Jets) 26-17-260-0-50t-3
Tommy Kramer (Minnesota) 25-15-258-1-40t-3
Neil Lomax (Phoenix) 13-10-148-0-25-0
Steve DeBerg (Kansas City) 35-21-259-0-26-2
Randy Wright (Green Bay) 23-18-184-0-25-0

backs, in succession, starter Jim McMahon, Mike Tomczak and apprentice Jim Harbaugh, could generate a total of just seven points.

The shake-out meant that only three teams remained undefeated. Against divisional rival Pittsburgh, for the third week in a row Cincinnati came up with a critical defensive play when cornerback Eric Thomas intercepted a pass at his own eight-yard line with under a minute remaining, preserving the Bengals' 17-12 victory. The Buffalo Bills still couldn't generate much offense, but a fourth-quarter, ten-point rally completed by Scott Norwood's late field goal – only 11 seconds remained – took them past the home-team Patriots. In retaining their unblemished record, the Rams also regained the bragging rights to the city of Los Angeles. The beaten Raiders felt that they had grounds for complaint when game film showed clearly that, on a crucial safety concession, quarterback Steve Beuerlein had been tripped. By way of consolation, Beuerlein had shown Raider-type grit, passing for 375 yards and two touchdowns despite being sacked a total of nine times – five were by Rams defensive end Gary Jeter. There was controversy, too, in the Giants' 12-10 win over Dallas. Cowboys kickoff returner Darryl Clack muffed the ball into the end zone and was tackled when trying to run it out. The ruling should have been a touchback but the Giants were awarded a safety. The opportunity to review the play was not taken by the replay official who, accepting his error and in the best of gentlemanly traditions, subsequently resigned.

STANDINGS

AFC East	W	L	T	PF	PA
Buffalo	3	0	0	38	30
N.Y. Jets	2	1	0	71	34
Miami	1	2	0	37	60
New England	1	2	0	48	55
Indianapolis	0	3	0	44	57
AFC Central					
Cincinnati	3	0	0	66	50
Cleveland	2	1	0	32	43
Houston	2	1	0	58	94
Pittsburgh	1	2	0	65	68
AFC West					
Seattle	2	1	0	58	41
Denver	1	2	0	61	44
Kansas City	1	2	0	33	50
L.A. Raiders	1	2	0	76	73
San Diego	1	2	0	33	64
NFC East	**W**	**L**	**T**	**PF**	**PA**
N.Y. Giants	2	1	0	56	50
Washington	2	1	0	67	66
Dallas	1	2	0	48	50
Philadelphia	1	2	0	75	59
Phoenix	1	2	0	58	62
NFC Central					
Chicago	2	1	0	58	51
Minnesota	2	1	0	77	26
Detroit	1	2	0	55	56
Tampa Bay	1	2	0	51	81
Green Bay	0	3	0	34	71
NFC West					
L.A. Rams	3	0	0	73	34
New Orleans	2	1	0	84	69
San Francisco	2	1	0	71	84
Atlanta	1	2	0	72	77

WEEK FOUR

American Football Conference
Cleveland 17 at Cincinnati 24
Los Angeles Raiders 30 at Denver 27 (OT)
Miami 13 at Indianapolis 15
New England 6 at Houston 31
Pittsburgh 28 at Buffalo 36
San Diego 24 at Kansas City 23

National Football Conference
Atlanta 20 at Dallas 26
Chicago 24 at Green Bay 6
Los Angeles Rams 45 at New York Giants 31
Philadelphia 21 at Minnesota 23
Tampa Bay 9 at New Orleans 13
Washington 21 at Phoenix 30

Interconference Games
New York Jets 17 at Detroit 10
San Francisco 38 at Seattle 7

Interconference Play
AFC 6 – NFC 6

Dean Biasucci kicked the Colts to victory over Miami.

One reason that the Raiders are selected so often for ABC's Monday Night Game - only Miami and Dallas have appeared more times - is that they give good value for money. And against Denver at Mile High Stadium they underlined their reputation by matching the third-greatest comeback for victory in NFL history as, led by new starting quarterback Jay Schroeder, they rallied from a 24-0 deficit to win by the score of 30-27 in overtime. It was in the extra period that Denver running back Tony Dorsett went beyond Jim Brown's career rushing total of 12,312 yards and into second place behind Walter Payton.

The previous day, Sunday, had seen the league's three undefeated teams, Buffalo, Cincinnati and the Rams, continue unchecked. For the Bills, place-kicker Scott Norwood landed five field goals, extending his successful streak to a Buffalo club-record 12. The Bengals turned to their powerful trio of runners, James Brooks, Stanley Wilson and rookie Ickey Woods, for victory over Cleveland. But the Browns could take heart in that, even with third-string quarterback Mike Pagel at the controls, they'd been beaten only narrowly. Of the three front-runners, the Rams were the most impressive with third-year quarterback Jim Everett throwing a personal, single-game best five touchdown passes.

Behind the leaders, the chasing pack was beginning to take shape as all three of San Francisco, Chicago and Houston won. With Joe Montana and Jerry Rice back in tune, the 49ers were particularly severe on Seattle, gaining a huge 580 net yards offense while restricting the Seahawks to just 154 on the way to a 38-7 scoreline. And though the Oilers were not quite as dominant against New England, the bottom line, 31-6, told the same story. The Bears returned to type as they rushed for 242 net yards in keeping Green Bay winless on the campaign. Indeed, following the Colts' first victory, a 15-13 thriller in which placekicker Dean Biasucci scored all their points with five field goals, the Packers were now alone with nothing to show.

Turning to the other contenders, Minnesota, New Orleans and the Jets each had logged their third straight wins after opening-day losses. The Vikings, who won on a Chuck Nelson 32-yard field goal with 15 seconds remaining, had done everybody a favour by handing the dangerous Philadelphia Eagles their third straight loss. This certainly was true in the NFC East, where the Cardinals' deserved victory over Washington meant that four .500 teams shared the divisional lead. In Kansas City, Lionel James' late touchdown gave San Diego a victory by the narrowest of margins and a share of the lead in the AFC West.

STANDINGS

AFC East	W	L	T	PF	PA
Buffalo	4	0	0	74	58
N.Y. Jets	3	1	0	88	44
Indianapolis	1	3	0	59	70
Miami	1	3	0	50	75
New England	1	3	0	54	86
AFC Central					
Cincinnati	4	0	0	90	67
Houston	3	1	0	89	100
Cleveland	2	2	0	49	67
Pittsburgh	1	3	0	93	104
AFC West					
L.A. Raiders	2	2	0	106	100
San Diego	2	2	0	57	87
Seattle	2	2	0	65	79
Denver	1	3	0	88	74
Kansas City	1	3	0	56	74

NFC East	W	L	T	PF	PA
Dallas	2	2	0	74	70
N.Y. Giants	2	2	0	87	95
Phoenix	2	2	0	88	83
Washington	2	2	0	88	96
Philadelphia	1	3	0	96	82
NFC Central					
Chicago	3	1	0	82	57
Minnesota	3	1	0	100	47
Detroit	1	3	0	65	73
Tampa Bay	1	3	0	60	94
Green Bay	0	4	0	40	95
NFC West					
L.A. Rams	4	0	0	118	65
New Orleans	3	1	0	97	78
San Francisco	3	1	0	109	91
Atlanta	1	3	0	92	103

Scott Norwood extended his successful streak to a Buffalo-record 12 field goals.

Earl Ferrell (# 31) punched for 108 yards in the Cardinals' win over Washington.

Outstanding Individual Performances

100 Yards Rushing
Gary Anderson (San Diego) 23-131-30t-1
Eric Dickerson (Indianapolis) 30-125-9-0
Tony Dorsett (Denver) 32-119-20-2
Greg Bell (L.A. Rams) 31-112-11-1
Earl Ferrell (Phoenix) 19-108-16-0
Roger Craig (San Francisco) 21-107-24-0
Neal Anderson (Chicago) 20-105-45t-2

100 Yards Pass Receiving
Stacey Bailey (Atlanta) 4-169-68t-1
Jerry Rice (San Francisco) 6-163-69t-3
Sterling Sharpe (Green Bay) 7-137-51-0
Vance Johnson (Denver) 7-134-86-0
Eddie Brown (Cincinnati) 4-127-46-0
Paul Palmer (Kansas City) 5-122-71t-2
Steve Smith (L.A. Raiders) 6-122-42t-2
Weegie Thompson (Pittsburgh) 4-118-42t-1
Anthony Carter (Minnesota) 6-113-27-0
Ray Alexander (Dallas) 6-107-29t-1

Passing
Jim Everett (L.A. Rams) 24-14-236-1-69t-5
Joe Montana (San Francisco) 29-20-302-1-69t-4
Steve Pelluer (Dallas) 26-17-216-1-29t-2
Mark Rypien (Washington) 41-26-303-1-26-3

WEEK FIVE

American Football Conference
Cincinnati 45 at Los Angeles Raiders 21
Cleveland 23 at Pittsburgh 9
Denver 12 at San Diego 0
Indianapolis 17 at New England 21
Kansas City 17 at New York Jets 17 (OT)

National Football Conference
Dallas 17 at New Orleans 20
Detroit 13 at San Francisco 20
Green Bay 24 at Tampa Bay 27
New York Giants 24 at Washington 23
Phoenix 41 at Los Angeles Rams 27

Interconference Games
Buffalo 3 at Chicago 24
Houston 23 at Philadelphia 32
Minnesota 7 at Miami 24
Seattle 31 at Atlanta 20

Interconference Play
AFC 8 – NFC 8

Week Five found the Bills facing their first major credibility test and they failed, going down to the Bears without breaking the plane of the end zone. Making matters worse, they lost their outstanding young inside linebacker, Shane Conlan, to injury. The Rams, too, lost their unbeaten record to a Phoenix club for whom the win was the third straight. Rams quarterback Jim Everett did little wrong, passing for 300 yards without an interception, but he was out-gunned by the Cardinals' Neil Lomax, while the rushing combination of Stump Mitchell and Earl Ferrell more than doubled the Rams' output. However, 20 miles north on I-5, in the Memorial Coliseum, the Bengals were in the process of crushing the Raiders. With the day's best passing show, Cincinnati quarterback Boomer Esiason victimised a Raiders defensive secondary which fielded only one regular starter, cornerback Mike Haynes.

Both San Francisco and New Orleans took advantage of the Rams' loss to move into a tie for first place in the NFC West, though neither team was impressive. The 49ers made hard work of beating Detroit while the Saints needed a last-second, 49-yard field goal by Morten Andersen to break a 17-17 deadlock with Dallas. Last-minute, game-winning field goals were becoming the speciality of Tampa Bay place-kicker Donald Igwebuike, whose late, 44-yard field goal enabled the Buccaneers to slip by the winless Packers. On Week Two, Igwebuike had beaten the same club with a 28-yarder as time expired. But there would be no late salvation for the Redskins, who lost by a single point. Against the Giants, for

whom all-pro outside linebacker Lawrence Taylor returned after a four-game suspension, placekicker Chip Lohmiller failed on a 36-yard field goal attempt with 2:54 remaining. Earlier, the poor lad had missed a touchdown conversion.

Elsewhere, two veteran quarterbacks, Dan Marino and Randall Cunningham, reminded us of their greatness while a newcomer made an opening statement. The youngster was rookie quarterback Kelly Stouffer, who didn't throw a touchdown pass but put together four smooth touchdown-scoring drives as the Seahawks kept the Falcons at arm's length. Despite being intercepted three times, Marino coaxed the Dolphins to victory with plenty to spare against the heavily favoured Vikings. But for pure theatre, the day belonged to Cunningham. With Philadelphia trailing Houston 16-0 in the first quarter, he unleashed a hail of passes for 289 yards and two touchdowns, and rushed for 59 yards, including a 33-yard touchdown run, in a 32-point scoring burst to which the Oilers made only one scoring response. Houston's loss enabled Cleveland to draw level after their gutsy win over Pittsburgh.

Left: Carlos Carson had an 80-yard touchdown catch.

Below: The Bears smothered Jim Kelly and the Bills.

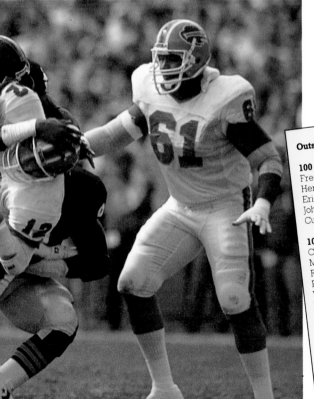

STANDINGS

AFC East	W	L	T	PF	PA
Buffalo	4	1	0	77	82
N.Y. Jets	3	1	1	105	61
Miami	2	3	0	74	82
New England	2	3	0	75	103
Indianapolis	1	4	0	76	91
AFC Central					
Cincinnati	5	0	0	135	88
Cleveland	3	2	0	72	76
Houston	3	2	0	112	132
Pittsburgh	1	4	0	102	127
AFC West					
Seattle	3	2	0	96	99
Denver	2	3	0	100	74
L.A. Raiders	2	3	0	127	145
San Diego	2	3	0	57	99
Kansas City	1	3	1	73	91

NFC East	W	L	T	PF	PA
N.Y. Giants	3	2	0	111	118
Phoenix	3	2	0	129	110
Dallas	2	3	0	91	90
Philadelphia	2	3	0	128	105
Washington	2	3	0	111	120
NFC Central					
Chicago	4	1	0	106	60
Minnesota	3	2	0	107	71
Tampa Bay	2	3	0	87	118
Detroit	1	4	0	78	93
Green Bay	0	5	0	64	122
NFC West					
L.A. Rams	4	1	0	145	106
New Orleans	4	1	0	117	95
San Francisco	4	1	0	129	104
Atlanta	1	4	0	112	134

Outstanding Individual Performances

100 Yards Rushing
Freeman McNeil (N.Y. Jets) 22-154-28-0
Herschel Walker (Dallas) 26-124-15-0
Eric Dickerson (Indianapolis) 29-118-17-1
John Settle (Atlanta) 21-115-20-0
Curt Warner (Seattle) 22-110-21-1

100 Yards Pass Receiving
Carlos Carson (Kansas City) 5-162-80t-1
Mickey Shuler (N.Y. Jets) 12-152-24-0
Ricky Sanders (Washington) 7-141-49t-2
Pete Mandley (Detroit) 7-116-23-1
Walter Stanley (Green Bay) 6-107-56-0
Mervyn Fernandez (L.A. Raiders) 4-104-59-1
Odessa Turner (N.Y. Giants) 8-103-28t-1
Willie Gault (L.A. Raiders) 4-102-44-0

Passing
Boomer Esiason (Cincinnati) 28-21-332-0-37-3
Jim Everett (L.A. Rams) 33-25-300-0-27-1
Jim McMahon (Chicago) 27-20-260-1-63t-2
Mark Rypien (Washington) 27-16-282-1-49t-2
Randall Cunningham (Philadelphia) 38-24-289-0-38t-2

WEEK SIX

American Football Conference
Indianapolis 23 at Buffalo 34
Kansas City 6 at Houston 7
Miami 24 at Los Angeles Raiders 14
New York Jets 19 at Cincinnati 36
Seattle 16 at Cleveland 10

National Football Conference
Chicago 24 at Detroit 7
Los Angeles Rams 33 at Atlanta 0
New York Giants 13 at Philadelphia 24
Tampa Bay 13 at Minnesota 14
Washington 35 at Dallas 17

Interconference Games
Denver 16 at San Francisco 13 (OT)
New England 3 vs Green Bay 45 (at Milwaukee)
New Orleans 23 at San Diego 17
Pittsburgh 14 at Phoenix 31

Interconference Play
AFC 9 – NFC 11

Rams outside linebacker Kevin Greene had three sacks and intercepted a pass.

On Week Six both the Rams and Buffalo returned to their winning ways and Cincinnati continued to roll. Against the Jets, with rookie running back Ickey Woods cutting and shearing for 139 yards, quarterback Boomer Esiason passed with caution, but he was no less devastating for that, throwing a brace of touchdowns to Eddie Brown, including a 60-yarder, and a third to Tim McGee. Their dual-purpose offensive showing was mirrored by the Rams, for whom running back Greg Bell gained 155 yards whilst quarterback Jim Everett passed for 234 yards and three touchdowns as they blanked Atlanta. Buffalo, meanwhile, dealt the Colts their fifth defeat of what, for a fancied club, already had become a disastrous campaign. And if the Browns had thought they'd already experienced their share of bad luck, there was yet more to come as third-string quarterback Mike Pagel separated his shoulder, forcing the introduction of 15th-year veteran Don Strock. Rubbing salt into the wound, on the injury play, Seattle's Paul Moyer returned a fumble 62 yards to set up a field goal. Subsequently, a pair of Strock errors – he fumbled and threw a pass interception – gave Seattle possession with which they established the points difference. Pagel was just one of seven quarterbacks who went down with injury. Houston lost second-stringer Cody Carlson, but, although third-stringer Brent Pease was intercepted three times, he atoned with the four-yard touchdown run which gave the Oilers victory over Kansas City.

In the NFC, Chicago lost starter Jim McMahon but had enough in hand to beat Detroit. However, their obvious challengers in the Central division, the Vikings, escaped with a one-point win when the Buccaneers couldn't quite assemble their field goal team for what would have been a simple chip-shot field goal as time ran out. Against San Diego, New Orleans trailed 14-0 but came back for the win which left them in a two-way tie on top of the NFC West. Another contender, San Francisco, went down to the Broncos in overtime on a Rich Karlis 22-yard field goal. In the NFC East, the Cardinals had emerged as the hot team with their fourth consecutive victory, in each one of which they had scored at least 30 points. This week's victim was Pittsburgh, who slumped to their fifth straight loss. Washington's win over traditional rival Dallas was a morale booster, but the key win in that division had to be that of the Eagles, who emerged from a titanic struggle with the Giants on Monday evening. Once again, Randall Cunningham was the chief destroyer as he completed 31 of 41 passes for 369 yards and three touchdowns, including an 80-yarder to wide receiver Cris Carter which stifled a Giants rally. Finally, after seven straight losses extending back into the 1987 season, Green Bay came out on top. And

STANDINGS

AFC East	W	L	T	PF	PA	NFC East	W	L	T	PF	PA
Buffalo	5	1	0	111	105	Phoenix	4	2	0	160	124
N.Y. Jets	3	2	1	124	97	N.Y. Giants	3	3	0	124	142
Miami	3	3	0	98	96	Philadelphia	3	3	0	152	118
New England	2	4	0	78	148	Washington	3	3	0	146	137
Indianapolis	1	5	0	99	125	Dallas	2	4	0	108	125
AFC Central						**NFC Central**					
Cincinnati	6	0	0	171	107	Chicago	5	1	0	130	67
Houston	4	2	0	119	138	Minnesota	4	2	0	121	84
Cleveland	3	3	0	82	92	Tampa Bay	2	4	0	100	132
Pittsburgh	1	5	0	116	158	Detroit	1	5	0	85	117
AFC West						Green Bay	1	5	0	109	125
Seattle	4	2	0	112	109	**NFC West**					
Denver	3	3	0	116	87	L.A. Rams	5	1	0	178	106
L.A. Raiders	2	4	0	141	169	New Orleans	5	1	0	140	112
San Diego	2	4	0	74	122	San Francisco	4	2	0	142	120
Kansas City	1	4	1	79	98	Atlanta	1	5	0	112	167

they did it in grand style, even allowing the Patriots to score first before unleashing a 45-point shower. It was good to have the Packers back.

An 80-yard touchdown reception by wide receiver Cris Carter helped Philadelphia to victory over the Giants.

Outstanding Individual Performances

100 Yards Rushing
Greg Bell (L.A. Rams) 21-155-44-1
Roger Craig (San Francisco) 26-143-14-0
Mike Rozier (Houston) 27-141-13-0
Ickey Woods (Cincinnati) 30-139-21-2
Kelvin Bryant (Washington) 23-118-17-1
Brent Fullwood (Green Bay) 14-118-33t-3
Sammy Winder (Denver) 17-100-35-0

100 Yards Pass Receiving
Cris Carter (Philadelphia) 5-162-80t-1
Mark Bavaro (N.Y. Giants) 9-148-33-0
Henry Ellard (L.A. Rams) 7-134-54t-1
Andre Reed (Buffalo) 7-124-58-2
Roy Green (Phoenix) 4-119-40-0
James Lofton (L.A. Raiders) 5-113-30-0
Eddie Brown (Cincinnati) 5-103-60t-2

Passing
Boomer Esiason (Cincinnati) 20-10-220-0-60t-3
Mark Rypien (Washington) 21-13-187-0-34-3
Randall Cunningham (Philadelphia) 41-31-369-0-80t-3
Neil Lomax (Phoenix) 26-17-291-1-40-3
Jim Everett (L.A. Rams) 24-15-234-1-54t-3
Don Majkowski (Green Bay) 26-18-210-0-35-1

WEEK SEVEN

American Football Conference
Buffalo 37 at New York Jets 14
Cincinnati 21 at New England 27
Houston 34 at Pittsburgh 14
Los Angeles Raiders 27 at Kansas City 17
San Diego 28 at Miami 31

National Football Conference
Dallas 7 at Chicago 17
Detroit 10 at New York Giants 30
Green Bay 34 at Minnesota 14
Phoenix 17 at Washington 33
San Francisco 24 at Los Angeles Rams 21

Interconference Games
Atlanta 14 at Denver 30
New Orleans 20 at Seattle 19
Philadelphia 3 at Cleveland 19
Tampa Bay 31 at Indianapolis 35

Interconference Play
AFC 12 – NFC 12

STANDINGS					
AFC East	**W**	**L**	**T**	**PF**	**PA**
Buffalo	6	1	0	148	119
Miami	4	3	0	129	124
N.Y. Jets	3	3	1	138	134
New England	3	4	0	105	169
Indianapolis	2	5	0	134	156
AFC Central					
Cincinnati	6	1	0	192	134
Houston	5	2	0	153	152
Cleveland	4	3	0	101	95
Pittsburgh	1	6	0	130	192
AFC West					
Denver	4	3	0	146	101
Seattle	4	3	0	131	129
L.A. Raiders	3	4	0	168	186
San Diego	2	5	0	102	153
Kansas City	1	5	1	96	125
NFC East	**W**	**L**	**T**	**PF**	**PA**
N.Y. Giants	4	3	0	154	152
Phoenix	4	3	0	177	157
Washington	4	3	0	179	154
Philadelphia	3	4	0	155	137
Dallas	2	5	0	115	142
NFC Central					
Chicago	6	1	0	147	74
Minnesota	4	3	0	135	118
Green Bay	2	5	0	143	139
Tampa Bay	2	5	0	131	167
Detroit	1	6	0	95	147
NFC West					
New Orleans	6	1	0	160	131
L.A. Rams	5	2	0	199	130
San Francisco	5	2	0	166	141
Atlanta	1	6	0	126	197

Against New England, Cincinnati's hot streak finally came to an end and yet, despite five interceptions thrown by Boomer Esiason, they were still in with every chance late in the third quarter after pulling back from a 20-point deficit to trail by only six. However, Patriots quarterback Doug Flutie engineered an 80-yard, touchdown-scoring drive which used up more than nine minutes, putting the result beyond sensible doubt. The Patriots had exploited the Bengals' weakness against the rush and the odds were that other clubs would now do the same. It was a formula used by the 49ers in their key victory over the Rams, with San Francisco running back Roger Craig

San Francisco's Roger Craig rushed for three touchdowns and a personal, single-game best of 190 yards.

Bucs quarterback Vinny Testaverde gave the Colts a scare.

Outstanding Individual Performances

100 Yards Rushing
Roger Craig (San Francisco) 22-190-46t-3
John Settle (Atlanta) 25-125-20-1
Kevin Mack (Cleveland) 16-100-65-0

100 Yards Pass Receiving
Bruce Hill (Tampa Bay) 7-162-34-2
Brian Blades (Seattle) 8-145-52-1
Bill Brooks (Indianapolis) 7-139-28t-1
Andre Reed (Buffalo) 7-132-65t-2
Ron Hall (Tampa Bay) 7-121-37-0
Mark Duper (Miami) 7-118-51-1
Louis Lipps (Pittsburgh) 8-109-22-0
Ernest Givins (Houston) 5-104-43t-1
Paul Palmer (Kansas City) 5-103-48t-1
Walter Stanley (Green Bay) 5-101-43-0

Passing
Mark Rypien (Washington) 27-15-303-1-60t-4
Phil Simms (N.Y. Giants) 32-23-320-0-51t-2
Warren Moon (Houston) 19-11-174-0-43t-2
Jim Kelly (Buffalo) 27-16-302-1-66t-3
Doug Flutie (New England) 14-10-165-0-38-0
Don Strock (Cleveland) 18-11-189-1-33-2
John Elway (Denver) 26-16-235-0-32-1

Elsewhere, important victories were logged by the Browns, who registered nine sacks to keep a tight rein on Philadelphia's Randall Cunningham, New Orleans, who overcame a 370-yard passing performance from Kelly Stouffer to edge past Seattle, and Denver, whose win was the third in a row and took them into a tie for first place in the AFC West. Washington rode a top-class performance by young quarterback Mark Rypien to halt the Cardinals' winning streak at four. The trade of Jay Schroeder to the Raiders and a subsequent abdominal illness suffered by Doug Williams had given Rypien his chance and, seven weeks into the campaign, he led the NFL in passing. The Oilers welcomed the return of quarterback Warren Moon after injury, and he showed few signs of his absence in a comfortable victory over Pittsburgh.

However, among several fine individual and team performances, for the second week in a row, pride of place had to go to the Packers, who followed up their beating of the Patriots with an equally impressive hammering of the mighty Minnesota Vikings. Quarterback Don Majkowski, who had replaced the injured Randy Wright and played a major role in the victory over New England, passed for 243 yards, and Max Zendejas equalled the Packers' single-game record with four field goals. With the defense recovering four of five Minnesota fumbles, this was looking more and more like the Green Bay of old.

rushing for a personal single-game best 190 yards and three touchdowns. The Bills used the passing combination of Jim Kelly and Andre Reed to consolidate their position at the expense of the Jets. Interestingly, four AFC East teams won, though Indianapolis was given a scare before surviving against Tampa Bay. With the Colts leading 35-10 entering the final quarter, the Buccaneers mounted a whirlwind 21-point comeback sparked by quarterback Vinny Testaverde, who passed for 226 yards in that one quarter alone on the way to the NFL's highest single-game total (469) of the campaign thus far.

WEEK EIGHT

American Football Conference
Denver 21 at Pittsburgh 39
Houston 21 at Cincinnati 44
Indianapolis 16 at San Diego 0
New England 20 at Buffalo 23
New York Jets 44 at Miami 30

National Football Conference
Dallas 23 at Philadelphia 24
Minnesota 49 at Tampa Bay 20
New York Giants 23 at Atlanta 16
San Francisco 9 at Chicago 10
Washington 20 vs Green Bay 17 (at Milwaukee)

Interconference Games
Cleveland 29 at Phoenix 21
Detroit 7 at Kansas City 6
L.A. Raiders 6 at New Orleans 20
Seattle 10 at L.A. Rams 31

Interconference Play
AFC 13 – NFC 15

Cincinnati took a major step towards the AFC Central division title by knocking off the Houston Oilers with surprising ease. After having moved easily to a 28-0 first-quarter lead, there was just the suggestion that they'd relaxed a little too early as the Oilers came back to trail by two touchdowns towards the end of the third quarter. But the Bengals had plenty in reserve and stretched out to a final scoreline of 44-21. Cleveland welcomed the return of quarterback Bernie Kosar and he slipped back into the groove immediately, passing for 314 yards and three touchdowns while the Browns defense was logging six sacks in a 29-21 win over Phoenix. For the second time in the season, Buffalo place-kicker Scott Norwood decided the issue against New England in the dying seconds. On Week Three his 41-yard field goal with 11 seconds remaining had overcome a one-point deficit. This time his 33-yarder with 13 seconds remaining broke a 20-20 deadlock. With a three-game lead and standing at 5-0 in intradivisional play, it would now take an accident of major proportions to keep Buffalo out of the playoffs. Behind them, the Dolphins had made a move with three consecutive victories, but, despite having quarterback Dan Marino pass for the second-highest single-game yardage total in NFL history, 521, they still came up two touchdowns short against the Jets. On the debit side of his performance, Marino's passes had been intercepted five times, three times by rookie free safety Erik McMillan. In the AFC West, all five teams lost, and there

were no hard-luck stories. Quarterback Jim Everett threw three touchdown passes for the third straight week as the Rams handed Seattle a 31-10 loss. San Diego was held scoreless by the Colts while the Broncos were blown out by Pittsburgh, for whom Gary Anderson kicked a club-record six field goals. In Kansas City, the Detroit Lions doubled their win total for the year. The Raiders outgained New Orleans but never recovered from the early second-half shock of having Saints rookie running back Craig (Ironhead) Heyward stomp all over them on a 73-yard touchdown run.

In the NFC there were signs of a pecking order emerging, one felt. Chicago had dealt a stunning, if not a knock-out, punch to the 49ers, who now trailed the Saints by two games and the Rams by one. The return of Doug Williams and another first-class, dual-purpose show by running back Kelvin Bryant helped the Redskins past Green Bay. Against the Giants, Atlanta went into self-destruct, allowing their opponents to come back with 14 points in the last two minutes. And a similar fate befell the Cowboys, against whom Randall Cunningham carved out fourth-quarter, touchdown-scoring drives of 99 and 85 yards. The killer blow, a two-yard touchdown pass to running back Anthony Toney, came with just four seconds left.

Above: It was a bitter-sweet day for Miami quarterback Dan Marino.

Right: Wade Wilson passed for 335 yards and three touchdowns as the Vikings rolled over Tampa Bay.

STANDINGS

AFC East	W	L	T	PF	PA	NFC East	W	L	T	PF	PA
Buffalo	7	1	0	171	139	N.Y. Giants	5	3	0	177	168
N.Y. Jets	4	3	1	182	164	Washington	5	3	0	199	171
Miami	4	4	0	159	168	Philadelphia	4	4	0	179	160
Indianapolis	3	5	0	150	156	Phoenix	4	4	0	198	186
New England	3	5	0	125	192	Dallas	2	6	0	138	166
AFC Central						**NFC Central**					
Cincinnati	7	1	0	236	155	Chicago	7	1	0	157	83
Cleveland	5	3	0	130	116	Minnesota	5	3	0	184	138
Houston	5	3	0	174	196	Detroit	2	6	0	102	153
Pittsburgh	2	6	0	169	213	Green Bay	2	6	0	160	159
AFC West						Tampa Bay	2	6	0	151	216
Denver	4	4	0	167	140	**NFC West**					
Seattle	4	4	0	141	160	New Orleans	7	1	0	180	137
L.A. Raiders	3	5	0	174	206	L.A. Rams	6	2	0	230	140
San Diego	2	6	0	102	169	San Francisco	5	3	0	175	151
Kansas City	1	6	1	102	132	Atlanta	1	7	0	142	220

Outstanding Individual Performances

100 Yards Rushing
Eric Dickerson (Indianapolis) 30-169-14-0
Kelvin Bryant (Washington) 27-140-25-0
John Stephens (New England) 25-134-17-1
Earl Ferrell (Phoenix) 18-110-21-1
Craig Heyward (New Orleans) 11-109-73t-1
Rodney Carter (Pittsburgh) 11-105-64t-1
Marcus Allen (L.A. Raiders) 20-102-20-0
James Brooks (Cincinnati) 16-102-18t-3

100 Yards Pass Receiving
Mervyn Fernandez (L.A. Raiders) 4-155-85t-1
Mark Clayton (Miami) 10-153-45t-2
Mark Duper (Miami) 6-132-56-0
Trumaine Johnson (Buffalo) 6-132-49-0
Anthony Carter (Minnesota) 6-123-39-1
Ray Alexander (Dallas) 8-112-26-1
Stephen Baker (N.Y. Giants) 6-104-23-0
Ricky Nattiel (Denver) 3-102-74t-1
Henry Ellard (L.A. Rams) 7-101-20-0

Passing
Jim Everett (L.A. Rams) 27-20-311-0-51-3
Wade Wilson (Minnesota) 30-22-335-0-49-3

WEEK NINE

American Football Conference
Cincinnati 16 at Cleveland 23
Denver 23 at Indianapolis 55
Kansas City 10 at Los Angeles Raiders 17
Pittsburgh 20 at New York Jets 24
San Diego 14 at Seattle 17

National Football Conference
Atlanta 27 at Philadelphia 24
Los Angeles Rams 12 at New Orleans 10
Minnesota 21 at San Francisco 24
New York Giants 13 at Detroit 10 (OT)
Phoenix 16 at Dallas 10

Interconference Games
Chicago 7 at New England 30
Green Bay 0 at Buffalo 28
Miami 17 at Tampa Bay 14
Washington 17 at Houston 41

Interconference Play
AFC 17 – NFC 15

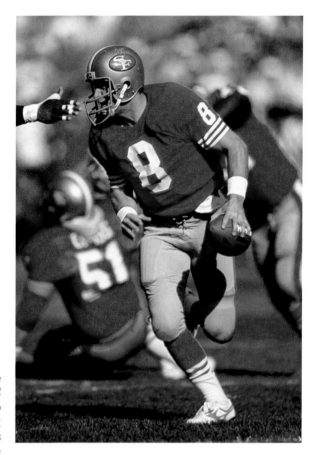

Week Nine saw all five AFC East teams win. Three of their victories were at the expense of the NFC Central and, with Minnesota losing to San Francisco and Detroit going down in overtime to the Giants, it meant that all five NFC Central teams lost. The Jets grabbed all the loot (dare one say?) thanks to rookie cornerback John Booty, who set up touchdowns by blocking a punt and recovering a muffed punt, and then intercepted a pass to snuff out the Steelers' final threat. The day's top rushing performance came from Eric Dickerson, who ran for 159 yards and four touchdowns as the Colts bullied Denver, 55-23. Dickerson's yardage total took him to 1,038 for the campaign, giving him his sixth straight 1,000-yards-rushing season and tying the NFL record held jointly by Walter Payton and Franco Harris.

Looking more closely at the interconference games, as expected the Bills overcame Green Bay, though a shutout always adds a little gloss. Again, Miami did appear to have an edge going into their game with Tampa Bay, and it was by that margin, just an edge, that they held on in the face of a fourth-quarter, 14-point rally by their intrastate rival. But the shock of the day had to be New England's win against Chicago. And they didn't simply win. With rookie John Stephens leading the way, they ran all over the Bears, who also suffered the loss of starting quarterback Jim McMahon for what was projected to be six weeks. In the one other interconference game, Houston wide receiver Drew Hill caught nine passes for 148 yards and three touchdowns as the

Oilers dismissed the Redskins and capitalised on an unexpected loss by the Bengals.

Up in Cleveland, a touchdown by Herman Fontenot on a one-yard blocked punt return was critical in the Browns' win over Cincinnati. The result meant that, despite having started by winning their first six games, the Bengals now stood only one game clear of both Cleveland and Houston. In the NFC West, too, the clubs took closer order as San Francisco moved to within one game of the lead which the Rams now shared with New Orleans, whom they had beaten 12-10. In the NFC East, the shuffling continued. Phoenix had rallied for victory against Dallas, with the game-clincher, the second of two fourth-quarter Earl Ferrell touchdowns, coming with only 50 seconds remaining. Despite outgaining Atlanta by 424 net offensive yards to 294, and logging 25 first downs to 11, Philadelphia had been upset by the Falcons, for whom second-year quarterback Chris Miller threw three touchdown passes. Slender though the Giants' victory over lowly Detroit had been, New York had emerged as the most likely to win that division. You could feel it in your bones.

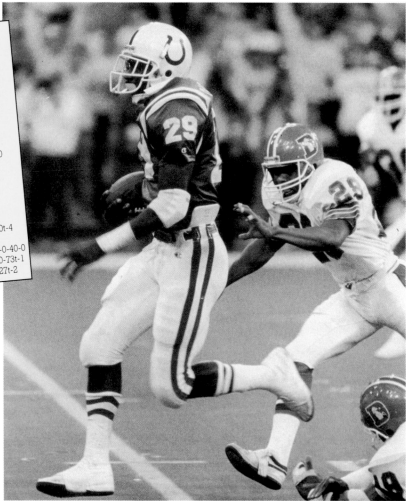

Outstanding Individual Performances

100 Yards Rushing
Eric Dickerson (Indianapolis) 21-159-41t-4
John Stephens (New England) 35-124-11-0
Thurman Thomas (Buffalo) 23-116-16-0
Earl Ferrell (Phoenix) 19-110-47-1

100 Yards Pass Receiving
Drew Hill (Houston) 9-148-33t-3
Mark Carrier (Tampa Bay) 9-142-23-0
Clarence Weathers (Cleveland) 7-140-49-0
Eric Martin (New Orleans) 6-132-31-0
Irving Fryar (New England) 3-122-80t-1
Bill Brooks (Indianapolis) 3-108-53t-1

Passing
Gary Kubiak (Denver) 16-12-138-0-48t-2
Doug Flutie (New England) 18-6-165-0-80t-4
Chris Miller (Atlanta) 23-10-235-0-49t-3
Chris Chandler (Indianapolis) 13-10-167-0-40-0
Steve Young (San Francisco) 25-14-232-0-73t-1
Joe Ferguson (Tampa Bay) 37-26-291-1-27t-2

Left: Backup quarterback Steve Young's late, 49-yard touchdown ramble gave the 49ers victory over Minnesota.

Right: Eric Dickerson ran for four touchdowns in the first half against Denver.

STANDINGS

AFC East	W	L	T	PF	PA	NFC East	W	L	T	PF	PA
Buffalo	8	1	0	199	139	N.Y. Giants	6	3	0	190	178
N.Y. Jets	5	3	1	206	184	Phoenix	5	4	0	214	196
Miami	5	4	0	176	182	Washington	5	4	0	216	212
Indianapolis	4	5	0	205	179	Philadelphia	4	5	0	203	187
New England	4	5	0	155	199	Dallas	2	7	0	148	182
AFC Central						**NFC Central**					
Cincinnati	7	2	0	252	178	Chicago	7	2	0	164	113
Cleveland	6	3	0	153	132	Minnesota	5	4	0	205	162
Houston	6	3	0	215	213	Detroit	2	7	0	112	166
Pittsburgh	2	7	0	189	237	Green Bay	2	7	0	160	187
AFC West						Tampa Bay	2	7	0	165	233
Seattle	5	4	0	158	174	**NFC West**					
Denver	4	5	0	190	195	L.A. Rams	7	2	0	242	150
L.A. Raiders	4	5	0	191	216	New Orleans	7	2	0	190	149
San Diego	2	7	0	116	186	San Francisco	6	3	0	199	172
Kansas City	1	7	1	112	149	Atlanta	2	7	0	169	244

WEEK TEN

American Football Conference
Buffalo 13 at Seattle 3
Cleveland 17 at Houston 24
Kansas City 11 at Denver 17
Los Angeles Raiders 13 at San Diego 3
Miami 10 at New England 21
New York Jets 14 at Indianapolis 38
Pittsburgh 7 at Cincinnati 42

National Football Conference
Dallas 21 at New York Giants 29
Detroit 17 at Minnesota 44
Green Bay 0 at Atlanta 20
Los Angeles Rams 24 at Philadelphia 30
New Orleans 24 at Washington 27
San Francisco 23 at Phoenix 24
Tampa Bay 10 at Chicago 28

Interconference Play
AFC 17 – NFC 15

The trial of strength on Week Ten pitted the NFC East against the leading three NFC West teams and, in each case, the East came out on top. With Randall Cunningham passing for 323 yards and three touchdowns, Philadelphia went out to a 27-10 lead over the Rams before withstanding a late charge led by the Rams' duo of quarterback Jim Everett and wide receiver Henry Ellard. Against Washington, New Orleans scored first and took a 24-17 lead into the final quarter, but a drive of 94 yards for a touchdown, and another of 64 yards for a late field goal, gave the Redskins a three-point advantage which held up when the Saints' Morten Andersen failed on a 49-yard field goal attempt with four seconds remaining. Leading by the score of 23-0 late in the third quarter, the 49ers, with Steve Young in at quarterback for the injured Joe Montana, were overhauled by an Al Del Greco field goal and three Neil Lomax touchdown passes, the final one to wide receiver Roy Green coming with three seconds left. The Giants stayed one game clear at the top by handing the Cowboys their sixth straight loss. In the NFC Central, Chicago and Minnesota stretched further out with victories which came against divisional rivals. Earlier in the week, Chicago head coach Mike Ditka had suffered a mild heart attack and defensive coordinator Vince Tobin was in charge for the win over Tampa Bay. For Minnesota's future rivals, the form of wide receiver Anthony Carter looked ominous. Carter caught eight passes for a regular-season, career-best 188 yards. He didn't catch a scoring pass but he did set up touchdowns with receptions of 32, 40, 28, 26 and 17 yards.

In the AFC, Cincinnati returned to their best with an emphatic victory over a Pittsburgh team which was now doomed to making up the numbers for the remainder of the way. For Cincinnati, rookie running back Ickey Woods, who logged his second 100-yards-rushing game of the season, was becoming an important factor. Behind Cincinnati, Houston moved into sole possession of second place by beating Cleveland with something to spare. The Oilers had 11 first downs rushing as they controlled possession for almost 36 minutes. By way of consolation, Cleveland tight end Ozzie Newsome became only the sixth player in league history to catch 600 or more passes. In the AFC East, the domestic competition saw the Colts claw back into a contending position as they maintained a charge which produced their fourth straight win. Together with New England and Miami, they were four games behind Buffalo, but they were up with the AFC pack in the

Anthony Carter played a big part in the Vikings' win over Detroit.

Defensive tackle Jerome Brown was dominant in Philadelphia's defeat of the Rams.

Outstanding Individual Performances

100 Yards Rushing
Roger Craig (San Francisco) 26-162-25-1
Ickey Woods (Cincinnati) 10-110-56-0
John Stephens (New England) 25-104-13t-1

100 Yards Pass Receiving
Eddie Brown (Cincinnati) 7-216-86t-2
Anthony Carter (Minnesota) 8-188-40-0
Henry Ellard (L.A. Rams) 7-166-68-1
Eric Martin (New Orleans) 10-146-33-1
Jim Jensen (Miami) 12-110-17-0
Lionel Manuel (N.Y. Giants) 5-106-46-0
Al Toon (N.Y. Jets) 13-106-17-0
Ray Alexander (Dallas) 8-103-23-1

Passing
Boomer Esiason (Cincinnati) 23-16-318-2-86t-3
Wade Wilson (Minnesota) 35-28-391-1-40-2
Warren Moon (Houston) 17-11-182-0-42-1
Doug Williams (Washington) 28-20-299-1-46-2
Mike Tomczak (Chicago) 26-18-269-1-46-2
Neil Lomax (Phoenix) 41-25-323-0-35t-3
Randall Cunningham (Philadelphia) 39-22-323-0-37t-3
Bobby Hebert (New Orleans) 32-19-279-0-35-2

STANDINGS

AFC East	W	L	T	PF	PA
Buffalo	9	1	0	212	142
N.Y. Jets	5	4	1	220	222
Indianapolis	5	5	0	243	193
Miami	5	5	0	186	203
New England	5	5	0	176	209
AFC Central					
Cincinnati	8	2	0	294	185
Houston	7	3	0	239	230
Cleveland	6	4	0	170	156
Pittsburgh	2	8	0	196	279
AFC West					
Denver	5	5	0	207	206
L.A. Raiders	5	5	0	204	219
Seattle	5	5	0	161	187
San Diego	2	8	0	119	199
Kansas City	1	8	1	123	166
NFC East	**W**	**L**	**T**	**PF**	**PA**
N.Y. Giants	7	3	0	219	199
Phoenix	6	4	0	238	219
Washington	6	4	0	243	236
Philadelphia	5	5	0	233	211
Dallas	2	8	0	169	211
NFC Central					
Chicago	8	2	0	192	123
Minnesota	6	4	0	249	179
Detroit	2	8	0	129	210
Green Bay	2	8	0	160	207
Tampa Bay	2	8	0	175	261
NFC West					
L.A. Rams	7	3	0	266	180
New Orleans	7	3	0	214	176
San Francisco	6	4	0	222	196
Atlanta	3	7	0	189	244

chase for a wild card spot. Buffalo's victory over Seattle had been secured with all the tension of a club which could feel those playoff nerves beginning to take hold. Meanwhile, Seattle's loss, coupled with victories for both Denver and the Raiders, left those three teams tied for first place in the AFC West.

WEEK ELEVEN

American Football Conference
Buffalo 31 at Miami 6
Cincinnati 28 at Kansas City 31
Cleveland 7 at Denver 30
Houston 24 at Seattle 27
New England 14 at New York Jets 13

National Football Conference
Chicago 34 at Washington 14
Minnesota 43 at Dallas 3
New Orleans 14 at Los Angeles Rams 10
New York Giants 17 at Phoenix 24
Tampa Bay 23 at Detroit 20

Interconference Games
Indianapolis 20 at Green Bay 13
Los Angeles Raiders 9 at San Francisco 3
Philadelphia 27 at Pittsburgh 26
San Diego 10 at Atlanta 7

Interconference Play
AFC 20 – NFC 16

Just when we'd all decided that the West was the AFC's weak division, all five teams won. Three of its teams beat the best three from the Central. With quarterback Dave Krieg back in harness and running back John L. Williams rushing for 102 yards, Seattle matched the visiting Oilers, score for score, before Krieg marched the offense 52 yards to set up Norm Johnson's last-second, 46-yard field goal. In Denver, the Browns barely raised a voice in anger as the Broncos, who converted four Cleveland turnovers into 20 first-half points, raced to a 30-point lead

before their first concession. But the major upset came in Cincinnati, where the home team might have been expected to win in a stroll. Yet the Bengals couldn't shake off a tenacious Chiefs team which rallied for 15 points, the last three coming on Nick Lowery's fifth field goal, a 39-yarder, with two seconds remaining. Both the Raiders and San Diego faced NFC West opponents, and while the Chargers' victory over Atlanta was not that shocking, the Raiders' triumph over San Francisco, and the manner of its making, had to vie for upset-of-the-day honours. The surprise was that they kept the 49ers, Joe Montana, Roger Craig, Jerry Rice and all, out of the end zone in handing their upstate rivals a 9-3 loss. It was the Raiders' third victory in a row and you just wondered if this could be the sign that Al Davis had put together a winner. Pittsburgh's loss to the Eagles completed a blank weekend for the AFC Central.

For Philadelphia, that win, coupled with the Giants' loss to Phoenix, for whom wide receiver Roy Green had the day's best receiving performance, left them trailing by only a game in the NFC East. The Redskins had missed their opportunity to go equal-top in the division by losing to Chicago. More accurately, rather than losing, they were well beaten by a Bears team which had the boost of having head coach Mike Ditka back on the sideline. Minnesota routed Dallas, thus extending to seven a Cowboys losing streak which was the longest since their first season in the NFL. There were signs that the Rams' charge was beginning to falter. Following their loss to Philadelphia, they were defeated by New Orleans in a tense struggle, with Saints quarterback Bobby Hebert out-passing his Rams

STANDINGS											
AFC East	W	L	T	PF	PA	**NFC East**	W	L	T	PF	PA
Buffalo	10	1	0	243	148	N.Y. Giants	7	4	0	236	223
Indianapolis	6	5	0	263	206	Phoenix	7	4	0	262	236
New England	6	5	0	190	222	Philadelphia	6	5	0	260	237
N.Y. Jets	5	5	1	233	236	Washington	6	5	0	257	270
Miami	5	6	0	192	234	Dallas	2	9	0	172	254
AFC Central						**NFC Central**					
Cincinnati	8	3	0	322	216	Chicago	9	2	0	226	137
Houston	7	4	0	263	257	Minnesota	7	4	0	292	182
Cleveland	6	5	0	177	186	Tampa Bay	3	8	0	198	281
Pittsburgh	2	9	0	222	306	Detroit	2	9	0	149	233
AFC West						Green Bay	2	9	0	173	227
Denver	6	5	0	237	213	**NFC West**					
L.A. Raiders	6	5	0	213	222	New Orleans	8	3	0	228	186
Seattle	6	5	0	188	211	L.A. Rams	7	4	0	276	194
San Diego	3	8	0	129	206	San Francisco	6	5	0	225	205
Kansas City	2	8	1	154	194	Atlanta	3	8	0	196	254

Outstanding Individual Performances

100 Yards Rushing
Gary Anderson (San Diego) 24-145-26-0
Lars Tate (Tampa Bay) 18-106-37-1
Merril Hoge (Pittsburgh) 21-102-17-0
Christian Okoye (Kansas City) 16-102-48-1
John L. Williams (Seattle) 13-102-44t-1

100 Yards Pass Receiving
Roy Green (Phoenix) 9-176-49-1
Louis Lipps (Pittsburgh) 6-171-89t-1
Drew Hill (Houston) 8-139-57t-1
Hassan Jones (Minnesota) 3-132-64t-2
Craig McEwen (Washington) 3-120-46-0
Dennis Gentry (Chicago) 5-116-45-1
John Settle (Atlanta) 10-106-27-0

Passing
John Elway (Denver) 30-21-207-0-21-2
Chris Chandler (Indianapolis) 17-9-98-0-24t-2
Jim Kelly (Buffalo) 26-18-211-0-28-1
Neil Lomax (Phoenix) 35-23-353-1-49-2

Left: Cardinals wide receiver Roy Green was back to his best against the Giants.

Below: Wide receiver Louis Lipps caught an 89-yard touchdown pass in the Steelers' one-point loss.

counterpart, Jim Everett. The Rams did have the chance to win but Saints safety Gene Atkins intercepted an end-zone pass inside the final minute. The victory gave New Orleans sole possession of the lead in the NFC West for the first time since Week Eight. At the other end of the football spec-trum, following Detroit's loss to Tampa Bay, head coach Darryl Rogers was fired and replaced by defensive coordinator Wayne Fontes. Curiously, all three of the Buccaneers' victories had come on Donald Igwebuike field goals inside the final 12 seconds.

WEEK TWELVE

American Football Conference
New England 6 at Miami 3
New York Jets 6 at Buffalo 9 (OT)
Pittsburgh 7 at Cleveland 27
Seattle 24 at Kansas City 27

National Football Conference
Chicago 27 at Tampa Bay 15
Detroit 19 vs Green Bay 9 (at Milwaukee)
Philadelphia 23 at New York Giants 17 (OT)
Washington 21 at San Francisco 37

Interconference Games
Atlanta 12 at Los Angeles Raiders 6
Cincinnati 38 at Dallas 24
Denver 0 at New Orleans 42
Indianapolis 3 at Minnesota 12
Phoenix 20 at Houston 38
San Diego 38 at Los Angeles Rams 24

Interconference Play
AFC 23 – NFC 19

Bernie Kosar guided the Browns to victory over Pittsburgh.

Nose tackle Fred Smerlas was the unlikely hero for the Bills, who clinched the AFC East title when they beat the Jets in overtime. Smerlas, a tenth-year veteran, had five tackles, a sack and blocked a field goal attempt to send the game into overtime. Neither team scored a touchdown and the issue was settled by the kickers, with Scott Norwood deciding it after 63 minutes and 47 seconds. For Buffalo the quest now would be to establish home-field advantage in the playoffs. Increasingly, it seemed likely that they would be joined by at least two AFC Central teams and perhaps a third, as all three of Cincinnati, Houston and Cleveland won. The Bengals had handed Dallas its eighth straight loss by a margin which, for Dallas, was made slightly less devastating by two fourth-quarter touchdowns. The task facing Houston, seemingly, was made easier by the absence of the Cardinals' starting quarterback, Neil Lomax. But with his replacement, Cliff Stoudt, passing for three touchdowns, it was as well for the Oilers that their starter, Warren Moon, passed for 266 yards and three touchdowns. The third AFC Central contender, the Browns, used a 77-yard touchdown reception by wide receiver Reginald Langhorne and scored on a blocked punt return as they defeated Pittsburgh 27-7.

In the unpredictable AFC West, the top three teams followed up their victories of Week Eleven by losing - wouldn't you just know it? Even in the windless Superdome, Denver was blown out by New Orleans in what was the biggest margin of victory in Saints history. With four weeks remaining, the Saints were two games clear of both San Francisco, who had beaten Washington comfortably, and the Rams, who had lost unexpectedly to San Diego. The Raiders were stifled by Atlanta, who scored the game's only touchdown after rookie linebacker Aundray Bruce had forced a fumble which he subsequently recovered on the Raiders' 12-yard line. Against Kansas City, Seattle came back with ten fourth-quarter points to tie the scores at 24-24. But Chiefs placekicker Nick Lowery settled that one from 40 yards out with 46 seconds left. It meant that three teams remained tied for the lead in the AFC West. And the same was true in the NFC East, where Philadelphia, which was the only team to win, moved alongside the Giants and Phoenix with victory coming in a most unusual manner. 4:28 remained when Eagles wide receiver Cris Carter recovered teammate Keith Jackson's fumble for the touchdown which took the game into overtime. Six minutes into the extra period, Giants linebacker Lawrence Taylor blocked a 31-yard field goal attempt. But the ball bounced into the arms of Philadelphia defensive end Clyde Simmons, who returned it 15 yards for the winning touchdown.

STANDINGS

AFC East	W	L	T	PF	PA	NFC East	W	L	T	PF	PA
Buffalo†	11	1	0	252	154	N.Y. Giants	7	5	0	253	246
New England	7	5	0	196	225	Philadelphia	7	5	0	283	254
Indianapolis	6	6	0	266	218	Phoenix	7	5	0	282	274
N.Y. Jets	5	6	1	239	245	Washington	6	6	0	278	307
Miami	5	7	0	195	240	Dallas	2	10	0	196	292
AFC Central						**NFC Central**					
Cincinnati	9	3	0	360	240	Chicago	10	2	0	253	152
Houston	8	4	0	301	277	Minnesota	8	4	0	304	185
Cleveland	7	5	0	204	193	Detroit	3	9	0	168	242
Pittsburgh	2	10	0	229	333	Tampa Bay	3	9	0	213	308
AFC West						Green Bay	2	10	0	182	246
Denver	6	6	0	237	255	**NFC West**					
L.A. Raiders	6	6	0	219	234	New Orleans	9	3	0	270	186
Seattle	6	6	0	212	238	L.A. Rams	7	5	0	300	232
San Diego	4	8	0	167	230	San Francisco	7	5	0	262	226
Kansas City	3	8	1	181	218	Atlanta	4	8	0	208	260

†Division Champion

Outstanding Individual Performances

100 Yards Rushing
James Brooks (Cincinnati) 16-148-51t-1
Herschel Walker (Dallas) 27-131-11t-1
Rueben Mayes (New Orleans) 25-115-19-1
Robb Riddick (Buffalo) 18-103-15-0

100 Yards Pass Receiving
Sterling Sharpe (Green Bay) 8-124-27-0
Ernest Givins (Houston) 5-118-46-2
J.T. Smith (Phoenix) 10-114-17-1
Eric Martin (New Orleans) 8-111-40t-2
Stephone Paige (Kansas City) 5-106-49-0
Jerry Rice (San Francisco) 3-105-80t-1
Drew Hill (Houston) 5-100-50t-1

Passing
Bobby Hebert (New Orleans) 23-20-194-0-40t-3
Warren Moon (Houston) 31-17-266-0-50t-3
Boomer Esiason (Cincinnati) 29-16-205-0-28-3
Bernie Kosar (Cleveland) 24-12-204-0-77t-2
Joe Montana (San Francisco) 23-15-218-1-80t-2
Steve Pelluer (Dallas) 23-16-185-1-31-2

Seattle kick returner Bobby Joe Edmonds is given a rough ride by Kansas City.

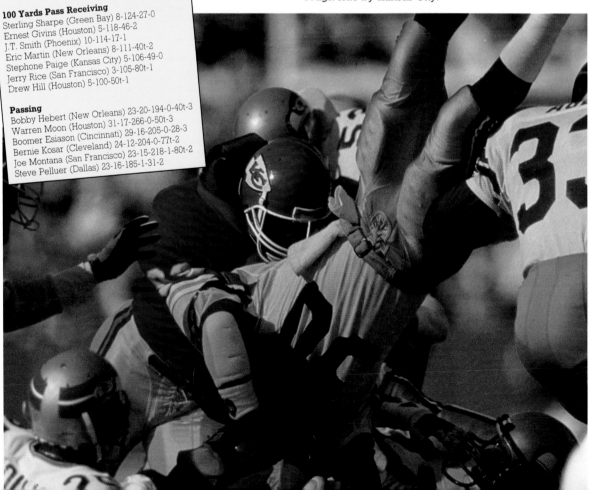

WEEK THIRTEEN

American Football Conference
Buffalo 21 at Cincinnati 35
Kansas City 10 at Pittsburgh 16
Los Angeles Raiders 27 at Seattle 35
Miami 34 at New York Jets 38
New England 21 at Indianapolis 24

National Football Conference
Green Bay 0 at Chicago 16
Minnesota 23 at Detroit 0
New York Giants 13 at New Orleans 12
Phoenix 21 at Philadelphia 31
Tampa Bay 10 at Atlanta 17

Interconference Games
Cleveland 17 at Washington 13
Houston 25 at Dallas 17
Los Angeles Rams 24 at Denver 35
San Francisco 48 at San Diego 10

Interconference Play
AFC 26 – NFC 20

STANDINGS

AFC East	W	L	T	PF	PA
Buffalo†	11	2	0	273	189
Indianapolis	7	6	0	290	239
New England	7	6	0	217	249
N.Y. Jets	6	6	1	277	279
Miami	5	8	0	229	278
AFC Central					
Cincinnati	10	3	0	395	261
Houston	9	4	0	326	294
Cleveland	8	5	0	221	206
Pittsburgh	3	10	0	245	343
AFC West					
Denver	7	6	0	272	279
Seattle	7	6	0	247	265
L.A. Raiders	6	7	0	246	269
San Diego	4	9	0	177	278
Kansas City	3	9	1	191	234
NFC East	**W**	**L**	**T**	**PF**	**PA**
N.Y. Giants	8	5	0	266	258
Philadelphia	8	5	0	314	275
Phoenix	7	6	0	303	305
Washington	6	7	0	291	324
Dallas	2	11	0	213	317
NFC Central					
Chicago*	11	2	0	269	152
Minnesota	9	4	0	327	185
Detroit	3	10	0	168	265
Tampa Bay	3	10	0	223	325
Green Bay	2	11	0	182	262
NFC West					
New Orleans	9	4	0	282	199
San Francisco	8	5	0	310	236
L.A. Rams	7	6	0	324	267
Atlanta	5	8	0	225	270

† Division Champion
* Clinched Playoff Spot

In the meeting of the AFC's 'big two', Buffalo lost possession on four turnovers and that may have made the difference. The crucial lapse came in the fourth quarter when, with the Bills driving for what could have been the tying touchdown, running back Robb Riddick spilled the ball on contact with Cincinnati nose tackle Tim Krumrie. The victorious Bengals hadn't yet clinched a playoff spot but, should they be involved in a head-to-head tie-breaker with Buffalo, they now held the upper hand. Buffalo was joined in the playoffs by the Bears, who clinched at least a wild card spot by blanking Green Bay. However, the victory was at the cost of all-pro defensive end Richard Dent, who broke his left leg, and second-string quarterback Mike Tomczak, who separated a shoulder and would be unavailable for the remainder of the regular season.

Two games adrift of Chicago, Minnesota kept in touch by shutting out Detroit. Over in the NFC East, even though being outplayed in almost every category, the Eagles did themselves a great deal of good by handing Phoenix its second loss in a row. While, then, Philadelphia was establishing a strong position should there be the need for a tie-breaker, the Cardinals were beginning to falter. Washington slipped further behind, losing to a late Earnest Byner 27-yard touchdown run. The Giants caused a little stir in the NFC West, with linebacker Lawrence Taylor putting on one of his irresistable displays in the Giants' one-point defeat of New Orleans. Taylor was involved in ten tackles, had three sacks,

forced two fumbles and, by his threatening presence, caused Saints placekicker Morten Andersen to miss what for him was an easy, 29-yard field goal attempt. The winning points came from Giants placekicker Paul McFadden, who was good from 35 yards out with 21 seconds left. With the Rams losing to Denver – it was their fourth loss in a row – and the 49ers breezing past San Diego, the race in the NFC West was now on again.

There were fireworks in East Rutherford where the Jets set an NFL single-game record with 39 first downs, and wide receiver Al Toon caught 14 passes for 181 yards against Miami. In a losing cause, Dan Marino threw five touchdown passes and the Dolphins had a pair of 100-yard receivers in Ferrell Edmunds and Mark Clayton. The Colts improved

Left: Jerry Rice of San Francisco scored touchdowns on plays covering 96 and 41 yards.

Right: Despite passing for five touchdowns, Miami quarterback Dan Marino was on the losing side.

Outstanding Individual Performances

100 Yards Rushing
Neal Anderson (Chicago) 17-139-80t-2
Curt Warner (Seattle) 27-130-26-0
Ickey Woods (Cincinnati) 26-129-17-3
Kevin Mack (Cleveland) 22-116-14-1
Greg Bell (L.A. Rams) 22-112-15-1
John L. Williams (Seattle) 17-105-24-0

100 Yards Pass Receiving
Al Toon (N.Y. Jets) 14-181-29-0
Jerry Rice (San Francisco) 6-171-96t-2
Henry Ellard (L.A. Rams) 11-167-54t-2
Mark Jackson (Denver) 6-140-58t-2
Stephen Baker (N.Y. Giants) 3-134-85t-1
Ferrell Edmunds (Miami) 2-117-80t-1
Mark Clayton (Miami) 7-116-31t-2
Tim Brown (L.A. Raiders) 4-114-49t-1
Drew Hill (Houston) 9-113-25-1

Passing
Joe Montana (San Francisco) 22-14-271-0-96t-3
Dan Marino (Miami) 35-17-353-0-80t-5
Boomer Esiason (Cincinnati) 25-18-238-0-31-1
Dave Krieg (Seattle) 28-16-220-2-48-5
Wade Wilson (Minnesota) 21-16-186-0-25-0

their position at the expense of their closest divisional rival, the Patriots, with whom they were now tied at 7-6. In the AFC West, Seattle dented the Raiders' impressive record in ABC Monday Night Game appearances. The final difference read only eight points but the victory was comprehensive and, even though the Seahawks remained tied with Denver, they did look the class team of a modest division.

WEEK FOURTEEN

American Football Conference
Denver 20 at Los Angeles Raiders 21
Indianapolis 31 at Miami 28
New York Jets 34 at Kansas City 38
Pittsburgh 37 at Houston 34
San Diego 10 at Cincinnati 27
Seattle 7 at New England 13

National Football Conference
Chicago 3 at Los Angeles Rams 23
Green Bay 14 at Detroit 30
New Orleans 3 at Minnesota 45
Phoenix 7 at New York Giants 44
San Francisco 13 at Atlanta 3
Washington 20 at Philadelphia 19

Interconference Games
Buffalo 5 at Tampa Bay 10
Dallas 21 at Cleveland 24

Interconference Play
AFC 27 – NFC 21

Outstanding Individual Performances

100 Yards Rushing
Eric Dickerson (Indianapolis) 31-169-19-1
Ickey Woods (Cincinnati) 19-141-30t-2
Herschel Walker (Dallas) 25-134-20-1
Joe Morris (N.Y. Giants) 32-122-27-1
John Stephens (New England) 31-121-21-0
Roger Craig (San Francisco) 23-103-14-0

100 Yards Pass Receiving
Louis Lipps (Pittsburgh) 4-166-80t-2
Mark Jackson (Denver) 6-138-63-0
Henry Ellard (L.A. Rams) 6-132-46-1
Ricky Sanders (Washington) 10-128-23-1
Stephone Paige (Kansas City) 4-113-41t-2
Al Toon (N.Y. Jets) 5-102-42-1

Passing
Bernie Kosar (Cleveland) 27-19-308-0-73t-3
Dan Marino (Miami) 32-26-304-1-55-3
Steve DeBerg (Kansas City) 25-16-267-1-41t-3
Chris Chandler (Indianapolis) 15-12-111-0-19t-1
Boomer Esiason (Cincinnati) 19-10-178-0-28-2
Wade Wilson (Minnesota) 22-13-215-1-68t-3
Phil Simms (N.Y. Giants) 20-11-149-0-36-2
Steve Pelluer (Dallas) 32-20-247-0-41-2
Bubby Brister (Pittsburgh) 36-17-311-0-80t-3
Pat Ryan (N.Y. Jets) 25-13-198-0-42t-2

On Week Fourteen, Cincinnati's comfortable win at home to San Diego, coupled with Houston's shock defeat at the hands of Pittsburgh, meant that the Bengals clinched a playoff spot, though the AFC Central division title still was not yet theirs. One fact which escaped most observers was that, despite beating Dallas, Cleveland's only possibility of reaching the playoffs now lay as a wild card.

Taking in the Steelers' defeat of Houston, it was a day of strange results. Who would have dared to predict that Tampa Bay would hold off the powerful Buffalo Bills? And they did it without their last-twelve-seconds specialist, injured kicker Donald Igwebuike, who was replaced by John Carney. The Bills rushed for only 39 net yards and were held on fourth-and-goal from the one in the third quarter. The Rams, losers of four straight games, re-entered the playoff race after restricting Chicago to just a field goal. In mitigation for the defeated Bears, third-string quarterback Jim Harbaugh completed only 11 of 30 passes. Kansas City beat the Jets. Indeed, with their third last-minute win in a four-week period, the Chiefs were establishing a reputation. Trailing the Jets 34-31 and in position, at the one-yard line, to make an easy field goal but with time for only one more play, Kansas City went for the touchdown. Lead blocker Christian Okoye broke his right hand on the play but he did enough to spring rookie running back James Saxon into the end zone for a memorable victory.

By the end of the day, in the AFC West it was 'as

STANDINGS

AFC East	W	L	T	PF	PA
Buffalo†	11	3	0	278	199
Indianapolis	8	6	0	321	267
New England	8	6	0	230	256
N.Y. Jets	6	7	1	311	317
Miami	5	9	0	257	309
AFC Central					
Cincinnati*	11	3	0	422	271
Cleveland	9	5	0	245	227
Houston	9	5	0	360	331
Pittsburgh	4	10	0	282	377
AFC West					
Denver	7	7	0	292	300
L.A. Raiders	7	7	0	267	289
Seattle	7	7	0	254	278
Kansas City	4	9	1	229	268
San Diego	4	10	0	187	305
NFC East	W	L	T	PF	PA
N.Y. Giants	9	5	0	310	265
Philadelphia	8	6	0	333	295
Phoenix	7	7	0	310	349
Washington	7	7	0	311	343
Dallas	2	12	0	234	341
NFC Central					
Chicago*	11	3	0	272	175
Minnesota	10	4	0	372	188
Detroit	4	10	0	198	279
Tampa Bay	4	10	0	233	330
Green Bay	2	12	0	196	292
NFC West					
New Orleans	9	5	0	285	244
San Francisco	9	5	0	323	239
L.A. Rams	8	6	0	347	270
Atlanta	5	9	0	228	283

† Division Champion
* Clinched Playoff Spot

Above left: Raiders defensive end Greg Townsend returned an interception 86 yards for a touchdown.

Above right: Washington's Ricky Sanders savours a ten-reception day against Philadelphia.

you were', with three teams once more tied for the lead. In losing to New England, Seattle had been restricted to just 65 net offensive yards and a mere two first downs. Against Denver, the Raiders opened up in fine style, careering to a 21-0, third-quarter lead. Their problems began with the casual acceptance of a penalty when rejection of that apparent bounty would have been the smart thing. With that possession Denver quarterback John Elway sparked a charge which left the Broncos, tantalisingly, only one point short of their goal.

Chicago's loss, coupled with Minnesota's ruthless disposing of New Orleans, left the Vikings trailing by only one game, with the return fixture against Chicago still to come. And if the Vikings had looked frighteningly good, so had the Giants, who pulverised Phoenix into third place and, one felt, out of contention. That win capitalised on the Eagles' loss to Washington and took New York into sole possession of the lead in the NFC East.

WEEK FIFTEEN

American Football Conference
Cincinnati 6 at Houston 41
Cleveland 31 at Miami 38
Denver 14 at Seattle 42
Indianapolis 16 at New York Jets 34
Los Angeles Raiders 21 at Buffalo 37
Pittsburgh 14 at San Diego 20

National Football Conference
Atlanta 7 at Los Angeles Rams 22
Dallas 24 at Washington 17
Detroit 12 at Chicago 13
Minnesota 6 at Green Bay 18
New Orleans 17 at San Francisco 30
Philadelphia 23 at Phoenix 17

Interconference Games
Kansas City 12 at New York Giants 28
Tampa Bay 7 at New England 10 (OT)

Interconference Play
AFC 28 – NFC 22

The Chicago Bears clinched their fifth NFC Central division title in a row but it was hardly in the style of a perennial champion, and they gained help from an unexpected source. Against the lowly Detroit Lions, the Bears struggled all the way and trailed by the score of 12-10 with only 5:48 remaining in the game. However, second-year quarterback Jim Harbaugh drove the Bears 55 yards to set up Kevin Butler's 32-yard field goal, which came with just four seconds left. More than just winning a game, Butler's score clinched a title, for the Packers were in the process of putting the Vikings out of the hunt with a memorable 18-6 victory. In the frozen conditions, the Vikings were unable to establish their rushing game and Packers linebacker Tim Harris had two sacks and trapped Vikings quarterback Wade Wilson for a fourth-quarter safety. The loss left Minnesota seeking a wild card slot in the playoffs. In San Francisco, the 49ers clinched at least a wild card berth with a performance which head coach Bill Walsh described as '. . . our best game of the season'. And even allowing for the euphoria of the moment, the 49ers did look good value in their 30-17 victory, which left the defeated New Orleans needing to beat Atlanta on the final weekend and hope that several other results went their way.

Of the ten other clubs still chasing their dreams, the Oilers had by far the most impressive outing as they routed the playoff-bound Cincinnati Bengals, 41-6. Victory over Cleveland in the final game,

coupled with a loss by Cincinnati, would give Houston the AFC Central division title. Against Miami on Monday Night, Don Strock, who had spent 15 years with the Dolphins before being released in August, 1988, came in for an injured Bernie Kosar and threw two fourth-quarter touchdown passes to bring the Browns into a 31-31 tie with 59 seconds remaining. But Dan Marino needed only 25 seconds to drive for the winning touchdown. Perhaps he didn't fancy playing in overtime. The Browns now needed to beat Houston to clinch a wild card spot. Another club, the Patriots, simply hates overtime – they'd lost all ten of their previous games which had gone into the extra period. More than halting that sequence and beating the Buccaneers, Jason Staurovsky's 27-yard overtime field goal meant that the Patriots

STANDINGS

AFC East	W	L	T	PF	PA
Buffalo†	12	3	0	315	220
New England	9	6	0	240	263
Indianapolis	8	7	0	337	301
N.Y. Jets	7	7	1	345	333
Miami	6	9	0	295	340
AFC Central					
Cincinnati*	11	4	0	428	312
Houston	10	5	0	401	337
Cleveland	9	6	0	276	265
Pittsburgh	4	11	0	296	397
AFC West					
Seattle	8	7	0	296	292
Denver	7	8	0	306	342
L.A. Raiders	7	8	0	288	326
San Diego	5	10	0	207	319
Kansas City	4	10	1	241	296
NFC East	**W**	**L**	**T**	**PF**	**PA**
N.Y. Giants	10	5	0	338	277
Philadelphia	9	6	0	356	312
Phoenix	7	8	0	327	372
Washington	7	8	0	328	367
Dallas	3	12	0	258	358
NFC Central					
Chicago†	12	3	0	285	187
Minnesota	10	5	0	378	206
Detroit	4	11	0	210	292
Tampa Bay	4	11	0	240	340
Green Bay	3	12	0	214	298
NFC West					
San Francisco*	10	5	0	353	256
L.A. Rams	9	6	0	369	277
New Orleans	9	6	0	302	274
Atlanta	5	10	0	235	305

†Division Champion
*Clinched Playoff Spot

Quarterback Steve Pelluer passed for 333 yards and three touchdowns as Dallas confounded the form against Washington.

needed only to win on the final weekend to be certain of a wild card spot. For the Giants, who beat Kansas City, victory against the Jets would bring them the title in the NFC East. The Eagles needed to win their final game and hope for help from somewhere. In the AFC West, where the Seahawks had eliminated Denver from any kind of contention, the title would be decided in the best possible way - a head-to-head confrontation between Seattle and the Raiders.

Outstanding Individual Performances

100 Yards Rushing
Gary Anderson (San Diego) 26-170-36-0
Joe Morris (N.Y. Giants) 31-140-16-0
Mike Rozier (Houston) 22-126-15t-3
Curt Warner (Seattle) 23-126-18-4
Roger Craig (San Francisco) 22-115-28-1
John L. Williams (Seattle) 20-109-12-0
Thurman Thomas (Buffalo) 14-106-37t-1
William Howard (Tampa Bay) 23-101-20-0
Freeman McNeil (N.Y. Jets) 23-100-13-1

100 Yards Pass Receiving
Ernie Jones (Phoenix) 6-166-93t-1
Michael Irvin (Dallas) 6-149-61t-3
Mark Jackson (Denver) 7-137-35-1
Pete Holohan (L.A. Rams) 8-126-29-0
Fred Banks (Miami) 6-118-46-0
Mark Clayton (Miami) 8-108-21-2
Perry Kemp (Green Bay) 6-108-29-0
Terry Orr (Washington) 3-104-55t-1
Art Monk (Washington) 7-103-41-0
Al Toon (N.Y. Jets) 7-103-33t-1

Passing
Dave Krieg (Seattle) 22-19-220-0-46-2
Jay Schroeder (L.A. Raiders) 24-14-227-0-57-2
Steve Pelluer (Dallas) 36-21-333-1-61t-3
Warren Moon (Houston) 25-14-254-1-42-2
Mark Malone (San Diego) 24-17-148-0-45-1

WEEK SIXTEEN

American Football Conference
Buffalo 14 at Indianapolis 17
Houston 23 at Cleveland 28
Kansas City 13 at San Diego 24
Miami 24 at Pittsburgh 40
New England 10 at Denver 21
Seattle 43 at Los Angeles Raiders 37

National Football Conference
Atlanta 9 at New Orleans 10
Chicago 27 at Minnesota 28
Detroit 10 at Tampa Bay 21
Green Bay 26 at Phoenix 17
Los Angeles Rams 38 at San Francisco 16
Philadelphia 23 at Dallas 7

Interconference Games
New York Giants 21 at New York Jets 27
Washington 17 at Cincinnati 20 (OT)

Interconference Play
AFC 30 – NFC 22

On Saturday of the final weekend, Cincinnati clinched the AFC Central division title by beating Washington in overtime on a Jim Breech, 20-yard field goal. With only five seconds remaining in regulation time, the Bengals had been let off when the Redskins' Chip Lohmiller hit the upright with a 29-yard field goal attempt. Later, on Saturday, the Patriots relinquished control of their own destiny by losing to Denver. Also, it opened a window for the Colts, who needed a win against Buffalo and then to have Houston beat Cleveland, to earn a wild card spot. And the first part came true, or rather, the Colts made it come true with Eric Dickerson rushing for 166 yards in their upset of the Bills. That result ensured two things, namely, that Cincinnati would have the home-field advantage throughout the playoffs and that New England definitely was out. A great deal rested on the Browns-Oilers game and it was an encounter befitting the occasion.

Way back in the playoffs following the 1981 season, against San Diego, Don Strock came in for starter David Woodley and completed 29 of 43 passes for 403 yards and four touchdowns as he rallied Miami from a 24-point deficit only to lose, 41-38, in overtime. In this 'must game' against Houston, he put on another show and this time he won. However, for Strock, the opening quarter was little short of disastrous as he threw three interceptions, one of which was returned directly for a touchdown. But then the 'old-timer' went to work, directing touchdown-scoring drives of 63, 78 and 89 yards as

the Browns clawed their way back from a 16-point deficit for the win which assured them of home-field advantage in the wild card game. Again they would entertain Houston, who had been assured of a wild-card spot by Denver's win. However, Houston's loss eliminated the Colts. The AFC playoff picture was completed when Seattle out-gunned the Raiders in Los Angeles to win the title in the West. Seahawks quarterback Dave Krieg passed for 410 yards and four touchdowns, and Norm Johnson tied his own club record with five field goals.

In the NFC, the Giants were within five minutes of victory and, with it, the Eastern division title, only to lose to the Jets on a late, Al Toon touchdown reception. Philadelphia duly took that title with a 23-7 win over Dallas, for whom the only consolation was that they'd have the first pick in the 1989 collegiate draft. The Vikings had secured a wild card spot even before they took to the field, but they won anyway and what better boost did they need than to beat the Bears? The 49ers were even better off, being certain of the title in the NFC West, thanks, curiously, to the Saints' win which meant that, at worst, there would be a three-way tie-breaker from which the 49ers had to come out on top. So the 49ers were in relaxed mood when they entertained a hungry Rams team on Sunday evening. The result, a Rams victory, was not unpredictable. It eliminated the Giants and gave the Rams the final wild card spot. The battle lines now were drawn.

Outstanding Individual Performances

100 Yards Rushing
Gary Anderson (San Diego) 34-217-36-1
Eric Dickerson (Indianapolis) 36-166-14-0
Jamie Morris (Washington) 45-152-12-0
John Stephens (New England) 17-130-52-1
Dalton Hilliard (New Orleans) 25-127-36-0
Neal Anderson (Chicago) 22-122-51t-1
Warren Williams (Pittsburgh) 16-117-33-0
Ickey Woods (Cincinnati) 18-115-24-0

100 Yards Pass Receiving
John L. Williams (Seattle) 7-180-75t-1
Webster Slaughter (Cleveland) 6-136-41-1
Brian Blades (Seattle) 4-123-55-2
Ricky Sanders (Washington) 6-120-45-1
Ernest Givins (Houston) 6-119-31-0
Eddie Brown (Cincinnati) 2-115-69t-1
Mervyn Fernandez (L.A. Raiders) 4-113-54t-1
Scott Schwedes (Miami) 4-110-42-0
Willie Gault (L.A. Raiders) 2-108-57-1
Dennis McKinnon (Chicago) 4-106-76t-1

Passing
Dave Krieg (Seattle) 32-19-410-1-75t-4
Gary Hogeboom (Indianapolis) 15-10-89-0-19-2
Boomer Esiason (Cincinnati) 19-10-187-0-69t-2
Doug Williams (Washington) 22-17-217-1-45-2
Ken O'Brien (N.Y. Jets) 26-16-214-0-49-2
Phil Simms (N.Y. Giants) 33-18-230-0-36-3
Jim Kelly (Buffalo) 29-17-204-0-26-2

STANDINGS

AFC East	W	L	T	PF	PA		NFC East	W	L	T	PF	PA
Buffalo†	12	4	0	329	237		Philadelphia†	10	6	0	379	319
Indianapolis	9	7	0	354	315		N.Y. Giants	10	6	0	359	304
New England	9	7	0	250	284		Washington	7	9	0	345	387
N.Y. Jets	8	7	1	372	354		Phoenix	7	9	0	344	398
Miami	6	10	0	319	380		Dallas	3	13	0	265	381
AFC Central							**NFC Central**					
Cincinnati†	12	4	0	448	329		Chicago†	12	4	0	312	215
Cleveland*	10	6	0	304	288		Minnesota*	11	5	0	406	233
Houston*	10	6	0	424	365		Tampa Bay	5	11	0	261	350
Pittsburgh	5	11	0	336	421		Detroit	4	12	0	220	313
AFC West							Green Bay	4	12	0	240	315
Seattle†	9	7	0	339	329		**NFC West**					
Denver	8	8	0	327	352		San Francisco†	10	6	0	369	294
L.A. Raiders	7	9	0	325	369		L.A. Rams*	10	6	0	407	293
San Diego	6	10	0	231	332		New Orleans	10	6	0	312	283
Kansas City	4	11	1	254	320		Atlanta	5	11	0	244	315

† Division Champion
* Wild Card

Fullback John L. Williams (right) and quarterback Dave Krieg (below) combined to clinch the AFC West title for Seattle.

WEEK SEVENTEEN – WILD CARD WEEKEND

AFC Houston 24 at Cleveland 23

Yet another cruel injury to a Browns starting quarterback and one or two doubtful official decisions which did not go Cleveland's way, were just some of the ingredients in a cauldron which boiled over on more than one occasion as the players engaged in the 'noble art'. But the Oilers can hardly be blamed for taking their chances as they came and, in the end, they were the deserved winners. The first sign of Houston power came after Cleveland had taken a three-point lead. Quarterback Warren Moon engineered a 91-yard drive which he finished off with a 14-yard touchdown pass to running back Allen Pinkett. Fifteen seconds later, on the very next play following a fumble by Cleveland quarterback Don Strock, Pinkett ran 16 yards for a touchdown.

With reserve Mike Pagel in at quarterback for the injured Strock, the Browns rallied, slowly at first on two Matt Bahr field goals, and then into the lead with Pagel's 14-yard touchdown pass to wide receiver Webster Slaughter. But when another team might have folded, the Oilers regrouped for a 76-yard drive culminating in Lorenzo White's one-yard touchdown scamper. A field goal by Houston's Tony Zendejas, with just under two minutes remaining, left Cleveland trailing by eight points and needing to score twice. As a final act of defiance, they managed one score, Pagel's second touchdown pass to Slaughter, but that was all.

Below: Browns quarterback Don Strock makes the critical fumble.

Right: Allen Pinkett rammed home the advantage for Houston.

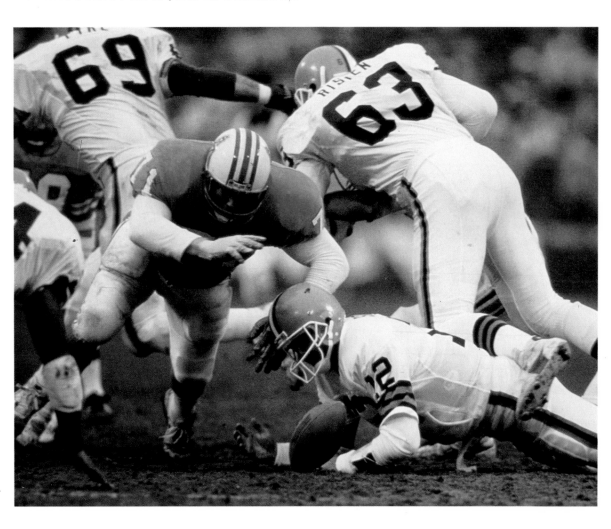

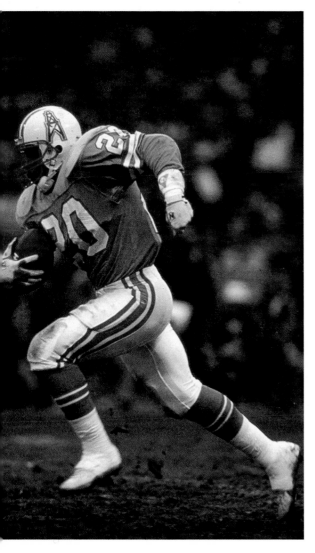

NFC   Los Angeles Rams 17 at Minnesota 28

Minnesota strong safety Joey Browner had two key interceptions.

After an early period during which they were adjusting to the occasion, the Vikings established a firm control and ran out the easy winners for the fifth time in the six-game playoff series involving these two great clubs. The opening minutes saw the Rams move smoothly into position for a touchdown strike, only for Minnesota strong safety Joey Browner to intercept a Jim Everett pass at the Vikings' one-yard line and return the ball 26 yards. That launched Minnesota on a drive which ended when running back Alfred Anderson ran seven yards for a touchdown. They scored again 21 seconds later. Once more Browner played a key role, swooping to intercept for the second time and returning the ball 14 yards. One play later, running back Allen Rice rumbled 17 yards into the end zone. Halfway through the second quarter the Rams burst into life, with running back Greg Bell tearing off gains of 22 and 20 yards to set up tight end Damone Johnson's three-yard touchdown reception. But the Vikings counter-punched, moving 84 yards for Anderson's second touchdown run. Had there been a point of slight doubt, it came early in the fourth quarter, with the Vikings protecting an 11-point lead but at third and ten. However, quarterback Wade Wilson confidently flipped the ball to wide receiver Anthony Carter for a 46-yard gain, setting up their fourth touchdown which came on tight end Carl Hilton's five-yard pass reception.

WEEK EIGHTEEN – DIVISIONAL PLAYOFFS

American Football Conference

Seattle 13 at Cincinnati 21

After threatening to overwhelm their opponents, the Bengals must have been just a little relieved to come out with this victory. Behind a dominating offensive line, helped by the crunching blocks of tight end Rodney Holman, Cincinnati drove inexorably for first-half touchdowns, two by Stanley Wilson and a third from Ickey Woods. Seattle's one great opportunity of the first half had gone begging when, after they'd recovered possession of a fumble by Cincinnati punt returner Ira Hillary on the Bengals' 25-yard line, running back John L. Williams fumbled inside the Cincinnati ten. Again, in the third quarter, they came up empty-handed at the Cincinnati three-yard line after being stopped on fourth down. Cincinnati's charge had evaporated while the Seahawks were gradually warming up. And by the final quarter they were hot as touchdowns by Williams, who caught 11 passes for 137 yards, and quarterback Dave Krieg left them trailing by eight points with over six minutes left. However, following Krieg's score, placekicker Norm Johnson missed the critical PAT. And with his failure went the Seahawks' momentum, enabling the Bengals to cruise the rest of the way to the second AFC title game in their history.

Houston 10 at Buffalo 17

The Bills used smothering defense and outstanding special teams play as they moved into their first title game since 1966. And it was as well that strong safety Leonard Smith blocked a punt, defensive end Bruce Smith blocked a field goal attempt and free safety Mark Kelso returned an interception 28 yards down to the Oilers' 18-yard line. The efforts of Leonard Smith and Kelso led to Buffalo points after the offense had failed to score from deep penetrations on its first two possessions. Also, the Bills were helped by a Houston club which repeatedly ran out of steam as it approached the end zone. One critical moment came on the first possession of the second half when the Oilers, who trailed by the score of 7-3, had driven down to the Buffalo two-yard line. Sadly, quarterback Warren Moon's pitchout went astray, eventually rolling out of bounds at the Buffalo 14. On the next play Tony Zendejas failed with a 31-yard field goal attempt. Early in the final quarter, Kelso's interception led to Scott Norwood's 27-yard field goal, which made the score 17-3, but the Oilers were not spent and Mike Rozier's late, one-yard touchdown run cut the deficit to seven points. They even

Cincinnati's Ickey Woods rushed for 126 yards and a touchdown.

forced Buffalo to punt, but returner Curtis Duncan fumbled away their one last possession.

National Football Conference

Philadelphia 12 at Chicago 20

The Eagles led the Bears in almost every category, including first downs by 22 to 14, net offensive yards by 430 to 341 and time of possession by 32:44 to 27:16. Astoundingly, ten times they reached the Chicago 26-yard line or beyond, and yet the most telling statistic of all shows their coming away with only four Luis Zendejas field goals. On a day of missed opportunities, then, Philadelphia saw two apparent touchdowns negated by infringements; they failed on fourth-and-inches at the Chicago four-yard line and brilliant rookie tight end Keith Jackson dropped a straightforward pass when under no pressure inside the Chicago end zone. The Bears had opened in dramatic style with wide receiver Dennis McKinnon catching a 64-yard touchdown pass. A 23-yard

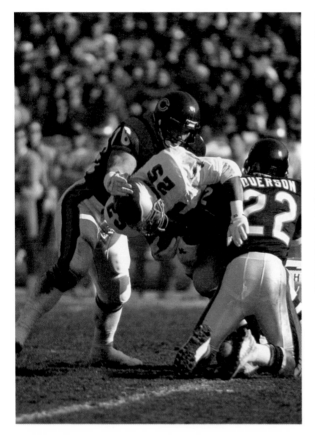

Steve McMichael and Dave Duerson (# 22) put the shackles on Philadelphia running back Anthony Toney.

kickoff return by Glen Kozlowski began the drive which ended with Neal Anderson's second-quarter, four-yard touchdown run, and Thomas Sanders' 58-yard run set up the 46-yard field goal which took the Bears' total to 17 points. In the worsening fog the Eagles came back to trail by only five points, before Kevin Butler's 27-yard field goal extended the margin to eight points. Philadelphia's final thrust foundered at the Bears' 17 when quarterback Randall Cunningham was intercepted for the third time in the game.

Minnesota 9 at San Francisco 34

In a rematch of last year's divisional playoff game, San Francisco overwhelmed Minnesota to march into a confrontation with Chicago for the NFC title. After conceding a 47-yard field goal just over six minutes into the game, the 49ers took control, with quarterback Joe Montana completing his first six passes on the way to combining with wide receiver Jerry Rice for three touchdowns. Each time, Rice had shown brilliant, close-quarter footwork to beat his marker. In the spaces between those scores,

Vikings quarterback Wade Wilson has nowhere to go but down.

Minnesota quarterback Wade Wilson had been controlled by a 49ers defense which went on to sack him a total of six times. Also, 49ers free safety Ronnie Lott intercepted two passes. A touchdown reception by wide receiver Hassan Jones on the Vikings' first possession of the second half suggested a recovery. But it was in the tone of the game that placekicker Chuck Nelson missed the PAT. And in the final quarter San Francisco motored further into the distance on Roger Craig touchdown runs covering four and 80 yards. More than completing a rout, those scores rounded off an offensive display of awesome power, signalling that the 49ers were back in business.

Roger Craig underlined the 49ers' superiority with an 80-yard touchdown run.

WEEK NINETEEN –
CONFERENCE CHAMPIONSHIPS

American Football Conference

Buffalo 10 at Cincinnati 21

Underlining the credibility of regular-season form, the AFC Championship Game brought together the two teams with the best records. They were separated only by the Bengals' Week-Thirteen, 35-21 victory against the Bills, a win which, in the final reckoning, earned Cincinnati the home-field advantage throughout the playoffs. Won-lost records apart, the teams were very different in character with the Bengals' clear strength lying in the AFC's best offense whereas the Bills' success had been built around the AFC's best defense. Looking back to the regular season, the Bills had been the first club to clinch a division title, following which they had gone into a mini-slump as they lost three of their final four games. But they regrouped for the divisional playoffs and had been worthy winners over a very good Houston team. Cincinnati had been in a dog-fight with Cleveland and Houston for most of the way, and they had needed every one of their four wins in the last five regular-season games to establish their position as the AFC's senior playoff team. In the divisional playoffs against Seattle, they had been troubled but not seriously threatened.

It was no real surprise when the Bengals used the rushing game which had been their developing style, and the Bills never quite managed to control rookie Ickey Woods, who carried 29 times for 102 yards. His one-yard run to open the scoring came after Eric Thomas had made one of the Bengals' three interceptions of Buffalo quarterback Jim Kelly. Despite the lack of an effective rushing offense, the Bills stayed in touch and went into half time trailing only by the score of 14-10. The key play of the game came late in the third quarter with the Bengals at 4th-and-4 on the Buffalo 33-yard line. After sending on the punting team, a cunning shift left reserve quarterback Turk Schonert unexpectedly standing over center, from where he took the snap and handed to Stanley Wilson who ran for a six-yard gain. Later in that drive, Woods scored his second touchdown to put the Bengals into the clear at 21-10 and on their way to the Super Bowl.

Boomer Esiason opens up against the Bills.

National Football Conference

Jerry Rice makes the critical move en route to the opening touchdown.

San Francisco 28 at Chicago 3

Despite uncertainty at quarterback and several personnel changes, the Chicago Bears had been no less mean than usual over a regular season for most of which they had been the NFC's leading club. Interestingly, two of their four losses had been against divisional rival Minnesota, though for the Bears there had been nothing resting on the final regular-season encounter when the Vikings had completed the double. At the divisional playoff stage they were not completely impressive against a Philadelphia team which had failed to take advantage of field position on many occasions. And Eagles quarterback Randall Cunningham had exposed their secondary with his 407 yards passing. But they did have a significant advantage over their NFC title-game opponent, San Francisco, who would need to adjust to the hostile conditions of Soldier Field. During the regular season the 49ers had sputtered, with just the odd blowout victory figuring among several close contests. With a record of 10-6, they had gained the title only by the narrow margin for which there was provision in the tie-breaking procedure. In the divisional playoff game, however, they had banished any doubts as they dismissed the talent-laden Vikings with clinical efficiency.

Unexpectedly, it was the Bears who couldn't make the adjustment to the icy conditions underfoot, whereas 49ers wide receiver Jerry Rice had no problem dodging Chicago cornerback Mike Richardson before sheering away for the balance of his 61-yard touchdown reception. Halfway through the second quarter Rice beat the other cornerback, Vestee Jackson, on a 27-yard score. Three minutes before half time, on one of only two occasions that Chicago penetrated the 49ers' 40-yard line, Kevin Butler kicked a 25-yard field goal. But any hopes of a Bears rally were dashed when the 49ers took the opening second-half possession 78 yards for tight end John Frank's five-yard touchdown reception. Tom Rathman's fourth-quarter, four-yard touchdown run only confirmed the inevitable as San Francisco coasted to the NFC Championship by the largest points margin since Dallas beat the Rams 28-0 in January, 1978.

SUPER BOWL XXIII

Cincinnati 16 – San Francisco 20
Joe Robbie Stadium, Miami, Florida,
January 22nd, 1989

How quickly things change. In 1987 the Bengals had gone 4-11 to finish last in the AFC Central and, together with three other clubs, next-to-bottom in the entire NFL. In the space of just one season, head coach Sam Wyche had transformed his charges into the AFC's premier team, a reputation they'd earned over the regular season and then confirmed by knocking off Buffalo in the AFC title game. It was easy to see why Cincinnati had scored more points, 448, than any other NFL team. Quarterback Boomer Esiason had come of age, winning his first NFL passing title with a rating of 97.4. He could call upon a fine trio of wide receivers out of which Eddie Brown and Tim McGee were expected to start ahead of the veteran, Cris Collinsworth. Of the NFL's top ten yardage receivers, Brown's average per reception was a huge 24.0, some 3.6 better than the next best by San Francisco's Jerry Rice. Over the last few weeks of the regular season and through the playoffs, the passing offense had lost its edge. But with running backs James Brooks and the remarkable rookie, Ickey Woods, coming to the boil, there were no worries. The latter certainly was true

Cincinnati's Ickey Woods made good progress in the early going.

about an immense offensive line which was, perhaps, the NFL's best. On defense, Cincinnati had shown uncharacteristic toughness. Indeed, it had been the defense which gave their season its early boost. Their clear strength lay in Tim Krumrie at nose tackle and David Fulcher at strong safety. Both players were original selections to the AFC-NFC Pro Bowl, while cornerback Eric Thomas was a reserve.

San Francisco could not have had a more impressive march through the playoffs, setting the tone with a handsome beating of Minnesota before crushing the Bears at Chicago's Soldier Field. Quarterback Joe Montana, who had entered the regular season not certain even to hold off the challenge of backup Steve Young, was now the unquestioned leader. And in wide receiver Jerry Rice and running back Roger Craig, he had the NFL's most effective one-two punch. In the two playoff games, Rice had caught five touchdown passes while, in the same period, one of Craig's two rushing touchdowns had covered 80 yards. The offensive line was not noted for its physical presence – it was never going to blow opponents away – but it lacked nothing in finesse, with veteran Randy Cross the foundation stone at center. On defense the 49ers were equally imposing, assembled around the backbone represented by nose tackle Michael Carter, inside linebackers Michael Walter and Riki Ellison, and safeties Ronnie Lott and Jeff Fuller. Overall, the 49ers were the more balanced team, in NFL terms ranking second on offense behind Cincinnati but third on defense, the latter being some way ahead of the Bengals, who ranked 15th. Throughout their one and only era of consistent success at the very highest level, the 49ers had been guided by head coach Bill Walsh. In what was a rematch of Super Bowl XVI, Walsh was attempting to become only the second head coach in NFL history to win three Super Bowls and, intriguingly, it was Walsh who gave Bengals head coach Sam Wyche his first coaching job in the pros.

When it came to the big game, rather than the much-anticipated clash of sabres the combatants spent the first half sparring, with the Bengals absorbing slightly more than they gave. And it was a fair reflection of events that the 49ers ended the first quarter with a 3-0 edge. A little into the second quarter, placekicker Mike Cofer should have increased the lead but his 19-yard field goal attempt, made more difficult by a poor snap from center, went wide to the left. Though still being outplayed,

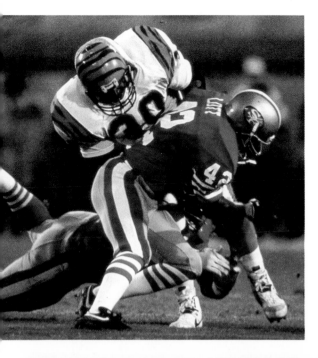

towards half time the Bengals did take advantage of good field position following a 37-yard punt by San Francisco's Barry Helton, when placekicker Jim Breech levelled the scores from 34 yards out.

In the second half Cincinnati began warming to the task, and with Esiason completing passes of 23, 20 and 11 yards, they drove 61 yards for Breech's second field goal. However, with the Bengals having held firm on the 49ers' next possession, Esiason's pass was intercepted by 49ers rookie linebacker Bill Romanowski. More than just setting up the game-tying field goal, Romanowski's theft sparked a scoring burst. For, on the ensuing kickoff following Cofer's 32-yard effort, Cincinnati's Stanford Jennings ran 93 yards unmolested on the second-longest touchdown play in Super Bowl

Left: San Francisco free safety Ronnie Lott bars the way for Ickey Woods.

Below: Stanford Jennings breaks into the clear on his 93-yard kickoff return for a touchdown.

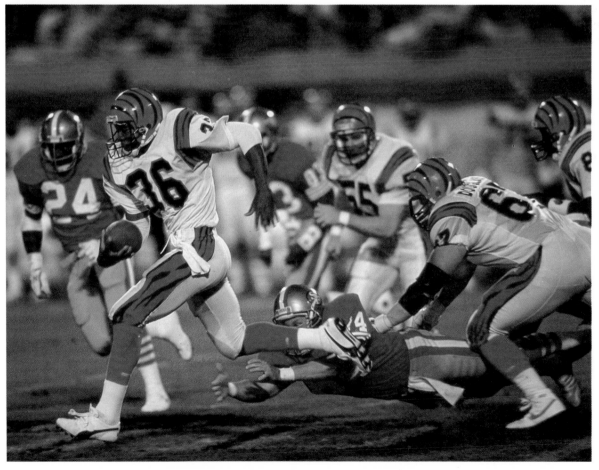

history. Back came the 49ers, as Montana completed passes of 31 yards to Rice and 40 yards to Craig, in a four-play drive which he rounded off with a 14-yard touchdown pass to Rice. After an exchange of possessions, Breech's third field goal left Cincinnati needing to protect a three-point lead with only 3:20 remaining. But Montana required just two minutes and 46 seconds to make the final statement which sealed the result. Completing eight of nine passes (one completion was nullified by a penalty), in an 11-play drive, he took the 49ers 82 yards down to the Cincinnati ten, from where he found unmarked wide receiver John Taylor with the game-icing, ten-yard touchdown pass.

Roger Craig sets off around left end.

In selecting the game's Most Valuable Player, the voters looked beyond both Montana and a first-class, dual-purpose display by Craig, and named Jerry Rice, whose 215 yards receiving established a new Super Bowl record. For the second time in their 21-year existence, then, the Cincinnati Bengals had to be content with the AFC Championship. And even in the harshly competitive world of American sports, where no one remembers who came second, that has to be worth something.

THE GAME

Scoring By Quarters

1st Quarter
San Francisco: Cofer, 41-yard field goal (11:46)
Cincinnati 0 – San Francisco 3

2nd Quarter
Cincinnati: Breech, 34-yard field goal (13:45)
Cincinnati 3 – San Francisco 3

3rd Quarter
Cincinnati: Breech, 43-yard field goal (9:21)
Cincinnati 6 – San Francisco 3
San Francisco: Cofer, 32-yard field goal (14:10)
Cincinnati 6 – San Francisco 6
Cincinnati: Jennings, 93-yard kickoff return; Breech kick (14:26)
Cincinnati 13 – San Francisco 6

4th Quarter
San Francisco: Rice, 14-yard pass from Montana; Cofer kick (0:57)
Cincinnati 13 – San Francisco 13
Cincinnati: Breech, 40-yard field goal (11:40)
Cincinnati 16 – San Francisco 13
San Francisco: Taylor, 10-yard pass from Montana; Cofer kick (14:26)
Cincinnati 16 – San Francisco 20

Below: Not for the first time did Joe Montana rise above the crowd.

Above: 'This is how you make a one-handed catch,' says 49ers wide receiver Jerry Rice.

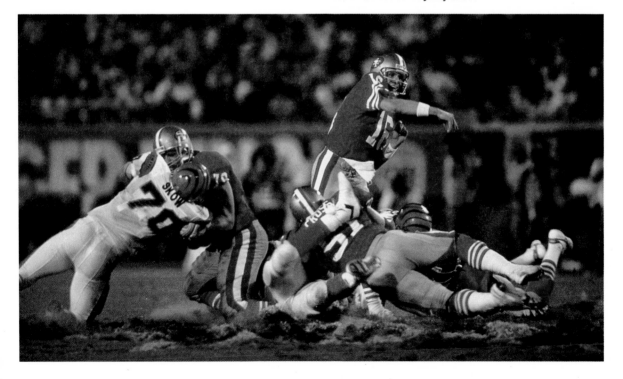

ANATOMY OF SUPER BOWL XXIII
– QUARTER BY QUARTER –

1st Quarter

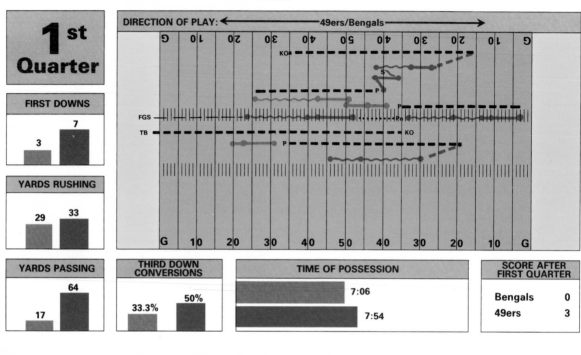

DIRECTION OF PLAY: ← 49ers/Bengals →

FIRST DOWNS

3 | 7

YARDS RUSHING

29 | 33

YARDS PASSING

17 | 64

THIRD DOWN CONVERSIONS

33.3% | 50%

TIME OF POSSESSION

7:06 | 7:54

SCORE AFTER FIRST QUARTER

Bengals 0
49ers 3

2nd Quarter

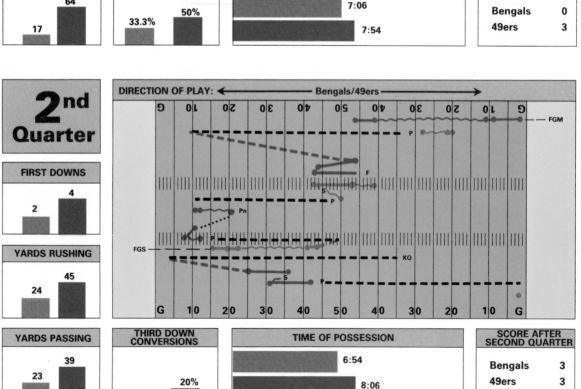

DIRECTION OF PLAY: ← Bengals/49ers →

FIRST DOWNS

2 | 4

YARDS RUSHING

24 | 45

YARDS PASSING

23 | 39

THIRD DOWN CONVERSIONS

0% | 20%

TIME OF POSSESSION

6:54 | 8:06

SCORE AFTER SECOND QUARTER

Bengals 3
49ers 3

KEY

Bengals
49ers

Kickoff/Punt/Interception/Fumble Return
Running Play
Passing play
Kickoff/Punt/Free Kick
Field Goal

Downs ● ●
Penalty yardage ··········

KO – Kickoff
P – Punt
FGS – Field Goal Scored
FGM – Field Goal Missed
S – Sack
TD – Touchdown
Pn – Penalty
TB – Touchback
I – Interception
F – Fumble

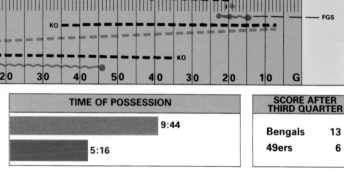

3rd Quarter

DIRECTION OF PLAY: ← Bengals/49ers →

FIRST DOWNS
4 | 3

YARDS RUSHING
22 | 22

YARDS PASSING
54 | 45

THIRD DOWN CONVERSIONS
66.6% | 0%

TIME OF POSSESSION
9:44
5:16

SCORE AFTER THIRD QUARTER
Bengals 13
49ers 6

4th Quarter

DIRECTION OF PLAY: ← 49ers/Bengals →

FIRST DOWNS
4 | 9

YARDS RUSHING
31 | 11

YARDS PASSING
29 | 195

THIRD DOWN CONVERSIONS
25% | 50%

TIME OF POSSESSION
8:59
6:01

FINAL SCORE
Bengals 16
49ers 20

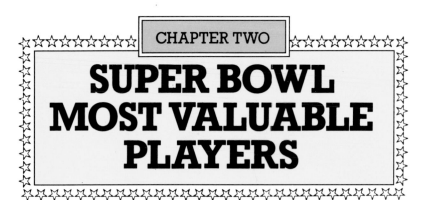

CHAPTER TWO

SUPER BOWL MOST VALUABLE PLAYERS

'Man is a gaming animal. He must always be trying to get the better in something or other.'

Charles Lamb, 1775-1834

He might have thrown footballs – picking out his targets from the maelstrom of bodies with a regularity which defied belief. Perhaps he carried a football into and through the teeth of hell. Maybe he broke spirits. Be it by polish or persuasion, style or stealth, bravery or bravado, cunning or collision, on that special day he was the finest player in the biggest game of all. He was the Super Bowl MVP.

It is hardly surprising that the title of Super Bowl MVP has gone most often to an offensive player – 12 times even to a quarterback – and, in all cases except one, the MVP was on the winning team. The odd man out was linebacker Chuck Howley, whose Dallas Cowboys lost to Baltimore on a late field goal in an error-filled game that came to be known as 'The Stupor Bowl'. A year later however, in Super Bowl VI, Howley was a factor as he set up a touchdown with a 41-yard interception return in the Cowboys' 24-3 victory over Miami.

BART STARR

Bart Starr was at the nerve centre as the quarterback of the Packers teams which won an unprecedented five NFL Championships in the space of seven years, beginning in 1961. It was the fourth of these championships which earned Green Bay the right to meet Kansas City in Super Bowl I. Outwardly, Starr was the least charismatic of many subsequent MVPs. Often described as a mechanic, his greatness lay in precision, field generalship and unswerving composure when under severe pressure. Super Bowl I might have been renamed 'third-down day' as, seven times, Starr converted third downs by passing, including four on a second-quarter drive culminating in the Jim Taylor touchdown run which gave Green Bay a 14-7 lead. The following year, against the physical Oakland Raiders, Starr played the perfect game, nudging the Packers into position for a pair of field goals before going for the jugular with a 62-yard scoring pass to split end Boyd Dowler. In the third quarter, the Packers built on a 16-7 lead with a touchdown-scoring drive which had been sparked by Starr's 35-yard pass completion to backup split end Max McGee. Typical of the man, there is no recorded post-game quote. He'd made his statement on the gridiron.

SUPER BOWL MOST VALUABLE PLAYERS

SUPER BOWL	MVP	POSITION	CLUB
I	Bart Starr	Quarterback	Green Bay
II	Bart Starr	Quarterback	Green Bay
III	Joe Namath	Quarterback	New York Jets
IV	Len Dawson	Quarterback	Kansas City
V	Chuck Howley	Linebacker	Dallas
VI	Roger Staubach	Quarterback	Dallas
VII	Jake Scott	Safety	Miami
VIII	Larry Csonka	Running Back	Miami
IX	Franco Harris	Running Back	Pittsburgh
X	Lynn Swann	Wide Receiver	Pittsburgh
XI	Fred Biletnikoff	Wide Receiver	Oakland
XII	Randy White and	Defensive Tackle	Dallas
	Harvey Martin	Defensive End	Dallas
XIII	Terry Bradshaw	Quarterback	Pittsburgh
XIV	Terry Bradshaw	Quarterback	Pittsburgh
XV	Jim Plunkett	Quarterback	Oakland
XVI	Joe Montana	Quarterback	San Francisco
XVII	John Riggins	Running Back	Washington
XVIII	Marcus Allen	Running Back	LA Raiders
XIX	Joe Montana	Quarterback	San Francisco
XX	Richard Dent	Defensive End	Chicago
XXI	Phil Simms	Quarterback	New York Giants
XXII	Doug Williams	Quarterback	Washington
XXIII	Jerry Rice	Wide Receiver	San Francisco

Bart Starr, MVP in Super Bowls I and II.

LEN DAWSON

A year earlier, the Jets' flamboyant quarterback, Joe Namath, had 'guaranteed' victory against the favoured Baltimore Colts. And he had been as good as his word – with a little help from the Colts who were not at their best – in a 16-7 upset which gave the AFL its first Super Bowl victory. In terms of personality, Len Dawson was altogether different from Namath. His warmth and easy charm would emerge much later from the TV commentary booth. Entering Super Bowl IV, Dawson was a quarterback – a very good quarterback who had won his most recent war with the rival Oakland Raiders – but nothing more than that. And it was perhaps for the lack of a story

Kansas City's Len Dawson underlined the AFL's credibility.

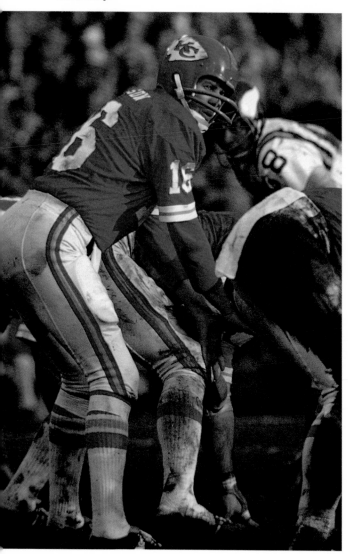

that, approaching the game, the newspapers were not slow to take up the strands of malicious gossip which linked Dawson to a gambling scandal. Added to a year of setbacks, including the death of his father, injuries which had kept him out of six early-season games and a lingering bout of strength-sapping 'flu, the so-called 'revelations' could have finished a man of lesser fibre. The charges were groundless – as Dawson knew – and they were long forgotten by the time he had orchestrated the AFL's second Super Bowl title in a row. The fearsome Minnesota Vikings were kept off-balance for most of the day by a series of finesse plays – feints, shifts, delays and reverses – and were never able to bring their power game into force. Three Jan Stenerud field goals and Mike Garrett's five-yard touchdown run gave Kansas City a 16-0 lead. Dave Osborn's touchdown run cut the Vikings' deficit to nine points but any hopes of a recovery were quashed on the Chiefs' next possession, when Dawson passed 46 yards for a touchdown to wide receiver Otis Taylor.

ROGER STAUBACH

Though in only their 12th NFL year, the Dallas Cowboys entered Super Bowl VI bearing the tag of perennial swooners for the number of times they'd fallen at the final hurdle. In the eyes of the image-destroyers, it counted for nothing that they owned their division, having won the title for the sixth straight time. In addition, in the 1966 and 1967 seasons, they had suffered close defeats in the NFL Championship Game, and they'd lost to a late field goal in Super Bowl V. 'Perennial contenders' would have been a more appropriate description. It was only midway through the 1971 season that head coach Tom Landry installed Roger Staubach as the starting quarterback, ahead of the player with whom Staubach had alternated, Craig Morton. The effect was dramatic as the Cowboys, after opening 4-3, closed out the campaign with seven straight wins. In subsequent years, Staubach would confirm the indications that he was a passer of extreme accuracy but, for the moment, he was still Roger (The Dodger) Staubach, whose scrambling added a new and key dimension to the Dallas offense. In Super Bowl VI, he took time adjusting to the complexities of the Dolphins' defense and, five times in the early going, he was reduced to scrambling on plays which called for a pass. But by the second quarter he was in tune, hitting wide receiver Lance Alworth with passes of 21 and seven yards, the latter for a touchdown. The Cowboys' second touchdown, a three-yard run by Duane Thomas, came after Staubach had used his own judgement and changed the play at the line of scrimmage. For the final touchdown he found tight end Mike Ditka with a seven-yard pass. By

Roger Staubach's poise helped Dallas to its first Super Bowl title.

comparison with the late 1980s, Staubach's statistics, 12 completions out of 19 attempts for 119 yards and two touchdowns, were modest. But he had made the Cowboys the ultimate winner.

FRANCO HARRIS

Canny play by Jake Scott and the earth-moving running of Larry Csonka helped the Miami Dolphins to win consecutive Super Bowl Championships. For three straight years, the Dolphins had been both the class and the power of the AFC. But there was a new force emerging from the industrial smog and grime of blue-collar Pittsburgh, Steeltown USA. Head coach Chuck Noll had been building his contender since the collegiate draft of 1969, when he had selected defensive tackle Joe Greene in the first round and the towering defensive end, L.C. Greenwood, as an outstanding bargain in round ten. Subsequent drafts had been bounteous, notably with the acquisition of quarterback Terry Bradshaw in 1970 and, in 1972, running back Franco Harris. Though

Franco Harris rushed for a Super Bowl-record 158 yards.

having passed a major credibility test by beating the Raiders in the AFC Championship Game, the squad was still some way short of its best and the NFC Champion Minnesota Vikings offered all the trouble any team needed. Throughout a low-scoring, tense, defensive struggle, it was the rushing of Harris which gave Pittsburgh its one consistent offensive weapon. Having seen their favourite trap plays effectively countered by the Vikings, the Steelers began sending Harris off-tackle to the outsides, putting his initial burst to its best use. He scored only one touchdown, winning a nine-yard race to the end zone, but his 34 rushes gained a Super Bowl-record 158 yards. In the end it was his contribution which made the difference.

LYNN SWANN and FRED BILETNIKOFF

Was there ever a greater contrast than between these two wide receivers who were voted MVP in Super Bowls X and XI respectively? Before any game, the urbane Lynn Swann, whose uniform might have carried the label of Saville Row, could be found in private meditation, perhaps contemplation of the flowing, graceful moves which would see him ghosting past his marker. Fred Biletnikoff, on the other hand, might well be the scruffiest wide receiver in

Wide receiver Lynn Swann brought grace to the Super Bowl.

Fred Biletnikoff's sure hands helped the Raiders to victory.

the history of the game – and that was with his helmet on! Wearing the tatters of a uniform, slit at the knees and cut away at the elbows, he was only just within the limits for dress established by the NFL. Adding to his bizarre appearance was a layer of 'stickum', a sickly yellow adhesive substance which subsequently has been banned by the league. Before a game, he'd ventilate his way through one, and into a second pack of cigarettes, at the same time chewing his nails to the quick. He maintained an uneasy co-existence with his stomach ulcer. Yet when it came time to play, each man in his own way could ravage a defense. Swann's advantage over Biletnikoff was speed allied with a barely discernable tremor as he shifted through his automatic gearbox. Biletnikoff had two speeds – not fast and slower – but he could catch a bullet in the dark. Against Dallas in Super Bowl X, Swann gained 161 yards on four catches, one coming on a majestic post pattern and producing a 64-yard touchdown reception. One year on, Biletnikoff's four receptions brought only 79 yards. But the catches were right out of the magician's hat, three of them taking the ball down to the

Minnesota two-yard line or closer and, each time, setting up touchdowns. Just a little more speed could have brought Biletnikoff three touchdowns but he had to settle for the award of MVP.

TERRY BRADSHAW

For the first and only time to date, in Super Bowl XII, two players, Harvey Martin and Randy White, shared the MVP award. And then there came Terry Bradshaw who, in his era, was the best 'money' quarterback in the game. Entering the NFL with the clamour which always accompanies the first pick

The Terry Bradshaw legend gathered substance in Super Bowl XIII.

overall, Bradshaw made a hesitant start, and very quickly the hyperbole turned to derision. The glamour boy had become the hick, the hayseed, the country boy who had no business being in the pros. But every jibe served only to fuel his will to succeed and, coming into Super Bowl XIII, already he had taken the Steelers to two NFL Championships. Facing Dallas for the second time in a Super Bowl, Bradshaw played a controlled game, but he established records for both passing yardage (318) and touchdown passes (4). It was as well since the Cowboys, urged on by Roger Staubach, came back with a flow of passes stemmed by the Steelers' prevent defense and staunched only when Rocky Bleier recovered the Cowboys' final onside kick. A year later, when they faced the Los Angeles Rams, there were some indications that the Steelers were on the wane and they quickly became embroiled in a nip-and-tuck struggle. In the third quarter, Bradshaw unfurled a 47-yard touchdown pass to Lynn Swann but, just under three minutes inside the fourth quarter, they trailed by the score of 19-17 and were in some trouble at third-and-eight on their own 27-yard line. It mattered little that '60 Prevent Slot Hook and Go' had not succeeded in practice during the week leading up to the Super Bowl. Bradshaw called the play anyway, and it was one of the great moments in Super Bowl history – an instant frozen in time – when wide receiver John Stallworth cradled the ball before completing the balance of a 73-yard touchdown play. A little later, Bradshaw found Stallworth with the 45-yard pass which set up a Franco Harris touchdown and sealed the result.

JIM PLUNKETT

The first pick overall in the 1971 draft, Jim Plunkett had five respectable years with the New England Patriots, starting in 56 straight games, but he never quite lived up to his promise. Sent to San Francisco in a trade, his career gently spiralled down and it was for backup insurance that the Raiders picked him up as a free agent in 1978. His big chance came six weeks into the 1980 season and he grabbed it with both hands. Starting quarterback Dante Pastorini had been injured on Week Five and, with the Raiders standing at a depressing 2-3, Plunkett catalysed a charge which saw nine wins and two close defeats. A record of 11-5 launched the Raiders into a playoff series which reached its climax in Super Bowl XV when they faced a powerful Philadelphia against which they had lost, 10-7, on Week Twelve. It was one of the major surprises, not that the Raiders

won but that they were able to handle the NFC's best team with such ease. On defense, outside linebacker Rod Martin intercepted three Ron Jaworski passes and, on offense, Plunkett did the rest. The time for nerves was long gone – he had used up all his disappointments. His opening touchdown pass to wide receiver Cliff Branch needed no more than the timing which, for Plunkett, was woven into the fabric of his being. Later, he needed just a little help from Branch, who stepped in front of Eagles cornerback Roynell Young for the 29-yard touchdown reception which put the result beyond doubt. Inbetween, Plunkett combined with running back Kenny King on what started out as a simple sideline pass but turned into a Super Bowl-record, 80-yard touchdown play. Plunkett, who had been born in the barrio of San Jose, California, the son of blind parents, accepted the MVP award with great dignity.

Super Bowl XV saw Jim Plunkett write the final lines to his fairy tale.

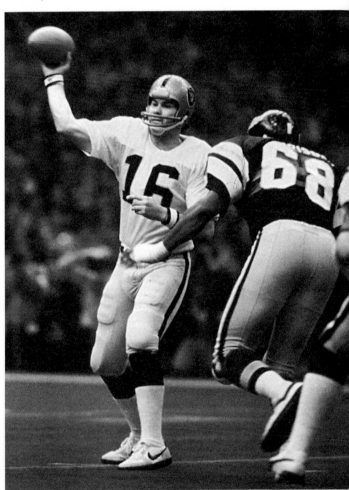

JOE MONTANA

After the 49ers had lost two of their first three games of the 1981 season, not too many heads turned their way until the midway point, at which time they'd won five in a row. Long before the end of that campaign they had clinched the title and, at 13-3, they finished with the best record in the NFL. Even then, more than a few experts needed convincing that here was a winner. In a game of big plays, they disposed of the Giants but that win only earned the most severe test of all – a title game against the playoff-hardened Dallas Cowboys. And it was perhaps in that gripping contest, with a memorable, game-winning 89-yard drive culminating in 'The Catch', wide receiver Dwight Clark's leaping touchdown reception, that the 49ers won hearts and convinced minds. The master at the controls had been quarterback Joe Montana. His first taste of Super Bowl action was anti-climactic, though the Bengals did fight their way back in the second half. A young Montana, who specialised in roll-out passes and throwing on the run, and was a dangerous scrambler, outmanoeuvred the heavy Cincinnati blitz to build up a 20-0 halftime lead. And when the Bengals did threaten with two touchdowns, he still had enough in

reserve to drive for a pair of Ray Wersching field goals. Three years later, a more mature Montana met a challenge of a different kind in the form of the NFL's latest passing sensation, Miami's Dan Marino. On the day, Montana matched everything Marino could muster and a great deal more, as he passed for 331 yards and three touchdowns, while rushing five times for 59 yards, including a six-yard touchdown.

JOHN RIGGINS and MARCUS ALLEN

After four straight years of domination by quarterbacks, there was a reversion to pro football's roots with running backs being voted MVP in successive years. John Riggins had been around for a while, having joined the NFL as the Jets' first-round pick in 1971. A respecter neither of reputation nor convention, it was inevitable that there would be trouble along the way and there was, not lots but enough, and he even sat out the entire 1980 season. He didn't care much either for 'those Xs and Os they show you in the coaching manuals'. 'Out there it just ain't like that,' he'd say. In the strike-shortened 1982 season he had been good but in the playoffs there seemed no heights that he could not scale. One-by-one he put Washington's opponents to the sword, rushing for 119, 185 and 140 yards in the games leading to Super Bowl XVII, where they would face Miami.

The Super Bowl arena was made for Joe Montana.

However, it was only in the final quarter that Riggins' incessant pressure began to tell. With the Redskins four points adrift and at fourth-and-one, he took a handoff and blasted around left end before raging, like no bull ever has, the distance on a 43-yard touchdown play. It was a blow to which the Dolphins could not respond. With Super Bowl records for rushing attempts (38), rushing yards (166) and the longest touchdown run from scrimmage, Riggins was a unanimous choice for MVP.

Marcus Allen could hardly have been more different. Charming, warm and every bit the polished product of USC, he was the perfect multi-purpose back. A fluid runner with a deceptively subtle side-step, also he rated as an excellent blocker and was a prolific receiver. The 1981 Heisman Trophy winner and owner of many collegiate records, Allen was a coach's dream and he had been a success immediately on joining the Raiders in 1982. Against

Above left: Miami finally succumbed to the power of John Riggins.

Above right: Marcus Allen put on a show in Super Bowl XVIII.

Washington in Super Bowl XVIII, Allen just ran and ran. For the first of his two touchdowns, he jinked five yards, untouched, past three bemused Redskins defenders. His second score came on a broken play. With nowhere to go on the left side, he reversed field, wrongfooting the entire Washington cover, before surging into the open acres on a Super Bowl-record, 74-yard touchdown run. A subsequent jaunt raised his total to 191 yards rushing, going beyond the mark set by Riggins a year earlier and earning him a well-deserved rest long before the gun brought down the curtain on a famous Raiders victory.

Phil Simms had perhaps the best title game ever played by a quarterback.

PHIL SIMMS

In the 1986 season, Phil Simms, the oft-injured quarterback of the New York Giants, gave signs that he was gathering for something extraordinary. On several occasions before then, he had edged close to some of the NFL's more expressive achievements, notably when strafing the Cardinals with five touchdown passes in only his second year as a pro and, in 1984, when throwing for 4,044 yards. In that 1986 campaign he led the Giants to 12 straight wins down the home stretch and such was his growing aura of invincibility that, when he completed a fourth-and-21 pass to set up the winning field goal against Minnesota in the regular season, it was not all that surprising. But the lingering feeling still was that Simms was not a championship winner. And in terms of consistency over a season, his record was modest, with a 1985 passer rating of just 78.6 his best to date. The playoffs put an end to all those doubts. A four-touchdown performance dismissed the 49ers, and astute ball-control saw the Giants defeat Washington 17-0 in the NFC Championship Game. But nothing he had achieved came close to his performance in the big one, which, by general consent, was the best Super Bowl game ever played by a quarterback. Three touchdowns and 268 yards came on an astounding 22 pass completions out of 25 attempts. More than simply earning Simms the award of MVP, those figures set a standard which could go unchallenged well into the 21st century.

DOUG WILLIAMS

Given the thread of a chance, Doug Williams grabbed hold and didn't let go until the Super Bowl Trophy was safely won. Drafted by Tampa Bay in the 1978 first round, Williams took the Buccaneers to the NFC Championship Game in only his second campaign as a pro. In the first five seasons, life was good for the man with the siege-gun arm who drove his team to the playoffs three times. But in early 1983 his world fell apart when he was widowed. Subsequently, an ill-advised move to the USFL would leave him isolated, almost a forgotten man, hidden away in the wreckage of that doomed upstart organisation. In 1986 his career was resurrected by the Redskins, who saw him as a solid backup to Jay Schroeder. After throwing only one pass in that first season with Washington, the following year he performed well in relief but, on his two outings as a starter, the Redskins lost. However, his poise in a final-week comeback win against Minnesota clinched his starting spot for the playoffs. The rest has a permanent place in pro football history. Having seen his team buckle under an early John Elway assault, Williams gathered himself before unleashing the most devastating fusillade of passes in Super Bowl annals. By the end, he owned or shared four of the most coveted records; yards passing (340), yards passing in one quarter (228), touchdown passes (4) and longest pass completion (80 yards).

Washington's Doug Williams came through in the end.

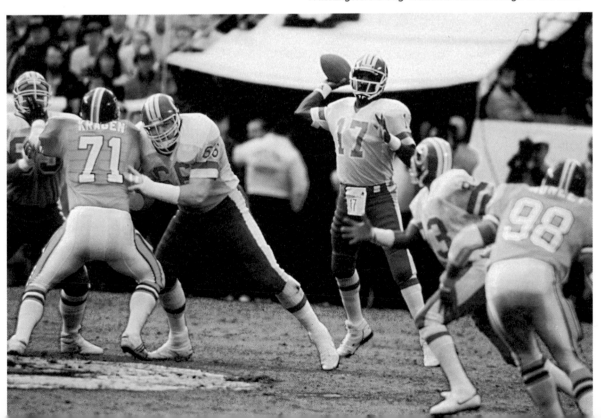

CHAPTER THREE

HOW THE SEASON WORKS

The National Football League consists of twenty-eight teams divided into two **Conferences**, the American Football Conference (AFC) and the National Football Conference (NFC). Each conference has fourteen teams, and is subdivided into two five-team **Divisions** and one four-team **Division**. These are essentially based on sensible geographical considerations but also take into account the traditional rivalries which were in existence when the expanded NFL was restructured in 1970. The teams are listed below in order of their final 1988 division standings since this is of importance in arriving at a team's schedule (fixture list) for 1989.

THE SCHEDULE

When considering a team's schedule, it's best to set aside the four teams who each finished the 1988 season in fifth place in their divisions. Looking at the remaining twenty-four, every team plays twelve games against others from its own conference. Again, excluding the four fifth-placed teams, every team will play four games against teams from the rival conference (known as Interconference games), specifically to allow fans in the cities of one conference the opportunity of seeing the star players and teams of the other conference. The structure of a team's schedule depends on whether it plays in a four-team or a five-team division.

AMERICAN FOOTBALL CONFERENCE

Eastern Division

		W	L	T
Buffalo	AE-1	12	4	0
Indianapolis	AE-2	9	7	0
New England	AE-3	9	7	0
N.Y. Jets	AE-4	8	7	1
Miami	AE-5	6	10	0

Central Division

		W	L	T
Cincinnati	AC-1	12	4	0
Cleveland	AC-2	10	6	0
Houston	AC-3	10	6	0
Pittsburgh	AC-4	5	11	0

Western Division

		W	L	T
Seattle	AW-1	9	7	0
Denver	AW-2	8	8	0
L.A. Raiders	AW-3	7	9	0
San Diego	AW-4	6	10	0
Kansas City	AW-5	4	11	1

NATIONAL FOOTBALL CONFERENCE

Eastern Division

		W	L	T
Philadelphia	NE-1	10	6	0
N.Y. Giants	NE-2	10	6	0
Washington	NE-3	7	9	0
Phoenix	NE-4	7	9	0
Dallas	NE-5	3	13	0

Central Division

		W	L	T
Chicago	NC-1	12	4	0
Minnesota	NC-2	11	5	0
Tampa Bay	NC-3	5	11	0
Detroit	NC-4	4	12	0
Green Bay	NC-5	4	12	0

Western Division

		W	L	T
San Francisco	NW-1	10	6	0
L.A. Rams	NW-2	10	6	0
New Orleans	NW-3	10	6	0
Atlanta	NW-4	5	11	0

Four-Team Division

A typical schedule, e.g., for the Atlanta Falcons, appears below. It is set out, deliberately not in chronological order but to emphasise that the schedule has a quite definite structure.

Atlanta Falcons (NFC West)

Los Angeles Rams	NFC West	Home
Los Angeles Rams	NFC West	Away
New Orleans Saints	NFC West	Home
New Orleans Saints	NFC West	Away
San Francisco 49ers	NFC West	Home
San Francisco 49ers	NFC West	Away
Detroit Lions	NFC Central	Home
Green Bay Packers	NFC Central	Away
Minnesota Vikings	NFC Central	Away
Dallas Cowboys	NFC East	Home
Phoenix Cardinals	NFC East	Away
Washington Redskins	NFC East	Home
Buffalo Bills	AFC East	Home
Indianapolis Colts	AFC East	Away
New England Patriots	AFC East	Home
New York Jets	AFC East	Away

The Falcons will always play their division rivals, the Rams, New Orleans and San Francisco, both home and away. The flavour of intra-conference competition is maintained by six games, every year, against teams from outside their division but within their conference. There will always be three games against the NFC East and three against the NFC Central. Again, every year, there will be four games against teams from a particular division of the rival conference, based on a three-year cycle. In 1989, they play against the AFC East; in 1990 they will play teams from the AFC Central and in 1991, the AFC West. For every team in the NFL, a complete list of opponents, other than those within a team's own division, is arrived at by applying the following formula. The letters and numbers refer to Conference, Division and final standing in that division. Thus the Philadelphia Eagles, who are in the National Conference Eastern Division and finished first in that division, are identified as NE-1. Equally, the Pittsburgh Steelers, who are in the American Conference Central Division and finished fourth in that division, are labelled AC-4.

AFC EAST-AE

AE-1		AE-2		AE-3		AE-4		AE-5	
H	**A**	**H**	**A**	**H**	**A**	**H**	**A**	**H**	**A**
AC-1	AC-3	AC-2	AC-1	AC-3	AC-4	AC-4	AC-2	AC-2	AC-1
AW-2	AW-1	AW-4	AW-2	AW-1	AW-3	AW-3	AW-4	AC-4	AC-3
NW-2	NW-1	NW-1	NW-2	NW-2	NW-1	NW-1	NW-2	AW-5	AW-5
NW-3	NW-4	NW-4	NW-3	NW-3	NW-4	NW-4	NW-3	NC-5	NE-5

AFC CENTRAL-AC

AC-1		AC-2		AC-3		AC-4	
H	**A**	**H**	**A**	**H**	**A**	**H**	**A**
AE-2	AE-1	AE-4	AE-2	AE-1	AE-3	AE-3	AE-4
AE-5	AW-3	AW-2	AE-5	AE-5	AW-4	AW-4	AE-5
AW-1	AW-5	AW-5	AW-1	AW-3	AW-5	AW-5	AW-2
NC-3	NC-1	NC-1	NC-3	NC-3	NC-1	NC-1	NC-3
NC-4	NC-2	NC-2	NC-4	NC-4	NC-2	NC-2	NC-4

AFC WEST-AW

AW-1		AW-2		AW-3		AW-4		AW-5	
H	**A**	**H**	**A**	**H**	**A**	**H**	**A**	**H**	**A**
AC-2	AC-1	AC-4	AC-2	AC-1	AC-3	AC-3	AC-4	AC-1	AC-2
AE-1	AE-3	AE-2	AE-1	AE-3	AE-4	AE-4	AE-2	AC-3	AC-4
NE-3	NE-1	NE-1	NE-3	NE-3	NE-1	NE-1	NE-3	AE-5	AE-5
NE-4	NE-2	NE-2	NE-4	NE-4	NE-2	NE-2	NE-4	NE-5	NC-5

NFC EAST-NE

NE-1		NE-2		NE-3		NE-4		NE-5	
H	**A**	**H**	**A**	**H**	**A**	**H**	**A**	**H**	**A**
NC-2	NC-1	NC-2	NW-1	NC-1	NW-3	NC-3	NC-4	NC-5	NC-5
NW-1	NW-3	NC-4	NW-2	NC-3	NW-4	NW-4	NW-2	NW-1	NW-3
AW-1	AW-2	AW-1	AW-2	AW-2	AW-1	AW-2	AW-1	NW-2	NW-4
AW-3	AW-4	AW-3	AW-4	AW-4	AW-3	AW-4	AW-3	AE-5	AW-5

NFC CENTRAL-NC

NC-1		NC-2		NC-3		NC-4		NC-5	
H	**A**	**H**	**A**	**H**	**A**	**H**	**A**	**H**	**A**
NE-1	NE-3	NW-2	NE-1	NW-1	NE-3	NE-4	NE-2	NE-5	NE-5
NW-2	NW-1	NW-4	NE-2	NW-3	NE-4	NW-3	NW-4	NW-3	NW-1
AC-1	AC-2	AC-1	AC-2	AC-2	AC-1	AC-2	AC-1	NW-4	NW-2
AC-3	AC-4	AC-3	AC-4	AC-4	AC-3	AC-4	AC-3	AW-5	AE-5

NFC WEST-NW

NW-1		NW-2		NW-3		NW-4	
H	**A**	**H**	**A**	**H**	**A**	**H**	**A**
NC-1	NC-3	NC-5	NC-1	NE-1	NC-3	NC-4	NC-2
NC-5	NE-1	NE-2	NC-2	NE-3	NC-4	NE-3	NC-5
NE-2	NE-5	NE-4	NE-5	NE-5	NC-5	NE-5	NE-4
AE-1	AE-2	AE-2	AE-1	AE-2	AE-1	AE-1	AE-2
AE-3	AE-4	AE-4	AE-3	AE-4	AE-3	AE-3	AE-4

Five-Team Division (Top Four Teams Only)

In the AFC East the schedules for the top four teams have identical structure and include home and away games against the other four teams in the division. Each of the top four teams plays two games against AFC Central teams and two against the AFC West. Also, they play the four teams in the NFC West as part of their three-year cycle of interconference games. In 1990, they will play teams from the NFC East and, in 1991, the NFC Central. Below is the schedule structure for the Buffalo Bills.

Buffalo Bills (AFC East)

Indianapolis Colts	AFC East	Home
Indianapolis Colts	AFC East	Away
Miami Dolphins	AFC East	Home
Miami Dolphins	AFC East	Away
New England Patriots	AFC East	Home
New England Patriots	AFC East	Away
New York Jets	AFC East	Home
New York Jets	AFC East	Away
Cincinnati Bengals	AFC Central	Home
Houston Oilers	AFC Central	Away
Denver Broncos	AFC West	Home
Seattle Seahawks	AFC West	Away
Atlanta Falcons	NFC West	Away
Los Angeles Rams	NFC West	Home
New Orleans Saints	NFC West	Home
San Francisco 49ers	NFC West	Away

Fifth-Placed Teams

In the AFC, the two fifth-placed teams will each play eight games against teams from their own division and will always play single games against each of the four AFC Central division teams. In the NFC, the two fifth-placed teams each play eight games against teams within their own division and will always play single games against the four NFC West teams. Each of the four fifth-placed teams is guaranteed home and away games against the other fifth-placed team in its own conference, and single games against the two fifth-placed teams from the rival conference. The schedule structures for all four teams are set out as follows:

Miami (AFC East)

AFC East		8 games
AFC Central		4 games
Kansas City	(AFC)	Home
Kansas City	(AFC)	Away
Dallas	(NFC)	Away
Green Bay	(NFC)	Home

Kansas City (AFC West)

AFC West		8 games
AFC Central		4 games
Miami	(AFC)	Home
Miami	(AFC)	Away
Dallas	(NFC)	Home
Green Bay	(NFC)	Away

Dallas (NFC East)

NFC East		8 games
NFC West		4 games
Green Bay	(NFC)	Home
Green Bay	(NFC)	Away
Kansas City	(AFC)	Away
Miami	(AFC)	Home

Green Bay (NFC Central)

NFC Central		8 games
NFC West		4 games
Dallas	(NFC)	Home
Dallas	(NFC)	Away
Kansas City	(AFC)	Home
Miami	(AFC)	Away

THE PLAYOFFS

On completion of the regular season, each conference holds an elimination competition known as the Playoffs. The teams involved are the three division winners and two Wild Card teams, namely those two, other than the division winners, who have the best won-lost-tied records. The two Wild Card teams play each other to decide which one advances to join the three division winners in the Divisional Playoffs (conference semi-final games). The results of the 1988 American Football Conference playoffs are set out as follows:

Wild Card Game
Houston 24 at Cleveland 23

Divisional Playoffs
Houston 10 at Buffalo 17
Seattle 13 at Cincinnati 21

AFC Championship Game
Buffalo 10 at Cincinnati 21
Cincinnati advanced to Super Bowl XXIII as AFC Champions.

Home-Field Advantage in the Playoffs
For the Wild Card game, the team with the better regular-season record is given the home-field advantage. Again, in the Divisional Playoffs, the home-field advantage goes to the team with the better regular-season record except in so far as the Wild Card winner can never play at home. For the AFC playoffs then, the pecking order was as follows:

	W	L	T
Cincinnati†	12	4	0
Buffalo†	12	4	0
Seattle†	9	7	0
Cleveland*	10	6	0
Houston*	10	6	0

† Division Champions
* Wild Card teams

TIE-BREAKING PROCEDURES

Ties are broken by the following list of criteria:

Teams in the same division
A: *Two teams*
1. Head-to-head (best record in games played between the two teams)
2. Best record in games played within the division
3. Best record in games played within the conference
4. Best record in common games
5. Best net points scored in division games (just like goal difference in soccer)
6. Best net points in all games

B: *Three or More Teams* (if two teams remain tied after all other teams are eliminated, the tie-breaking procedure reverts to A:1.)
1. Head-to-head (best record in games played between the teams)
2. Best record in games played within the division
3. Best record in games played within the conference
4. Best record in common games
5. Best net points in division games
6. Best net points in all games

Tie-Breakers for the Wild Card places
(a) If the teams are from the same division, the division tie-breaker is applied.
(b) If the teams are from different divisions, the following procedure is adopted:
C: *Two Teams*
1. Head-to-head (if they have played each other)
2. Best record in games played within the conference
3. Best record in common games (minimum of four)
4. Best average net points in conference games
5. Best net points in all games

D: *Three or More Teams* (If two teams remain tied after all other teams are eliminated, the tie-breaking procedure reverts to A:1, or C:1, whichever is applicable.)
1. Head-to-head sweep (this applies only if one team has either beaten or lost to all the others)
2. Best record in games played within the conference
3. Best record in common games (minimum of four)
4. Best average net points in conference games
5. Best net points in all games

1988 Tie-Breakers
Cleveland-Houston (Home-field advantage):
A:2; Order: Cleveland (4-2), Houston (3-3)
Cincinnati-Buffalo (Home-field advantage):
C:1; Cincinnati 35 – Buffalo 21
Philadelphia-New York Giants (Division title):
A:1; Philadelphia beat the Giants twice.
49ers-Rams-Saints (Division title):
B:1; Order: 49ers (3-1), Rams (2-2), Saints (1-3)
Giants-Rams-Saints (Final NFC wild card spot):
D:2; Order: Rams (8-4), Giants (9-5), Saints (6-6)
San Francisco-Philadelphia (Home-field advantage):
C:3; Order: 49ers (5-3), Eagles (5-4)

THE SUPER BOWL

Though the obvious comparison is with the FA Cup final, the Super Bowl is best seen as the culmination of an end-of-season knockout competition, involving the champions of six mini-leagues together with the Wild Card teams, the latter being considered, perhaps, as potential giant killers. (Only one team, the Oakland Raiders, has won the Super Bowl Championship starting out as a Wild Card.) Unlike for the FA Cup final, the Super Bowl venue changes from year to year and, since the site is chosen some three years in advance, it is possible for one team to be playing 'at home'. This has never occurred, though both the Los Angeles Rams and the San Francisco 49ers were close to home when they played in Super Bowls XIV and XIX respectively. In selecting the venue, great importance is placed on the likelihood of good weather. Consequently, with the exception of the Pontiac Silverdome (this is a domed stadium), all past Super Bowl stadia have been in the 'sunshine belt', stretching from Florida to California. Super Bowl XXIV will be played at the Louisiana Superdome, New Orleans, and XXV at Tampa Stadium, Tampa, Florida.

THE PRO BOWL

At the end of the season, the best players from each conference fly off to Hawaii to give the fans out there a treat. The teams are selected by a ballot of head coaches and players in each conference. Each team has two equal votes, those being the head coach's and a consensus of the players' selections. Coaches and players vote only for players in their own conference and may not vote for players from their own teams. Last year, led by Most Valuable Player Randall Cunningham, the NFC won a one-sided encounter, 34-3, extending its lead in the series to 11-8.

Randall Cunningham (# 12) has a step on Andre Tippett.

AFC-NFC Pro Bowl Results – NFC leads series 11-8

YEAR	DATE	WINNER	LOSER	SITE	ATTENDANCE
1989	Jan. 29	NFC 34	AFC 3	Honolulu	50,113
1988	Feb. 7	AFC 15	NFC 6	Honolulu	50,113
1987	Feb. 1	AFC 10	NFC 6	Honolulu	50,101
1986	Feb. 2	NFC 28	AFC 24	Honolulu	50,101
1985	Jan. 27	AFC 22	NFC 14	Honolulu	50,385
1984	Jan. 29	NFC 45	AFC 3	Honolulu	50,445
1983	Feb. 6	NFC 20	AFC 19	Honolulu	49,883
1982	Jan. 31	AFC 16	NFC 13	Honolulu	50,402
1981	Feb. 1	NFC 21	AFC 7	Honolulu	50,360
1980	Jan. 27	NFC 37	AFC 7	Honolulu	49,800
1979	Jan. 29	NFC 13	AFC 13	Los Angeles	46,281
1978	Jan. 23	NFC 14	AFC 13	Tampa	51,337
1977	Jan. 17	AFC 24	NFC 14	Seattle	64,752
1976	Jan. 26	NFC 23	AFC 20	New Orleans	30,546
1975	Jan. 20	NFC 17	AFC 10	Miami	26,484
1974	Jan. 20	AFC 15	NFC 13	Kansas City	66,918
1973	Jan. 21	AFC 33	NFC 28	Dallas	37,091
1972	Jan. 23	AFC 26	NFC 13	Los Angeles	53,647
1971	Jan. 24	NFC 27	AFC 6	Los Angeles	48,222

PRO BOWL ROSTERS
(Original selections – starters in Capitals)

OFFENSE	AMERICAN FOOTBALL CONFERENCE		NATIONAL FOOTBALL CONFERENCE	
Wide Receivers	AL TOON	N.Y. Jets	JERRY RICE	San Francisco
	EDDIE BROWN	Cincinnati	ANTHONY CARTER	Minnesota
	Drew Hill	Houston	Henry Ellard	L.A. Rams
	Mark Clayton	Miami	Eric Martin	New Orleans
Tight Ends	MICKEY SHULER	N.Y. Jets	KEITH JACKSON	Philadelphia
	Rodney Holman	Cincinnati	Steve Jordan	Minnesota
Tackles	ANTHONY MUNOZ	Cincinnati	JACKIE SLATER	L.A. Rams
	CHRIS HINTON	Indianapolis	GARY ZIMMERMAN	Minnesota
	Tunch Ilkin	Pittsburgh	Luis Sharpe	Phoenix
Guards	BRUCE MATTHEWS	Houston	BILL FRALIC	Atlanta
	MAX MONTOYA	Cincinnati	TOM NEWBERRY	L.A. Rams
	Mike Munchak	Houston	Mark May	Washington
Centers	RAY DONALDSON	Indianapolis	JAY HILGENBERG	Chicago
	Kent Hull	Buffalo	Doug Smith	L.A. Rams
Quarterbacks	BOOMER ESIASON	Cincinnati	RANDALL	
	Warren Moon	Houston	CUNNINGHAM	Philadelphia
			Wade Wilson	Minnesota
Running Backs	ERIC DICKERSON	Indianapolis	ROGER CRAIG	San Francisco
	JOHN STEPHENS	New England	HERSCHEL WALKER	Dallas
	Mike Rozier	Houston	Neal Anderson	Chicago
	James Brooks	Cincinnati	John Settle	Atlanta

DEFENSE

Defensive Ends	BRUCE SMITH	Buffalo	REGGIE WHITE	Philadelphia
	LEE WILLIAMS	San Diego	CHRIS DOLEMAN	Minnesota
	Ray Childress	Houston	Charles Mann	Washington
Interior Linemen	TIM KRUMRIE	Cincinnati	KEITH MILLARD	Minnesota
	Fred Smerlas	Buffalo	Michael Carter	San Francisco
Outside Linebackers	CORNELIUS BENNETT	Buffalo	LAWRENCE TAYLOR	N.Y. Giants
	ANDRE TIPPETT	New England	MIKE COFER	Detroit
	Clay Matthews	Cleveland	Charles Haley	San Francisco
Inside Linebackers	SHANE CONLAN	Buffalo	MIKE SINGLETARY	Chicago
	JOHN OFFERDAHL	Miami	SAM MILLS	New Orleans
	Dino Hackett	Kansas City	Scott Studwell	Minnesota
	John Grimsley*	Houston		
Cornerbacks	ALBERT LEWIS	Kansas City	JERRY GRAY	L.A. Rams
	FRANK MINNIFIELD	Cleveland	CARL LEE	Minnesota
	Hanford Dixon	Cleveland	Scott Case	Atlanta
Safeties	DERON CHERRY	Kansas City	JOEY BROWNER	Minnesota
	DAVID FULCHER	Cincinnati	RONNIE LOTT	San Francisco
	Erik McMillan	N.Y. Jets	Dave Duerson	Chicago
			Terry Kinard*	N.Y. Giants

SPECIAL TEAMS

Placekicker	SCOTT NORWOOD	Buffalo	MORTEN ANDERSEN	New Orleans
Punter	MIKE HORAN	Denver	JIM ARNOLD	Detroit
Kick Returner	TIM BROWN	L.A. Raiders	JOHN TAYLOR	San Francisco
Specialist	RUFUS PORTER	Seattle	RON WOLFLEY	Phoenix
Head Coach	MARV LEVY	Buffalo	MIKE DITKA	Chicago

* Special selection made by head coach

AN ALL-PRO TEAM

Anyone can pick his or her own All-Pro team and just about everyone does. Here's my dream team.

Wide Receivers	Jerry Rice	San Francisco
	Anthony Carter	Minnesota
Tight End	Mark Bavaro	N.Y. Giants
Tackles	Anthony Munoz	Cincinnati
	Gary Zimmerman	Minnesota
Guards	Mike Munchak	Houston
	Bill Fralic	Atlanta
Center	Jay Hilgenberg	Chicago
Quarterback	Joe Montana	San Francisco
Running Backs	Eric Dickerson	Indianapolis
	Herschel Walker	Dallas
Defensive Ends	Bruce Smith	Buffalo
	Reggie White	Philadelphia
Defensive Tackles	Tim Krumrie	Cincinnati
	Keith Millard	Minnesota
Outside Linebackers	Lawrence Taylor	N.Y. Giants
	Andre Tippett	New England
Inside Linebackers	Mike Singletary	Chicago
	Shane Conlan	Buffalo
Safeties	Joey Browner	Minnesota
	Ronnie Lott	San Francisco
Cornerbacks	Frank Minnifield	Cleveland
	Carl Lee	Minnesota
Placekicker	Dean Biasucci	Indianapolis
Punter	Mike Horan	Denver
Punt Returner	John Taylor	San Francisco
Kickoff Returner	Tim Brown	L.A. Raiders
Special-team Specialist	Steve Tasker	Buffalo
Head Coach	Bill Walsh	San Francisco

Jay Hilgenberg has become the NFL's premier center.

Mike Munchak takes good care of quarterback Warren Moon.

CHAPTER FOUR

ALL-TIME RECORDS

CHAMPIONS 1920-1988

National Football League 1920-1969
(Until 1933 based solely on regular-season play)

1920 Akron Pros
1921 Chicago Staleys
1922 Canton Bulldogs
1923 Canton Bulldogs
1924 Cleveland Bulldogs
1925 Chicago Cardinals
1926 Frankford Yellow Jackets
1927 New York Giants
1928 Providence Steam Roller
1929 Green Bay Packers
1930 Green Bay Packers
1931 Green Bay Packers
1932 Chicago Bears 9 – Portsmouth Spartans 0
       (Championship Playoff)

NFL Championship Games 1933-69
1933 Chicago Bears 23 – New York Giants 21
1934 New York Giants 30 – Chicago Bears 13
1935 Detroit Lions 26 – New York Giants 7
1936 Green Bay Packers 21 – Boston Redskins 6
1937 Washington Redskins 28 – Chicago Bears 21
1938 New York Giants 23 – Green Bay Packers 17
1939 Green Bay Packers 27 – New York Giants 0
1940 Chicago Bears 73 – Washington Redskins 0
1941 Chicago Bears 37 – New York Giants 9
1942 Washington Redskins 14 – Chicago Bears 6
1943 Chicago Bears 41 – Washington Redskins 21
1944 Green Bay Packers 14 – New York Giants 7
1945 Cleveland Rams 15 – Washington Redskins 14
1946 Chicago Bears 24 – New York Giants 14
1947 Chicago Cardinals 28 – Philadelphia Eagles 21
1948 Philadelphia Eagles 7 – Chicago Cardinals 0
1949 Philadelphia Eagles 14 – Los Angeles Rams 0
1950 Cleveland Browns 30 – Los Angeles Rams 28
1951 Los Angeles Rams 24 – Cleveland Browns 17
1952 Detroit Lions 17 – Cleveland Browns 7
1953 Detroit Lions 17 – Cleveland Browns 16
1954 Cleveland Browns 56 – Detroit Lions 10
1955 Cleveland Browns 38 – Los Angeles Rams 14
1956 New York Giants 47 – Chicago Bears 7

1957 Detroit Lions 59 – Cleveland Browns 14
1958 Baltimore Colts 23 – New York Giants 17 (OT)
1959 Baltimore Colts 31 – New York Giants 16
1960 Philadelphia Eagles 17 – Green Bay Packers 13
1961 Green Bay Packers 37 – New York Giants 0
1962 Green Bay Packers 16 – New York Giants 7
1963 Chicago Bears 14 – New York Giants 10
1964 Cleveland Browns 27 – Baltimore Colts 0
1965 Green Bay Packers 23 – Cleveland Browns 12
1966 Green Bay Packers 34 – Dallas Cowboys 27
1967 Green Bay Packers 21 – Dallas Cowboys 17
1968 Baltimore Colts 34 – Cleveland Browns 0
1969 Minnesota Vikings 27 – Cleveland Browns 7

American Football League Championship Games 1960-1969

1960 Houston Oilers 24 – Los Angeles Chargers 16
1961 Houston Oilers 10 – San Diego Chargers 3
1962 Dallas Texans 20 – Houston Oilers 17 (OT)
1963 San Diego Chargers 51 – Boston Patriots 10
1964 Buffalo Bills 20 – San Diego Chargers 7
1965 Buffalo Bills 23 – San Diego Chargers 0
1966 Kansas City Chiefs 31 – Buffalo Bills 7
1967 Oakland Raiders 40 – Houston Oilers 7
1968 New York Jets 27 – Oakland Raiders 23
1969 Kansas City Chiefs 17 – Oakland Raiders 7

CONFERENCE CHAMPIONSHIP GAMES 1970-1988

NFC
1970 Dallas Cowboys 17 – San Francisco 49ers 10
1971 Dallas Cowboys 14 – San Francisco 49ers 3
1972 Washington Redskins 26 – Dallas Cowboys 3
1973 Minnesota Vikings 27 – Dallas Cowboys 10
1974 Minnesota Vikings 14 – Los Angeles Rams 10
1975 Dallas Cowboys 37 – Los Angeles Rams 7
1976 Minnesota Vikings 24 – Los Angeles Rams 13
1977 Dallas Cowboys 23 – Minnesota Vikings 6
1978 Dallas Cowboys 28 – Los Angeles Rams 0
1979 Los Angeles Rams 9 – Tampa Bay Buccaneers 0
1980 Philadelphia Eagles 20 – Dallas Cowboys 7
1981 San Francisco 49ers 28 – Dallas Cowboys 27
1982 Washington Redskins 31 – Dallas Cowboys 17
1983 Washington Redskins 24 – San Francisco 49ers 21

1984   San Francisco 49ers 23 – Chicago Bears 0
1985   Chicago Bears 24 – Los Angeles Rams 0
1986   New York Giants 17 – Washington Redskins 0
1987   Washington Redskins 17 – Minnesota Vikings 10
1988   San Francisco 49ers 28 – Chicago Bears 3

AFC
1970   Baltimore Colts 27 – Oakland Raiders 17
1971   Miami Dolphins 21 – Baltimore Colts 0
1972   Miami Dolphins 21 – Pittsburgh Steelers 17
1973   Miami Dolphins 27 – Oakland Raiders 10
1974   Pittsburgh Steelers 24 – Oakland Raiders 13
1975   Pittsburgh Steelers 16 – Oakland Raiders 10
1976   Oakland Raiders 24 – Pittsburgh Steelers 7
1977   Denver Broncos 20 – Oakland Raiders 17
1978   Pittsburgh Steelers 34 – Houston Oilers 5
1979   Pittsburgh Steelers 27 – Houston Oilers 13
1980   Oakland Raiders 34 – San Diego Chargers 27
1981   Cincinnati Bengals 27 – San Diego Chargers 7
1982   Miami Dolphins 14 – New York Jets 0
1983   Los Angeles Raiders 30 – Seattle Seahawks 14
1984   Miami Dolphins 45 – Pittsburgh Steelers 28
1985   New England Patriots 31 – Miami Dolphins 14
1986   Denver Broncos 23 – Cleveland Browns 20 (OT)
1987   Denver Broncos 38 – Cleveland Browns 33
1988   Cincinnati Bengals 21 – Buffalo Bills 10

Walter Payton, all-time king of the rushers, will go unchallenged for several years.

Super Bowl 1966-1988

Season	SB	Winner		Loser		Stadium	Attendance
1966	I	Green Bay	35	Kansas City	10	Los Angeles Coliseum	61,946
1967	II	Green Bay	33	Oakland	14	Miami Orange Bowl	75,546
1968	III	N.Y. Jets	16	Baltimore	7	Miami Orange Bowl	75,389
1969	IV	Kansas City	23	Minnesota	7	New Orleans Tulane Stadium	80,562
1970	V	Baltimore	16	Dallas	13	Miami Orange Bowl	79,204
1971	VI	Dallas	24	Miami	3	New Orleans Tulane Stadium	81,023
1972	VII	Miami	14	Washington	7	Los Angeles Coliseum	90,182
1973	VIII	Miami	24	Minnesota	7	Houston Rice Stadium	71,882
1974	IX	Pittsburgh	16	Minnesota	6	New Orleans Tulane Stadium	80,997
1975	X	Pittsburgh	21	Dallas	17	Miami Orange Bowl	80,187
1976	XI	Oakland	32	Minnesota	14	Pasadena Rose Bowl	103,438
1977	XII	Dallas	27	Denver	10	New Orleans Superdome	75,583
1978	XIII	Pittsburgh	35	Dallas	31	Miami Orange Bowl	79,484
1979	XIV	Pittsburgh	31	L.A. Rams	19	Pasadena Rose Bowl	103,985
1980	XV	Oakland	27	Philadelphia	10	New Orleans Superdome	76,135
1981	XVI	San Francisco	26	Cincinnati	21	Pontiac Silverdome	81,270
1982	XVII	Washington	27	Miami	17	Pasadena Rose Bowl	103,667
1983	XVIII	L.A. Raiders	38	Washington	9	Tampa Stadium	72,920
1984	XIX	San Francisco	38	Miami	16	Stanford Stadium	84,059
1985	XX	Chicago	46	New England	10	New Orleans Superdome	73,818
1986	XXI	N.Y. Giants	39	Denver	20	Pasadena Rose Bowl	101,063
1987	XXII	Washington	42	Denver	10	San Diego Jack Murphy Stadium	73,302
1988	XXIII	San Francisco	20	Cincinnati	16	Miami Joe Robbie Stadium	75,179

ALL-TIME INDIVIDUAL RECORDS
(Regular Season only – New Records and Records tied are in bold type)

CAREER BEST

SEASONS PLAYED	26	George Blanda
GAMES PLAYED	340	George Blanda
POINTS	2,002	George Blanda (9-TD, 943-EP, 335-FG)
EXTRA POINTS	943	George Blanda
FIELD GOALS	373	Jan Stenerud
TOUCHDOWNS		
Rushing and Pass Receiving	126	Jim Brown (106-R, 20-P)
Rushing	110	Walter Payton
Pass Receiving	99	Don Hutson
Passes Thrown	342	Fran Tarkenton
By Interception Return	9	Ken Houston
By Punt Return	8	Jack Christiansen
		Rick Upchurch
By Kickoff Return	6	Ollie Matson
		Gale Sayers
		Travis Williams
By Fumble Recovery Return	4	Billy Thompson
YARDAGE		
Rushing	16,726	Walter Payton
Pass Receiving	**12,686**	**Steve Largent**
Passing	47,003	Fran Tarkenton
HOW MANY TIMES		
Pass Receptions	**791**	**Steve Largent**
Passes Completed	3,686	Fran Tarkenton
Interceptions	81	Paul Krause
100-Yard Rushing Games	77	Walter Payton
100-Yard Pass Receiving Games	50	Don Maynard
1,000-Yard Rushing Seasons	10	Walter Payton
1,000-Yard Pass Receiving Seasons	8	Steve Largent
MOST SEASONS LEADING LEAGUE		
Points	5	Don Hutson, Green Bay 1940-44
		Gino Cappelletti, Boston 1961, 1963-66
Extra Points	8	George Blanda, Chicago Bears 1956, Houston 1961-62,
		Oakland 1967-69, 1972, 1974
Field Goals	5	Lou Groza, Cleveland Browns 1950, 1952-54, 1957
Touchdowns	8	Don Hutson, Green Bay 1935-38, 1941-44
Touchdowns, Rushing	5	Jim Brown, Cleveland Browns 1957-59, 1963, 1965
Touchdowns, Pass Receiving	9	Don Hutson, Green Bay 1935-38, 1940-44
Touchdowns, Passes Thrown	4	Johnny Unitas, Baltimore 1957-60
		Len Dawson, Dallas Texans 1962, Kansas City 1963, 1965-66
Yards, Rushing	8	Jim Brown, Cleveland Browns 1957-61, 1963-65
Yards, Pass Receiving	7	Don Hutson, Green Bay 1936, 1938-39, 1941-44
Yards, Passing	5	Sonny Jurgensen, Philadelphia 1961-62, Washington 1966-67, 1969
Pass Receptions	8	Don Hutson, Green Bay 1936-37, 1939, 1941-45
Passes Completed	5	Sammy Baugh, Washington 1937, 1943, 1945, 1947-48
Pass Interceptions	3	Everson Walls, Dallas 1981-82, 1985

SEASON BEST

POINTS	176	Paul Hornung, Green Bay 1960 (15-TD, 41-EP, 15-FG)
EXTRA POINTS	66	Uwe von Schamann, Miami 1984
FIELD GOALS	35	Ali Haji-Sheikh, N.Y. Giants 1983
TOUCHDOWNS		
Rushing and Pass Receiving	24	John Riggins, Washington 1983 (24-R)
Rushing	24	John Riggins, Washington 1983
Pass Receiving	22	Jerry Rice, San Francisco 1987

Passes Thrown	48	Dan Marino, Miami 1984
By Interception Return	4	Ken Houston, Houston 1971
		Jim Kearney, Kansas City 1972
By Punt Return	4	Jack Christiansen, Detroit 1951
		Rick Upchurch, Denver 1976
By Kickoff Return	4	Travis Williams, Green Bay 1967
		Cecil Turner, Chicago 1970
By Fumble Recovery Return	2	By many players
YARDAGE		
Rushing	2,105	Eric Dickerson, L.A. Rams 1984
Pass Receiving	1,746	Charley Hennigan, Houston 1961
Passing	5,084	Dan Marino, Miami 1984
HOW MANY TIMES		
Pass Receptions	106	Art Monk, Washington 1984
Passes Completed	378	Dan Marino, Miami 1986
Interceptions	14	Dick 'Night Train' Lane, L.A. Rams 1952

GAME BEST

POINTS	40	Ernie Nevers (6-TD, 4-EP), Chicago Cardinals v Chicago Bears 1929
EXTRA POINTS	9	Pat Harder, Chicago Cardinals v N.Y. Giants 1948
		Bob Waterfield, L.A. Rams v Baltimore 1950
		Charlie Gogolak, Washington v N.Y. Giants 1966
FIELD GOALS	7	Jim Bakken, St Louis v Pittsburgh 1967
TOUCHDOWNS		
All methods of scoring	6	Ernie Nevers (6-R), Chicago Cardinals v Chicago Bears 1929
		Dub Jones (4-R, 2-P), Cleveland v Chicago Bears 1951
		Gale Sayers (4-R, 1-P, 1-Ret), Chicago Bears v San Francisco 1965
Rushing	6	Ernie Nevers, Chicago Cardinals v Chicago Bears 1929
Pass Receiving	5	Bob Shaw, Chicago Cardinals v Baltimore 1950
		Kellen Winslow, San Diego v Oakland 1981
Passes Thrown	7	Sid Luckman, Chicago Bears v N.Y. Giants 1943
		Adrian Burk, Philadelphia v Washington 1954
		George Blanda, Houston v N.Y. Titans 1961
		Y.A. Tittle, N.Y. Giants v Washington 1962
		Joe Kapp, Minnesota v Baltimore 1969
YARDAGE		
Rushing	275	Walter Payton, Chicago v Minnesota 1977
Pass Receiving	309	Stephone Paige, Kansas City v San Diego 1985
Passing	554	Norm Van Brocklin, L.A. Rams v N.Y. Yanks 1951
HOW MANY TIMES		
Rushing Attempts	**45**	**Jamie Morris, Washington v Cincinnati 1988**
Pass Receptions	18	Tom Fears, L.A. Rams v Green Bay 1950
Passes Completed	42	Richard Todd, N.Y. Jets v San Francisco 1980
Interceptions	4	By many players
LONGEST		
Touchdown Rushing	99 yds	Tony Dorsett, Dallas v Minnesota 1983
Touchdown Pass Receiving	99 yds	Andy Farkas (from Filchock), Washington v Pittsburgh 1939
		Bobby Mitchell (from Izo), Washington v Cleveland 1963
		Pat Studstill (from Sweetan), Detroit v Baltimore 1966
		Gerry Allen (from Jurgensen), Washington v Chicago 1968
		Cliff Branch (from Plunkett), L.A. Raiders v Washington 1983
		Mike Quick (from Jaworski), Philadelphia v Atlanta 1985
Field Goal	63 yds	Tom Dempsey, New Orleans v Detroit 1970
Punt Return (All TDs)	98 yds	Gil LeFebvre, Cincinnati v Brooklyn 1933
		Charlie West, Minnesota v Washington 1968
		Dennis Morgan, Dallas v St Louis 1974
Kickoff Return (All TDs)	106 yds	Al Carmichael, Green Bay v Chicago Bears 1956
		Noland Smith, Kansas City v Denver 1967
		Roy Green, St Louis v Dallas 1979

Interception Return (TD)	103 yds	Vencie Glenn, San Diego v Denver 1987
Fumble Recovery Return (TD)	104 yds	Jack Tatum, Oakland v Green Bay 1972

TEAM RECORDS

Most Championships	11	Green Bay, 1929-31, 1936, 1939, 1944, 1961-62, 1965-67
	9	Chicago Staleys/Bears, 1921, 1932-33, 1940-41, 1943, 1946, 1963, 1985
	5	N.Y. Giants, 1927, 1934, 1938, 1956, 1986
	4	Detroit, 1935, 1952-53, 1957
		Cleveland Browns, 1950, 1954-55, 1964
		Baltimore, 1958-59, 1968, 1970
		Pittsburgh, 1974-75, 1978-79
		Oakland/L.A. Raiders, 1967, 1976, 1980, 1983
		Washington, 1937, 1942, 1982, 1987
Most Consecutive Games Won (inc. playoffs)	18	Chicago Bears, 1933-34 and 1941-42 Miami, 1972-73
Most Consecutive Games Won (exc. playoffs)	17	Chicago Bears, 1933-34
Most Consecutive Games Lost	26	Tampa Bay, 1976-77
Most Points in a Season	541	Washington, 1983
Fewest Points in a Season (Since 1932)	37	Cincinnati-St Louis, 1934
Most Points in a Game	72	Washington v N.Y. Giants, 1966
Most Points (Both Teams) in a Game	113	Washington v N.Y. Giants, 1966
Fewest Points (Both Teams) in a Game	0	Many teams; last time N.Y. Giants v Detroit, 1943

ALL-TIME TOP TWENTY
(1988 Active players in capitals)

All-Time Leading Rushers

		Yrs.	Att.	Yards	Ave.	TDs
1.	Walter Payton	13	3,838	16,726	4.4	110
2.	TONY DORSETT	12	2,936	12,739	4.3	77
3.	Jim Brown	9	2,359	12,312	5.2	106
4.	Franco Harris	13	2,949	12,120	4.1	91
5.	John Riggins	14	2,916	11,352	3.9	104
6.	O.J. Simpson	11	2,404	11,236	4.7	61
7.	ERIC DICKERSON	6	2,136	9,915	4.6	75
8.	Earl Campbell	8	2,187	9,407	4.3	74
9.	Jim Taylor	10	1,941	8,597	4.4	83
10.	Joe Perry	14	1,737	8,378	4.8	53
11.	OTTIS ANDERSON	10	1,949	8,294	4.3	55
12.	Larry Csonka	11	1,891	8,081	4.3	64
13.	Mike Pruitt	11	1,844	7,378	4.0	51
14.	Leroy Kelly	10	1,727	7,274	4.2	74
15.	George Rogers	7	1,692	7,176	4.2	54
16.	MARCUS ALLEN	7	1,712	6,982	4.1	61
17.	John Henry Johnson	13	1,571	6,803	4.3	48
18.	FREEMAN McNEIL	8	1,525	6,794	4.5	28
19.	Wilbert Montgomery	9	1,540	6,789	4.4	45
20.	Chuck Muncie	9	1,561	6,702	4.3	71

All-Time Leading Receivers

		Yrs.	No.	Yards	Ave.	TDs
1.	STEVE LARGENT	13	791	12,686	16.0	97
2.	Charlie Joiner	18	750	12,146	16.2	65
3.	Charley Taylor	13	649	9,110	14.0	79
4.	Don Maynard	15	633	11,834	18.7	88
5.	Raymond Berry	13	631	9,275	14.7	68
6.	OZZIE NEWSOME	11	610	7,416	12.2	44
7.	JAMES LOFTON	11	599	11,085	18.5	54
8.	Harold Carmichael	14	590	8,985	15.2	79
9.	Fred Biletnikoff	14	589	8,974	15.2	76
10.	Harold Jackson	15	579	10,372	17.9	76
11.	ART MONK	9	576	7,979	13.9	39
12.	Lionel Taylor	10	567	7,195	12.7	45
13.	WES CHANDLER	11	559	8,966	16.0	56
14.	Lance Alworth	11	542	10,266	18.9	85
15.	Kellen Winslow	9	541	6,741	12.5	45
16.	John Stallworth	14	537	8,723	16.2	63
17.	Bobby Mitchell	11	521	7,954	15.3	65
18.	Nat Moore	13	510	7,546	14.8	74
19.	Dwight Clark	9	506	6,750	13.3	48
	STANLEY MORGAN	12	506	9,866	19.5	64

All-Time Leading Scorers

		Yrs.	TDs	EPs	FGs	Total
1.	George Blanda	26	9	943	335	2,002
2.	Jan Stenerud	19	0	580	373	1,699
3.	Jim Turner	16	1	521	304	1,439
4.	Mark Moseley	16	0	482	300	1,382
5.	Jim Bakken	17	0	534	282	1,380
6.	Fred Cox	15	0	519	282	1,365
7.	Lou Groza	17	1	641	234	1,349
8.	PAT LEAHY	15	0	467	241	1,190
9.	Gino Cappelletti*	11	42	350	176	1,130
10.	CHRIS BAHR	13	0	459	223	1,128
11.	Ray Wersching	15	0	456	222	1,122
12.	Don Cockroft	13	0	432	216	1,080
13.	Garo Yepremian	14	0	444	210	1,074
14.	Bruce Gossett	11	0	374	219	1,031
15.	Sam Baker	15	2	428	179	977
16.	Rafael Septien	10	0	420	180	960
17.	Lou Michaels**	13	1	386	187	955
18.	NICK LOWERY	10	0	304	201	907
19.	Roy Gerela	11	0	351	184	903
20.	JIM BREECH	10	0	381	172	897

* Includes four two-point conversions
** Includes a safety recorded in 1965 when Michaels played as a defensive end.

New England wide receiver Stanley Morgan edged into the all-time top twenty.

Chicago quarterback Jim McMahon entered the passer rating list in equal-13th spot.

All-Time Passer Ratings (Minimum 1,500 attempts)

		Yrs.	Att.	Comp.	Yards	TDs	Int.	Rating
1.	JOE MONTANA	10	3,673	2,322	27,533	190	99	92.0
2.	DAN MARINO	6	3,100	1,866	23,856	196	103	91.5
3.	BOOMER ESIASON	5	1,830	1,038	14,825	98	65	86.2
4.	DAVE KRIEG	9	2,344	1,358	17,549	148	96	85.5
5.	KEN O'BRIEN	6	1,990	1,183	14,243	84	50	85.0
6.	Roger Staubach	11	2,958	1,685	22,700	153	109	83.4
7.	NEIL LOMAX	8	3,153	1,817	22,771	136	90	82.7
8.	Len Dawson	19	3,741	2,136	28,711	239	183	82.6
	Sonny Jurgensen	18	4,262	2,433	32,224	255	189	82.6
10.	Ken Anderson	16	4,475	2,654	32,838	197	160	81.9
11.	DANNY WHITE	13	2,950	1,761	21,959	155	132	81.7
12.	Bart Starr	16	3,149	1,808	24,718	152	138	80.5
13.	JIM McMAHON	7	1,513	874	11,203	67	56	80.4
	Fran Tarkenton	18	6,467	3,686	47,003	342	266	80.4
15.	Dan Fouts	15	5,604	3,297	43,040	254	242	80.2
16.	Otto Graham	6	1,565	872	13,499	88	94	78.2
	Bert Jones	10	2,551	1,430	18,190	124	101	78.2
	Johnny Unitas	18	5,186	2,830	40,239	290	253	78.2
19.	Frank Ryan	13	2,133	1,090	16,042	149	111	77.6
20.	Joe Theismann	12	3,602	2,044	25,206	160	138	77.4

PASSES COMPLETED	No.	YARDS PASSING	Yards	TOUCHDOWN PASSES	No.
1. Fran Tarkenton	3,686	1. Fran Tarkenton	47,003	1. Fran Tarkenton	342
2. Dan Fouts	3,297	2. Dan Fouts	43,040	2. Johnny Unitas	290
3. Johnny Unitas	2,830	3. Johnny Unitas	40,239	3. Sonny Jurgensen	255
4. Ken Anderson	2,654	4. Jim Hart	34,665	4. Dan Fouts	254
5. Jim Hart	2,593	5. John Hadl	33,503	5. John Hadl	244
6. John Brodie	2,469	6. Ken Anderson	32,838	6. Len Dawson	239
7. Sonny Jurgensen	2,433	7. Sonny Jurgensen	32,224	7. George Blanda	236
8. Roman Gabriel	2,366	8. John Brodie	31,548	8. John Brodie	214
9. John Hadl	2,363	9. Norm Snead	30,797	9. Terry Bradshaw	212
10. JOE FERGUSON	2,323	10. Roman Gabriel	29,444	Y.A. Tittle	212
11. JOE MONTANA	2,322	11. JOE FERGUSON	29,263	11. Jim Hart	209
12. Norm Snead	2,276	12. Len Dawson	28,711	12. Roman Gabriel	201
13. Ken Stabler	2,270	13. Y.A. Tittle	28,339	13. Ken Anderson	197
14. RON JAWORSKI	2,151	14. Terry Bradshaw	27,989	14. Bobby Layne	196
15. Len Dawson	2,136	15. Ken Stabler	27,938	DAN MARINO	196
16. Y.A. Tittle	2,118	16. Craig Morton	27,908	Norm Snead	196
17. Craig Morton	2,053	17. RON JAWORSKI	27,805	17. Ken Stabler	194
18. Joe Theismann	2,044	18. Joe Namath	27,663	18. JOE FERGUSON	193
19. Terry Bradshaw	2,025	19. JOE MONTANA	27,533	19. Bob Griese	192
20. Archie Manning	2,011	20. George Blanda	26,920	20. JOE MONTANA	190

INDEX OF RETIRED PLAYERS
LISTED IN THE ALL-TIME STATISTICS

ALLEN Gerry, Baltimore (1966), Washington (1967-69)

ALWORTH Lance, San Diego (1962-70), Dallas (1971-72)

ANDERSON Ken, Cincinnati (1971-86)

BAKER Sam, Washington (1953 and 1956-59), Cleveland (1960-61), Dallas Cowboys (1962-63), Philadelphia (1964-69)

BAKKEN Jim, St Louis (1962-78)

BAUGH Sammy, Washington (1937-52)

BERRY Raymond, Baltimore (1955-67)

BILETNIKOFF Fred, Oakland (1965-78)

BLANDA George, Chicago Bears (1949 and 1950-58), Baltimore (1950), Houston (1960-66), Oakland (1967-75)

BRADSHAW Terry, Pittsburgh (1970-83)

BRANCH Cliff, Oakland/L.A. Raiders (1972-85)

BRODIE John, San Francisco (1957-73)

BROWN Jim, Cleveland (1957-65)

BURK Adrian, Baltimore (1950), Philadelphia (1951-56)

CAMPBELL Earl, Houston (1978-84), New Orleans (1984-85)

CAPPELLETTI Gino, Boston Patriots (1960-70)

CARMICHAEL Al, Green Bay (1953-58), Denver (1960-61)

CARMICHAEL Harold, Philadelphia (1971-83), Dallas (1984)

CHRISTIANSEN Jack, Detroit (1951-58)

CLARK Dwight, San Francisco (1979-87)

COCKROFT Don, Cleveland (1968-80)

COX Fred, Minnesota (1963-77)

CSONKA Larry, Miami (1968-74 and 1979), N.Y. Giants (1976-78)

DAWSON Len, Pittsburgh (1957-59), Cleveland (1960-61), Dallas Texans/Kansas City (1962-75)

DEMPSEY Tom, New Orleans (1969-70), Philadelphia (1971-74), L.A. Rams (1975-76), Houston (1977), Buffalo (1978-79)

FARKAS Andy, Washington (1938-44), Detroit (1945)

FEARS Tom, L.A. Rams (1948-56)

FILCHOCK Frank, Pittsburgh (1938), Washington (1938-41 and 1944-45), N.Y. Giants (1946), Baltimore (1950)

FOUTS Dan, San Diego (1973-87)

GABRIEL Roman, L.A. Rams (1962-72), Philadelphia (1973-77)

GERELA Roy, Houston (1969-70), Pittsburgh (1971-78), San Diego (1979)

GOGOLAK Charlie, Washington (1966-68), Boston/New England (1970-72)

GOSSETT Bruce, L.A. Rams (1964-69), San Francisco (1970-74)

GRAHAM Otto, Cleveland Browns (1946-55)

GRIESE Bob, Miami (1967-80)

GROZA Lou, Cleveland Browns (1946-59 and 1961-67)

HADL John, San Diego (1962-72), L.A. Rams (1973-74), Green Bay (1974-75), Houston (1976-77)

HARDER Pat, Chicago Cardinals (1946-50), Detroit (1951-53)

HARRIS Franco, Pittsburgh (1972-83), Seattle (1984)

HART Jim, St Louis (1966-83), Washington (1984)

HENNIGAN Charley, Houston (1960-66)

HORNUNG Paul, Green Bay (1957-62 and 1964-66)

HOUSTON Ken, Houston (1967-72), Washington (1973-80)

HUTSON Don, Green Bay (1935-45)

IZO George, St Louis (1960), Washington (1961-64), Detroit (1965), Pittsburgh (1966)

JACKSON Harold, L.A. Rams (1968 and 1973-77), Philadelphia (1969-72), New England (1978-81), Minnesota (1982), Seattle (1983)

JOHNSON John Henry, San Francisco (1954-56), Detroit (1957-59), Pittsburgh (1960-65), Houston (1966)

JOINER Charlie, Houston (1969-72), Cincinnati (1972-75), San Diego (1976-86)

JONES Bert, Baltimore (1973-81), L.A. Rams (1982)

JONES Dub, Miami (AAFC) (1946), Brooklyn (AAFC) (1946-48), Cleveland (1948-55)

JURGENSEN Sonny, Philadelphia (1957-63), Washington (1964-74)

KAPP Joe, Minnesota (1967-69), Boston Patriots (1970)

KEARNEY Jim, Detroit (1965-66), Kansas City (1967-75), New Orleans (1976)

KELLY Leroy, Cleveland (1964-73)

KRAUSE Paul, Washington (1964-67), Minnesota (1968-79)

LANE Dick 'Night Train', L.A. Rams (1952-53), Chicago Cardinals (1954-59), Detroit (1960-65)

LAYNE Bobby, Chicago Bears (1948), N.Y. Bulldogs (1949), Detroit (1950-58), Pittsburgh (1958-62)

LeFEBVRE Gil, Cincinnati Reds (1933-34), Detroit (1935)

LUCKMAN Sid, Chicago Bears (1939-50)

MANNING Archie, New Orleans (1971-75 and 1977-82), Houston (1982-83), Minnesota (1983-84)

MATSON Ollie, Chicago Cardinals (1952 and 1954-58), L.A. Rams (1959-62), Detroit (1963), Philadelphia (1964-66)

MAYNARD Don, N.Y. Giants (1958), N.Y. Titans/Jets (1960-72), St Louis (1973)

MICHAELS Lou, L.A. Rams (1958-60), Pittsburgh (1961-63), Baltimore (1964-69), Green Bay (1971)

MITCHELL Bobby, Cleveland (1958-61), Washington (1962-68)

MONTGOMERY Wilbert, Philadelphia (1977-84), Detroit (1985)

MOORE Nat, Miami (1974-86)

MORGAN Dennis, Dallas (1974), Philadelphia (1975)

MORTON Craig, Dallas (1965-74), N.Y. Giants (1974-76), Denver (1977-82)

MOSELEY Mark, Philadelphia (1970), Houston (1971-72), Washington (1974-86), Cleveland (1986)

MUNCIE Chuck, New Orleans (1976-80), San Diego (1980-84)

NAMATH Joe, N.Y. Jets (1965-76), L.A. Rams (1977)

NEVERS Ernie, Duluth Eskimos (1926-27), Chicago Cardinals (1929-31)

PAYTON Walter, Chicago (1975-87)

PERRY Joe, San Francisco (1948-60 and 1963), Baltimore (1961-62)

PLUNKETT Jim, New England (1971-75), San Francisco (1976-77), Oakland/L.A. Raiders (1978-85)

PRUITT Mike, Cleveland (1976-84), Buffalo (1985), Kansas City (1985-86)

RIGGINS John, N.Y. Jets (1971-75), Washington (1976-79 and 1981-85)

ROGERS George, New Orleans (1981-84), Washington (1985-87)

RYAN Frank, L.A. Rams (1958-61), Cleveland (1962-68), Washington (1969-70)

SAYERS Gale, Chicago (1965-71)

SEPTIEN Rafael, L.A. Rams (1977), Dallas (1978-86)

SHAW Bob, Cleveland/L.A. Rams (1945-49), Chicago Cardinals (1950)

SIMPSON O.J., Buffalo (1969-77), San Francisco (1978-79)

SMITH Noland, Kansas City (1967-69), San Francisco (1969)

SNEAD Norm, Washington (1961-63), Philadelphia (1964-70), Minnesota (1971), N.Y. Giants (1972-74 and 1976), San Francisco (1974-75)

STABLER Ken, Oakland (1970-79), Houston (1980-81), New Orleans (1982-84)

STARR Bart, Green Bay (1956-71)

STAUBACH Roger, Dallas (1969-79)

STENERUD Jan, Kansas City (1967-79), Green Bay (1980-83), Minnesota (1984-85)

STUDSTILL Pat, Detroit (1961-62 and 1964-67), L.A. Rams (1968-71), New England (1972)

SWEETAN Karl, Detroit (1966-67), New Orleans (1968), L.A. Rams (1969-70)

TARKENTON Fran, Minnesota (1961-66 and 1972-78), N.Y. Giants (1967-71)

TATUM Jack, Oakland (1971-79), Houston (1980)

TAYLOR Charley, Washington (1964-75 and 1977)

TAYLOR Jim, Green Bay (1958-66), New Orleans (1967)

TAYLOR Lionel, Chicago Bears (1959), Denver (1960-66), Houston (1967-68)

THEISMANN Joe, Washington (1974-85)

THOMPSON Billy, Denver (1969-81)

TITTLE Y.A., Baltimore (1948-50), San Francisco (1951-60), N.Y. Giants (1961-64)

TODD Richard, N.Y. Jets (1976-83), New Orleans (1984-85)

TURNER Cecil, Chicago (1968-73)

TURNER Jim, N.Y. Jets (1964-70), Denver (1971-79)

UNITAS Johnny, Baltimore (1956-72), San Diego (1973)

UPCHURCH Rick, Denver (1975-83)

VAN BROCKLIN Norm, L.A. Rams (1949-57), Philadelphia (1958-60)

von SCHAMANN Uwe, Miami (1979-84)

WATERFIELD Bob, Cleveland/L.A. Rams (1945-52)

WERSCHING Ray, San Diego (1973-76), San Francisco (1977-87)

WEST Charlie, Minnesota (1968-73), Detroit (1974-77), Denver (1978-79)

WILLIAMS Travis, Green Bay (1967-70), L.A. Rams (1971)

WINSLOW Kellen, San Diego (1979-87)

YEPREMIAN Garo, Detroit (1966-67), Miami (1970-78), New Orleans (1979), Tampa Bay (1980-81)

CHAPTER FIVE

FUTURE STARS OF THE NFL

It is one of the certainties of every NFL season that there will appear new young stars or veterans may unexpectedly blossom. The 1987 playoffs saw the sudden and dramatic impact of running back Timmy Smith while, in the 1988 season, rookie Tim Brown was the NFL leading kickoff returner and another rookie, free safety Erik McMillan, led the AFC in interceptions. Last year saw the best of Minnesota's eight-year veteran quarterback, Wade Wilson, who led the NFC in passing. It is always fun to try to anticipate the names of the players who are just a step or two away from the very top. Here are a few suggestions.

It is remarkable that the Buffalo Bills reached the AFC Championship Game and yet did not have one player who ranked in the NFL top ten in any of the categories of rushing, passing and pass receiving. And it probably was the lack of a consistently top-class performer on offense which proved to be the Bills' undoing in the end. It could be that **Thurman Thomas** is the man who will fill that slot. A prolific running back at Oklahoma State, Thomas was drafted in the 1988 second round. As a rookie he was the Bills' leading rusher, logging 100-yard games against Green Bay and the Raiders. He was not spectacular, and no one is claiming that he is in the Eric Dickerson class, but he's the kind of player who could gain 1,200 yards in a season if the Bills are prepared to use him as the cornerstone of their offense.

Not since Bert Jones and, before him, Johnny Unitas, have the Colts had a quarterback of genuine top class. And while, at this stage, it would be premature even to think of **Chris Chandler** as being in that company, as a rookie he did show a great deal of composure and more than a little promise. His

Chris Chandler made a steady start for the Colts.

collegiate reputation suffered during a disappointing 1987 senior year with the University of Washington, and he was drafted only in the third round. However, after losing their first three games and with Chandler in at quarterback because of injury to Jack Trudeau, the Colts went 9-4 over the remainder of the season, failing only narrowly to reach the playoffs. The Colts have a solid offensive line and, with Eric Dickerson exploding from the backfield, with the correct play selection Chandler has an excellent opportunity to establish himself in the NFL's upper echelons.

It was only a preseason game but . . . Miami quarterback Ron Jaworski dropped back and dumped a short pass over the middle, where rookie **Ferrell Edmunds** made a simple reception before running 71 yards, outpacing the entire Washington defense, for a touchdown. So what? Miami receivers have been doing that for some years. But this receiver was a tight end, all 6ft 6in, 245lb of him. Yes, the TV replay showed him easing away, even from the defensive secondary. And to demonstrate that it was no fluke, Edmunds went even better in the regular season, against the New York Jets, with an 80-yard touchdown reception, the longest ever by a Dolphins tight end. He's still raw and drops too many catchable passes. He needs to work on his blocking techniques and he is said to lose concentration. But he has great size and, with his blazing speed, Edmunds could develop into the best big-play tight end in the game.

Coming into the 1988 season it was a little surprising that the Cincinnati Bengals released one of their former first-round picks, center Dave Rimington. But the Bengals knew something we didn't. In his four starts of the previous year, **Bruce Kozerski** had shown that he could take over permanently. A lowly ninth-round pick in 1984, Kozerski served his apprenticeship, playing center, guard and tackle as necessary when the regular starters were injured. Last year was his first full campaign as a starter and he was outstanding, pass-blocking for Boomer Esiason and clearing the middle for the Bengals' superb rushing offense. Following the gradual decline of Mike Webster and with the great Miami center, Dwight Stephenson, unlikely ever to be at his former best after suffering a serious knee injury, Kozerski could mount a serious challenge to the Colts' Ray Donaldson and Buffalo's Kent Hull for supremacy in the AFC.

Ask most people to name all 28 starting free safeties and they're unlikely to get much further than half-a-dozen players. The name of **Felix Wright**, who

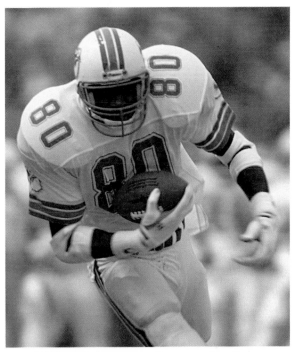

Ferrell Edmunds has outstanding natural attributes.

Felix Wright's talents are not widely recognised.

joined the Browns in 1985 as a walk-on free agent, probably will not be among them. Indeed, even in the Cleveland defensive secondary, Wright plays in the shadow cast by his more expressive teammates, cornerbacks Frank Minnifield and Hanford Dixon. Never having missed a game and gaining a starting spot in 1987 because of injuries to Al Gross, Wright's has been a much underestimated contribution in what has become one of the best units in the NFL. In 1987 he had four interceptions to tie for the club lead with Minnifield. Last year, with a club-leading five interceptions, a club second-best total of 120 tackles and coming equal-third with ten passes defensed, he staked a claim to be the leader of the back four-some.

A change often can bring dramatic results, and while **Simon Fletcher's** conversion to outside linebacker did not meet with instant success, he now is to be regarded as one of the AFC's best in that position, with plenty of improvement to come. Fletcher, who was a second-round draft pick in 1985, was used as a backup defensive end in his first two campaigns before shifting to play the strong outside linebacker spot the following year. In a moderate Broncos defense he quickly adjusted and, last year, he logged nine quarterback sacks to lead the team and rank equal-sixth in the AFC. Had there been a key indicator of his importance to the Broncos' defense, it lies in the total number of plays for which

he was on the field during the regular season, 1,039. It is a figure which placed him second in the club, behind multi-purpose defensive back Mike Harden, and way ahead of the number logged by any other Denver linebacker. Interestingly, and confirming his cover speed, he defensed six passes. It is a profile which has all the features required of a future Pro Bowler.

With such depth at wide receiver, it was just a little surprising when the Raiders used their high position in the draft to pick **Tim Brown**, even accepting that he won the 1987 Heisman Trophy. There even were those observers who felt that Brown had been overhyped in college and that he'd been plain lucky when his two punt returns for touchdowns against Michigan State had been shown live on national television. But a closer look revealed a player who was extremely versatile; one who had played wide receiver and tailback in the Wishbone formation, and had excelled both as a punt and kickoff returner. Al Davis was picking far more than just a wide receiver and the proof of that was evident when, on opening day, with his first NFL regular-season kickoff return, he ran 97 yards for a touchdown. Against Denver on Week Four, in overtime, he had a 74-yard punt return for a touchdown nullified by a penalty. In one sense, Brown may be regarded as a star already, for he went on to win the NFL kickoff return title. But that is not unusual – in the years since records in this category were first kept (48), a rookie has won the kickoff return title 25 times – and many of those winners have not fulfilled their promise.

Looking at San Diego it is difficult not to think of **Jamie Holland**, **Anthony Miller** and the picture of what could be a very productive future for the man who eventually settles in as the Chargers' permanent quarterback. Miller's NFL debut was no surprise. Coming as he did from the University of Tennessee, his searing pace was taken for granted and, as things transpired, he played up to expectations, fully justifying the Chargers' decision to use their first-round option to draft him. In contrast, Holland caught passes only sparingly at Ohio State, a college known for its run-oriented offenses, but his blazing speed was never in doubt. After having been given little opportunity to show his paces as a rookie, in 1988 he steadily was given greater playing time and he responded, leading the Chargers with 39 receptions, three better than the second-placed Miller. A technical factor – the possibility that the Chargers may use an offense featuring just one wide receiver – could restrict their game time. But that would be a pity, for each has the possibility of

Simon Fletcher could breathe new life into the Broncos' defense.

securing a spot on a San Diego honour roll which lists the likes of wide receivers Lance Alworth, Charlie Joiner Gary Garrison and Wes Chandler.

The name of **John L. Williams** is not unfamiliar, but it is used most often in the context of what he has accomplished 'playing as a foil for the great Curt Warner'. But, increasingly, Williams is carving out a reputation in his own right, and the signs are that he may be ready to take over – even from Warner – as the Seahawks' main offensive weapon. Last year, he trailed Warner in rushing yardage by 148, but his 877 yards were gained at an average of 4.6 compared with Warner's 3.9. A late-season burst, in which he caught 19 passes in the final three regular-season games, boosted his total to a club-best 58 receptions. For trivia buffs he became the first player in Seahawks history to better wide receiver Steve Largent. Against Cincinnati in the divisional playoffs, he caught 11 passes for 137 yards and a touchdown. The quintessential modern fullback – he also throws a shuddering block – in his favour he stays healthy. It is almost certain that only the requirement of playing in support of Warner has kept Williams outside the NFL's elite group of superstars.

The Cowboys are close to a low point in their illustrious history but no one expects them to stay there for long, and when, five years down the line, we analyse a Super Bowl champion, it may be seen that the

Right: Anthony Miller has game-breaking speed.

Below: The Cowboys expect greatness from defensive tackle Danny Noonan.

new beginning had its origins in the 1987 draft when they picked **Danny Noonan** in the first round. Nicknamed 'Schwarzenegger' or 'Danny the Barbarian' by his teammates, last year Noonan took over as the starting defensive right tackle and is fully expected to continue the peerless quality in that position established by the retired Bob Lilly and the man Noonan has replaced, Randy White. Exceptionally powerful – he is the Cowboys' strongest player able to bench press 505 lb – also he is very fast. He bears the stamp of one of those 'lucky' players who always seem to be around to take advantage of chances. Against Atlanta on Week Four he returned his one interception for a touchdown and registered the Cowboys' only safety of the campaign. Again, in his first full season as a starter, he tied for the club lead with 7.5 sacks – a title which more often goes to a defensive end or outside linebacker.

In only one year as a pro, Philadelphia tight end **Keith Jackson** already has achieved star quality, and this was confirmed by his selection to start in the AFC-NFC Pro Bowl. So what more is there and why does he appear in a section devoted to 'future stars'? The plain fact is that we may only have been given a brief glimpse of Jackson's talents and, fine receiver that he is, by sheer inexperience at pro level he drops passes which he soon will be gobbling up. It all means that we can anticipate with great pleasure numbers of astronomical proportions coming out of Philadelphia. Certainly, with Randall Cunningham

at quarterback, Jackson has all the potential to eclipse the astonishing feat of Raiders tight end Todd Christensen, who is the only player in NFL history to catch 80-or-more passes in four consecutive regular seasons. In 1988 Jackson made a start, catching 81 passes for 869 yards and six touchdowns. Ironically, his rookie year will be remembered most for the pass he dropped in the end zone against the Bears in the NFC divisional playoffs. One imagines that he'll erase the memory of that one in double-quick time.

If there is one player in the NFL who has been almost totally overlooked by the media, it is **Freddie Joe Nunn**, whose performances over the last two seasons truly have earned him a spot amongst the group which chases the incomparable Reggie White of Philadelphia. The Cardinals' first-round pick in 1985, Nunn played for two years at outside linebacker and was steady without being spectacular. The quantum leap came in 1987 when he was moved forward to defensive end. In the 12 games played by the regulars during that strike-shortened campaign, Nunn had 11 sacks and followed up with 14 in 1988, the latter being a total surpassed by only one defensive lineman in the entire league – you guessed it – Reggie White. 25 sacks in his last 28 games can't be bad. Perhaps he ought to be a little more flashy – dance around a bit – and maybe we'll see him in the AFC-NFC Pro Bowl where many fans feel that he belongs.

The Cardinals' **Tim McDonald** is another player whose outstanding 1988 season went largely unnoticed outside Phoenix. Just listen to this catalogue of achievements and wonder. After playing sparingly in his rookie year because of injury, in 1988, his second season, McDonald laid claim to the starting spot at strong safety, left vacant by the trade of Leonard Smith to Buffalo, and had an immediate impact. Despite having virtually no pro playing experience, he led the club with 115 total tackles, almost double the number of the next best, Niko Noga, who had 62. Again he topped the club by forcing four fumbles. He came third behind the starting cornerbacks in passes defensed. But the contribution which says perhaps everything about his enthusiasm came on special teams, when he blocked or deflected three kicks, a field goal attempt, a punt and a PAT. Defensive left tackle Bob Clasby was the only other Cardinals player to block a kick. This young man could make more than a few headlines in 1989.

Keith Jackson could define new standards for the tight end position.

Cardinals head coach Gene Stallings has the enviable problem of whom to feature as his premier tight end. The arrival of 1987 third-round draftee

Left: Tim McDonald gives direction to the Cardinals' defense.

Below: Jay Novacek could play at either tight end or wide receiver.

Robert Awalt, a cultivated player of great poise who settled in immediately, coincided with the emergence of the man he replaced because of injury in midseason, **Jay Novacek**. Entering the 1988 season, Novacek could not regain his starting spot after Awalt's six-touchdown, rookie campaign but, by season's end, the two had shared playing time to similar effect. Confirming that there is little to choose between them, in both 1987 and 1988, their figures were remarkably similar on an average-per-reception basis, though Novacek represents the deeper threat. The problem may be resolved by matters of detail, such as Awalt's extra size and presence on the line of scrimmage, and Novacek's ability to play the role of wide receiver. Given the chance of playing a full season at tight end, either man could challenge for all-star honours, and it is only the probable need to share time which would keep them out of the hunt.

It remains one of the mysteries of the Washington Redskins' strategy that **Kelvin Bryant** has been used sparingly and, at that, mostly for his pass receiving. For whatever reason, only towards the middle of last season did the Redskins see him as the centre-piece of their offense. In a purple patch, Bryant rushed for 331 yards and a touchdown, and caught 18 passes including three for touchdowns as the Redskins won three games in a row. Two games later a knee injury brought a premature end to his season. Sadly, the lack of durability has been a feature of Bryant's three-year NFL career, and we can only guess at what he could achieve given a full season. A dual-purpose impact rivalling the likes of Roger Craig and Herschel Walker is not out of the question. With head coach Joe Gibbs looking for 'balance' as the flavour of his offense, the versatile Bryant will be given every opportunity to play a significant role in 1989.

Coming into the campaign, top draftee **Bennie Blades** was expected to have an instant impact on the Lions' defense and he did. But he may even have been upstaged by **Chris Spielman**, who was the 29th player selected in the same draft. Both players have a common destiny – they are future all-pros. After some consideration by the Lions' coaches, Blades was installed at strong safety, a position which would give full scope to his multiple talents. He covered well and tackled like a demon. As for versatility, he was the only Lions defensive back to have at least one sack, an interception and a fumble recovery, the latter category in which he had four to tie for the club lead with cornerback Bruce McNorton. In college, Spielman was known for his inspirational effect and his physical talents were beyond question. But no one could have predicted that he would have such an immediate impact in the pros. Starting all 16 games at inside linebacker, Spielman established a new Detroit club record with 153 total tackles, 118 of them solos, and still found time to defense seven passes. He had a team, single-game high of 16 tackles against Minnesota and, for consistency, logged ten or more tackles on six occasions. After the disappointments associated with the selection of defensive end Reggie Rogers in 1987, the Lions deserved a slice of luck and they've had a double dose.

Tim Harris must rue his misfortune to be playing at a time when the NFC has an abundance of top-class outside linebackers. Of course, the Giants' Lawrence Taylor has a lock on one Pro Bowl spot, meaning that several good players are left fighting it out for the other. As a 1986, fourth-round draft pick, Harris went on to be voted the club's Rookie of the Year and, without much doubt, he has become the Packers' premier player on defense. After two solid years playing at outside linebacker, he tore through the 1988 season with all the ferocity of a chainsaw, 'logging' 13.5 sacks to rank fifth in a tough conference. He was two sacks clear of the AFC leader, Greg Townsend. Also, he led the club in tackles with 97, which is, incidentally, his jersey number. On Week Seven, he was particularly severe on the Vikings, when he registered two sacks, one for a safety, blocked a punt and returned the ball ten yards for a touchdown and had five tackles as the Packers upset Minnesota 34-14. If Harris has an advantage over his competition it lies in his youth – he will be 25 in September, 1989.

Offensive linemen rarely are given the accolades they deserve. They're just there in the background – the sort of players on whom you can rely but, even looking at the great ones such as Cincinnati's

Anthony Munoz, Atlanta's Bill Fralic and the Colts' Chris Hinton, always taking a rear seat to the glamour players. As groups, the story is a little different. It is always easy to visualise the great offensive lines which have characterised the modern L.A. Rams. Again, much of the Raiders' success came behind one of the best offensive lines in the history of the game. Remember those lines which began with Art Shell, Gene Upshaw and Jim Otto? For the moment, **Paul Gruber** will have to settle for the quiet life. He received greater media attention before he was drafted, but the moment he was picked, outside of Tampa he became just another promising lineman. In reality, he is almost as important to the Buccaneers as quarterback Vinny Testaverde. Gruber, an overpowering tackle, represents instant authority at a position in which there is no room for doubts. If he fails in his job, there is very little on the offense that can work. Importantly, too, Gruber is the rock around which a great offensive line can be built. Perhaps then we'll think of 'those great Bucs lines' and, maybe even of Paul Gruber.

The fine print of any season can be very revealing. It was interesting to note that, over the final four games of the 1987 season, Tampa Bay wide receiver **Bruce Hill** showed himself to be an exciting prospect by catching 17 passes and not failing to gain at least 73 yards in any of those appearances. Well, he carried on, and while not quite at such a prolific level, last year he led the Bucs in each of receptions (58), yards receiving (1,040) and touchdown receptions (9). He'll be pressed by his starting partner, **Mark Carrier**, whose progress came at a similarly impressive rate. In just the space of one season, the Bucs have brought through their ranks both an actual and a potential 1,000-yard receiver. We may have to begin keeping a careful eye on developments over on Florida's west coast.

It will be the coming season before the full impact of the Falcons' 1988 draft will begin to be felt. They needed outside linebackers and while, in first-round pick **Aundray Bruce**, they knew they were obtaining an outstanding prospect, the possibility that second-rounder **Marcus Cotton** might come through was almost too exciting to contemplate. Bruce, who started in all 16 games, was slowed by an injury in training camp. But he did gather pace in the second half of the season, finishing up as the Falcons' leading sacker with six. In contrast, Cotton blew out of the starting gate, even out-performing Bruce in the early going. But ankle and knee injuries brought an early end to his season. Thankfully, Cotton is expected to recover fully after arthroscopic surgery. In the future, with Bruce and Cotton playing

Already, wide receiver Bruce Hill has reeled off some impressive numbers.

in tandem, victories over San Francisco, Philadelphia and the Raiders, all three of whom they beat last year, might not appear quite so shocking.

One disappointing feature of the 1988 season was that the New Orleans Saints could not maintain the charge which saw them win seven games in a row early in the campaign. As they slipped away, the TV cameras focused on events elsewhere. Had they been leading the pack in the closing stages, media coverage would have ensured that we were treated to an analysis of their strengths. We'd have seen that outside linebacker **Pat Swilling** was not that far

behind the man on the other side, Rickey Jackson, who receives much more of the acclaim. They shared the team lead with seven sacks. Looking at the inside positions, Sam Mills was voted to the Pro Bowl and yet his inside partner, **Vaughan Johnson**, led the team in tackles for the second year in a row and generally was more effective. When the Saints' opposition has the ball, it might be illuminating to have a closer look at numbers 56 and 53.

CHAPTER SIX

AMERICAN FOOTBALL CONFERENCE

TEAM RANKINGS

	OFFENSE						DEFENSE					
	Total Yds.	Rushing	Passing	Points For	No. Intercepted	No. Sacked	Total Yds.	Rushing	Passing	Points Against	Interceptions	Sacks
Buffalo	4	5	5	7	3 =	5 =	1	3	3	1	13 =	1
Cincinnati	1	1	4	1	2	5 =	6	6	6	6 =	2 =	3 =
Cleveland	8	13	3	11	3 =	10	3	5	4	3	5 =	6
Denver	3	11	2	8	11 =	8	10	13	5	9	10 =	7
Houston	6	2 =	10	2	5	3	4	1	8	11	2 =	3 =
Indianapolis	10	2 =	12	4	11 =	9	7	2	13	4	13 =	9 =
Kansas City	11	12	6	12	10	13	5	14	1	5	8	13
L.A. Raiders	9	10	7	9	6 =	14	8	10	7	12	9	5
Miami	2	14	1	10	13	1	13	12	9	13	10 =	12
New England	14	7	14	13	14	2	2	7	2	2	5 =	11
N.Y. Jets	5	6	8	3	1	11 =	11	8	12	10	1	2
Pittsburgh	7	4	9	6	6 =	11 =	14	4	14	14	5 =	14
San Diego	13	9	13	14	6 =	7	9	9	10	8	10 =	8
Seattle	12	8	11	5	6 =	4	12	11	11	6 =	2 =	9 =

AFC PASSERS

	Att	Comp	% Comp	Yards	Ave Gain	TD	% TD	Long	Int	% Int	Rating Points
Esiason, Boomer, *Cin.*	388	223	57.5	3572	9.21	28	7.2	t86	14	3.6	97.4
Krieg, Dave, *Sea.*	228	134	58.8	1741	7.64	18	7.9	t75	8	3.5	94.6
Moon, Warren, *Hou.*	294	160	54.4	2327	7.91	17	5.8	t57	8	2.7	88.4
Kosar, Bernie, *Clev.*	259	156	60.2	1890	7.30	10	3.9	t77	7	2.7	84.3
Marino, Dan, *Mia.*	606	354	58.4	4434	7.32	28	4.6	t80	23	3.8	80.8
O'Brien, Ken, *Jets*	424	236	55.7	2567	6.05	15	3.5	t50	7	1.7	78.6
Kelly, Jim, *Buff.*	452	269	59.5	3380	7.48	15	3.3	t66	17	3.8	78.2
DeBerg, Steve, *K.C.*	414	224	54.1	2935	7.09	16	3.9	t80	16	3.9	73.5
Elway, John, *Den.*	496	274	55.2	3309	6.67	17	3.4	86	19	3.8	71.4
Chandler, Chris, *Ind.*	233	129	55.4	1619	6.95	8	3.4	54	12	5.2	67.2
Beuerlein, Steve, *Raiders*	238	105	44.1	1643	6.90	8	3.4	57	7	2.9	66.6
Brister, Bubby, *Pitt.*	370	175	47.3	2634	7.12	11	3.0	t89	14	3.8	65.3
Schroeder, Jay, *Raiders*	256	113	44.1	1839	7.18	13	5.1	t85	13	5.1	64.6
Malone, Mark, *S.D.*	272	147	54.0	1580	5.81	6	2.2	59	13	4.8	58.8
Non-qualifiers											
Kubiak, Gary, *Den.*	69	43	62.3	497	7.20	5	7.2	t68	3	4.3	90.1
Strock, Don, *Clev.*	91	55	60.4	736	8.09	6	6.6	41	5	5.5	85.2
Ryan, Pat, *Jets*	113	63	55.8	807	7.14	5	4.4	t42	4	3.5	78.3
Hogeboom, Gary, *Ind.*	131	76	58.0	996	7.60	7	5.3	58	7	5.3	77.7
Stouffer, Kelly, *Sea.*	173	98	56.6	1106	6.39	4	2.3	53	6	3.5	69.2
Pagel, Mike, *Clev.*	134	71	53.0	736	5.49	3	2.2	28	4	3.0	64.1
Flutie, Doug, *N.E.*	179	92	51.4	1150	6.42	8	4.5	t80	10	5.6	63.3
Blackledge, Todd, *Pitt.*	79	38	48.1	494	6.25	2	2.5	34	3	3.8	60.8
Laufenberg, Babe, *S.D.*	144	69	47.9	778	5.40	4	2.8	t47	5	3.5	59.3
Carlson, Cody, *Hou.*	112	52	46.4	775	6.92	4	3.6	t51	6	5.4	59.2
Kenney, Bill, *K.C.*	114	58	50.9	549	4.82	0	0.0	25	5	4.4	46.3
Grogan, Steve, *N.E.*	140	67	47.9	834	5.96	4	2.9	t41	13	9.3	37.6

t = Touchdown
Leader based on rating points, minimum 224 attempts

AFC RECEIVERS – Most Receptions

	No	Yards	Ave	Long	TD
Toon, Al, *Jets*	93	1067	11.5	42	5
Clayton, Mark, *Mia.*	86	1129	13.1	t45	14
Hill, Drew, *Hou.*	72	1141	15.8	t57	10
Reed, Andre, *Buff.*	71	968	13.6	t65	6
Shuler, Mickey, *Jets*	70	805	11.5	t42	5
Johnson, Vance, *Den.*	68	896	13.2	86	5
Paige, Stephone, *K.C.*	61	902	14.8	49	7
Givins, Ernest, *Hou.*	60	976	16.3	46	5
Byner, Earnest, *Clev.*	59	576	9.8	t39	2
Jensen, Jim, *Mia.*	58	652	11.2	31	5
Williams, John L., *Sea.*	58	651	11.2	t75	3
Langhorne, Reggie, *Clev.*	57	780	13.7	t77	7
Stradford, Troy, *Mia.*	56	426	7.6	36	1
Brooks, Bill, *Ind.*	54	867	16.1	t53	3
Brown, Eddie, *Cin.*	53	1273	24.0	t86	9
Palmer, Paul, *K.C.*	53	611	11.5	t71	4
Lipps, Louis, *Pitt.*	50	973	19.5	t89	5
Hoge, Merril, *Pitt.*	50	487	9.7	40	3
Jackson, Mark, *Den.*	46	852	18.5	63	6
Carson, Carlos, *K.C.*	46	711	15.5	t80	3
Brennan, Brian, *Clev.*	46	579	12.6	33	1
Nattiel, Ricky, *Den.*	46	574	12.5	t74	1
Brown, Tim, *Raiders*	43	725	16.9	t65	5
Blades, Brian, *Sea.*	40	682	17.1	55	8
Largent, Steve, *Sea.*	39	645	16.5	46	2
Duper, Mark, *Mia.*	39	626	16.1	56	1
Holland, Jamie, *S.D.*	39	536	13.7	45	1
Holman, Rodney, *Cin.*	39	527	13.5	33	3
Sewell, Steve, *Den.*	38	507	13.3	t68	5
Johnson, Trumaine, *Buff.*	37	514	13.9	49	0
Harmon, Ronnie, *Buff.*	37	427	11.5	36	3
McGee, Tim, *Cin.*	36	686	19.1	t78	6
Miller, Anthony, *S.D.*	36	526	14.6	49	3
Dickerson, Eric, *Ind.*	36	377	10.5	t50	1
James, Lionel, *S.D.*	36	279	7.8	31	1

t = Touchdown

AFC RECEIVERS – Most Yards

	Yards	No	Ave	Long	TD
Brown, Eddie, *Cin.*	1273	53	24.0	t86	9
Hill, Drew, *Hou.*	1141	72	15.8	t57	10
Clayton, Mark, *Mia.*	1129	86	13.1	t45	14
Toon, Al, *Jets*	1067	93	11.5	42	5
Givins, Ernest, *Hou.*	976	60	16.3	46	5
Lipps, Louis, *Pitt.*	973	50	19.5	t89	5
Reed, Andre, *Buff.*	968	71	13.6	t65	6
Paige, Stephone, *K.C.*	902	61	14.8	49	7
Johnson, Vance, *Den.*	896	68	13.2	86	5
Brooks, Bill, *Ind.*	867	54	16.1	t53	3
Jackson, Mark, *Den.*	852	46	18.5	63	6
Fernandez, Mervyn, *Raiders*	805	31	26.0	t85	4
Shuler, Mickey, *Jets*	805	70	11.5	t42	5
Langhorne, Reggie, *Clev.*	780	57	13.7	t77	7
Brown, Tim, *Raiders*	725	43	16.9	t65	5
Carson, Carlos, *K.C.*	711	46	15.5	t80	3
McGee, Tim, *Cin.*	686	36	19.1	t78	6
Blades, Brian, *Sea.*	682	40	17.1	55	8
Jensen, Jim, *Mia.*	652	58	11.2	31	5
Williams, John L., *Sea.*	651	58	11.2	t75	3
Largent, Steve, *Sea.*	645	39	16.5	46	2
Duper, Mark, *Mia.*	626	39	16.1	56	1
Palmer, Paul, *K.C.*	611	53	11.5	t71	4
Brennan, Brian, *Clev.*	579	46	12.6	33	1
Byner, Earnest, *Clev.*	576	59	9.8	t39	2
Edmunds, Ferrell, *Mia.*	575	33	17.4	t80	3
Nattiel, Ricky, *Den.*	574	46	12.5	t74	1
Walker, Wesley, *Jets*	551	26	21.2	t50	7
Lofton, James, *Raiders*	549	28	19.6	57	0
Holland, Jamie, *S.D.*	536	39	13.7	45	1
Holman, Rodney, *Cin.*	527	39	13.5	33	3
Miller, Anthony, *S.D.*	526	36	14.6	49	3
Johnson, Trumaine, *Buff.*	514	37	13.9	49	0
Sewell, Steve, *Den.*	507	38	13.3	t68	5
Morgan, Stanley, *N.E.*	502	31	16.2	32	4

t = Touchdown

Cincinnati wide receiver Eddie Brown had the season's highest single-game total of 216 yards receiving on Week Ten.

AFC RUSHERS

	Att	Yards	Ave	Long	TD
Dickerson, Eric, *Ind.*	388	1659	4.3	t41	14
Stephens, John, *N.E.*	297	1168	3.9	52	4
Anderson, Gary, *S.D.*	225	1119	5.0	36	3
Woods, Ickey, *Cin.*	203	1066	5.3	56	15
Warner, Curt, *Sea.*	266	1025	3.9	29	10
Rozier, Mike, *Hou.*	251	1002	4.0	28	10
McNeil, Freeman, *Jets*	219	944	4.3	28	6
Brooks, James, *Cin.*	182	931	5.1	t51	8
Thomas, Thurman, *Buff.*	207	881	4.3	t37	2
Williams, John L., *Sea.*	189	877	4.6	t44	4
Allen, Marcus, *Raiders*	223	831	3.7	32	7
Hoge, Merril, *Pitt.*	170	705	4.1	20	3
Dorsett, Tony, *Den.*	181	703	3.9	26	5
Jackson, Bo, *Raiders*	136	580	4.3	25	3
Byner, Earnest, *Clev.*	157	576	3.7	t27	3
Hector, Johnny, *Jets*	137	561	4.1	19	10
Winder, Sammy, *Den.*	149	543	3.6	35	4
Vick, Roger, *Jets*	128	540	4.2	17	3
Pinkett, Allen, *Hou.*	122	513	4.2	27	7
Mack, Kevin, *Clev.*	123	485	3.9	65	3
Okoye, Christian, *K.C.*	105	473	4.5	48	3
Highsmith, Alonzo, *Hou.*	94	466	5.0	42	2
Palmer, Paul, *K.C.*	134	452	3.4	t26	2
Perryman, Bob, *N.E.*	146	448	3.1	16	6
Heard, Herman, *K.C.*	106	438	4.1	20	0
Riddick, Robb, *Buff.*	111	438	3.9	21	12
Hampton, Lorenzo, *Mia.*	117	414	3.5	33	9
Williams, Warren, *Pitt.*	87	409	4.7	33	0
Wilson, Stanley, *Cin.*	112	398	3.6	19	2
Manoa, Tim, *Clev.*	99	389	3.9	34	2
Stradford, Troy, *Mia.*	95	335	3.5	18	2
Jackson, Earnest, *Pitt.*	74	315	4.3	t29	3
Mueller, Jamie, *Buff.*	81	296	3.7	20	0
Davenport, Ron, *Mia.*	55	273	5.0	64	0
Esiason, Boomer, *Cin.*	43	248	5.8	24	1
Saxon, James, *K.C.*	60	236	3.9	14	2
Elway, John, *Den.*	54	234	4.3	26	1
Bentley, Albert, *Ind.*	45	230	5.1	20	2
Carter, Rodney, *Pitt.*	36	216	6.0	t64	3
Spencer, Tim, *S.D.*	44	215	4.9	24	0
Harmon, Ronnie, *Buff.*	57	212	3.7	32	1
Brister, Bubby, *Pitt.*	45	209	4.6	20	6
Flutie, Doug, *N.E.*	38	179	4.7	16	1
Malone, Mark, *S.D.*	37	169	4.6	t36	4
Smith, Steve, *Raiders*	38	162	4.3	21	3
Kelly, Jim, *Buff.*	35	154	4.4	20	0
Dupard, Reggie, *N.E.*	52	151	2.9	15	2
Adams, Curtis, *S.D.*	38	149	3.9	14	1
Chandler, Chris, *Ind.*	46	139	3.0	t29	3
Sewell, Steve, *Den.*	32	135	4.2	26	1
Lipps, Louis, *Pitt.*	6	129	21.5	t39	1
Stone, Dwight, *Pitt.*	40	127	3.2	11	0
Laufenberg, Babe, *S.D.*	31	120	3.9	23	0

t = Touchdown

AFC SCORING – Kickers

	XP	XPA	FG	FGA	PTS
Norwood, Scott, *Buff.*	33	33	32	37	129
Anderson, Gary, *Pitt.*	34	35	28	36	118
Biasucci, Dean, *Ind.*	39	40	25	32	114
Zendejas, Tony, *Hou.*	48	50	22	34	114
Leahy, Pat, *Jets*	43	43	23	28	112
Johnson, Norm, *Sea.*	39	39	22	28	105
Karlis, Rich, *Den.*	36	37	23	36	105
Bahr, Matt, *Clev.*	32	33	24	29	104
Lowery, Nick, *K.C.*	23	23	27	32	104
Bahr, Chris, *Raiders*	37	39	18	29	91
Breech, Jim, *Cin.*	56	59	11	16	89
Reveiz, Fuad, *Mia.*	31	32	8	12	55
Abbott, Vince, *S.D.*	15	15	8	12	39
Staurovsky, Jason, *N.E.*	14	15	7	11	35

AFC SCORING – Touchdowns

	TD	TDR	TDP	TDM	PTS
Dickerson, Eric, *Ind.*	15	14	1	0	90
Woods, Ickey, *Cin.*	15	15	0	0	90
Brooks, James, *Cin.*	14	8	6	0	84
Clayton, Mark, *Mia.*	14	0	14	0	84
Riddick, Robb, *Buff.*	14	12	1	1	84
Hampton, Lorenzo, *Mia.*	12	9	3	0	72
Warner, Curt, *Sea.*	12	10	2	0	72
Rozier, Mike, *Hou.*	11	10	1	0	66
Hector, Johnny, *Jets*	10	10	0	0	60
Hill, Drew, *Hou.*	10	0	10	0	60
Brown, Eddie, *Cin.*	9	0	9	0	54
Pinkett, Allen, *Hou.*	9	7	2	0	54
Smith, Steve, *Raiders*	9	3	6	0	54
Allen, Marcus, *Raiders*	8	7	1	0	48
Blades, Brian, *Sea.*	8	0	8	0	48
Langhorne, Reggie, *Clev.*	8	1	7	0	48

AFC KICKOFF RETURNERS

	No	Yards	Ave	Long	TD
Brown, Tim, *Raiders*	41	1098	26.8	t97	1
Holland, Jamie, *S.D.*	31	810	26.1	t94	1
Miller, Anthony, *S.D.*	25	648	25.9	t93	1
Humphery, Bobby, *Jets*	21	510	24.3	48	0
Martin, Sammy, *N.E.*	31	735	23.7	t95	1
Woodson, Rod, *Pitt.*	37	850	23.0	t92	1
Edmonds, Bobby Joe, *Sea.*	40	900	22.5	65	0
Young, Glen, *Clev.*	29	635	21.9	34	0
Allen, Marvin, *N.E.*	18	391	21.7	30	0
Jennings, Stanford, *Cin.*	32	684	21.4	t98	1
Bell, Ken, *Den.*	36	762	21.2	38	0
Cribbs, Joe, *Mia.*	41	863	21.0	44	0
Stone, Dwight, *Pitt.*	29	610	21.0	t92	1
Fontenot, Herman, *Clev.*	21	435	20.7	84	0
Harris, Leonard, *Hou.*	34	678	19.9	56	0
Bentley, Albert, *Ind.*	39	775	19.9	40	0
Townsell, JoJo, *Jets*	31	601	19.4	40	0
Palmer, Paul, *K.C.*	23	364	15.8	23	0

t = Touchdown
Leader based on average return, minimum 18 returns

Left: San Diego's Gary Anderson had the season's highest single-game total of 217 yards rushing on Week Sixteen.

Above: Eric Dickerson evades a tackle and gathers himself for yet another surge.

AFC PUNTERS

	No	Yards	Long	Ave	Total Punts	TB	Blk	Opp Ret	Ret Yds	In 20	Net Ave
Newsome, Harry, *Pitt.*	65	2950	62	45.4	71	10	6	40	418	9	32.8
Mojsiejenko, Ralf, *S.D.*	85	3745	62	44.1	86	11	1	56	558	22	34.5
Horan, Mike, *Den.*	65	2861	70	44.0	65	2	0	33	364	19	37.8
Stark, Rohn, *Ind.*	64	2784	65	43.5	64	8	0	37	418	15	34.5
Roby, Reggie, *Mia.*	64	2754	64	43.0	64	9	0	35	318	18	35.3
Gossett, Jeff, *Raiders*	91	3804	58	41.8	91	8	0	47	397	27	35.7
Rodriguez, Ruben, *Sea.*	70	2858	68	40.8	70	4	0	36	202	14	36.8
Goodburn, Kelly, *K.C.*	76	3059	59	40.3	76	8	0	48	473	10	31.9
Runager, Max, *S.F.-Clev.*	49	1959	52	40.0	51	2	2	25	201	13	33.7
Kidd, John, *Buff.*	62	2451	60	39.5	62	2	0	36	222	13	35.3
Prokop, Joe, *Jets*	85	3310	64	38.9	85	10	0	34	201	26	34.2
Montgomery, Greg, *Hou.*	65	2523	61	38.8	65	5	0	35	206	12	34.1
Feagles, Jeff, *N.E.*	91	3482	74	38.3	91	8	0	37	217	24	34.1
Fulhage, Scott, *Cin.*	44	1672	53	38.0	46	5	2	24	220	13	29.4

Leader based on gross average, minimum 36 punts

AFC SACKERS

	No
Townsend, Greg, *Raiders*	11.5
Smith, Bruce, *Buff.*	11.0
Williams, Lee, *S.D.*	11.0
Bennett, Cornelius, *Buff.*	9.5
Skow, Jim, *Cin.*	9.5
Fletcher, Simon, *Den.*	9.0
Green, Jacob, *Sea.*	9.0
Childress, Ray, *Hou.*	8.5
Fuller, William, *Hou.*	8.5
Meads, Johnny, *Hou.*	8.0
Williams, Brent, *N.E.*	8.0
Jones, Sean, *Hou.*	7.5
Lyons, Marty, *Jets*	7.5
Gastineau, Mark, *Jets*	7.0
Tippett, Andre, *N.E.*	7.0
Buck, Jason, *Cin.*	6.0
Matthews, Clay, *Clev.*	6.0
Perry, Michael Dean, *Clev.*	6.0
Still, Art, *Buff.*	6.0
Davis, Scott, *Raiders*	5.5
Townsend, Andre, *Den.*	5.5
Buchanan, Charles, *Clev.*	5.0
Grant, David, *Cin.*	5.0
Grayson, Dave, *Clev.*	5.0
Hand, Jon, *Ind.*	5.0
Jones, Rulon, *Den.*	5.0
Pickel, Bill, *Raiders*	5.0
Rose, Ken, *Jets*	5.0
Turner, T.J., *Mia.*	5.0
Wise, Mike, *Raiders*	5.0
Woods, Tony, *Sea.*	5.0
Wright, Jeff, *Buff.*	5.0
Clancy, Sam, *Clev.*	4.5
Mersereau, Scott, *Jets*	4.5
Sochia, Brian, *Mia.*	4.5
Bussey, Barney, *Cin.*	4.0
Cline, Jackie, *Mia.*	4.0
Johnson, Tim, *Pitt.*	4.0
Maas, Bill, *K.C.*	4.0
O'Neal, Leslie, *S.D.*	4.0
Smerlas, Fred, *Buff.*	4.0
Bickett, Duane, *Ind.*	3.5
Bryant, Jeff, *Sea.*	3.5
Carr, Gregg, *Pitt.*	3.5
Cofield, Tim, *K.C.*	3.5
Nickerson, Hardy, *Pitt.*	3.5
Ryan, Jim, *Den.*	3.5
Williams, Gerald, *Pitt.*	3.5

Denver punter Mike Horan had the NFL's highest net average.

Special Teams

Dean Biasucci, who was successful with six of eight field goal attempts from 50-or-more yards was unlucky not to be voted to his second Pro Bowl. Punter Rohn Stark, too, was high in the voting after averaging an NFL, fourth-best 43.5-yard gross average. On punt return duty, Clarence Verdin ranked fourth in the league with an excellent 10.9-yard average which included a 73-yard touchdown return. Albert Bentley is a steady kickoff returner without ever looking likely to go all the way.

1989 DRAFT

Round	Name	Pos.	Ht.	Wt.	College
1.	Rison, Andre	WR	5-10	185	Michigan State
3.	Benson, Mitchell	DT	6-3	294	Texas Christian
4.	Tomberlin, Pat	T-G	6-2	299	Florida
6.	McDonald, Quintus	LB	6-3	241	Penn State
7.	Hunter, Ivy Joe	RB	6-0	218	Kentucky
7.	Washington, Charles	S	6-0	205	Cameron, Oklahoma
8.	Larson, Kurt	LB	6-3	230	Michigan State
9.	Mackall, William	WR	5-8	180	Tennessee-Martin
10.	Thompson, Jim	T	6-6	268	Auburn
11.	Johnson, Wayne	QB	6-4	213	Georgia
12.	DuBose, William	RB	5-11	220	South Carolina State
12.	Taylor, Steve	QB	5-11	200	Nebraska

VETERAN ROSTER

No.	Name	Pos.	Ht.	Wt.	NFL Year	College
97	Alston, O'Brien	LB	6-6	246	2	Maryland
79	Armstrong, Harvey	NT-DE	6-3	268	7	Southern Methodist
62	Baldinger, Brian	G-C	6-4	268	7	Duke
31	Ball, Michael	S	6-0	216	2	Southern
86	Banks, Roy	WR	5-10	193	2	Eastern Illinois
36	Baylor, John	CB	6-0	195	1	Southern Mississippi
81	Beach, Pat	TE	6-4	252	7	Washington State
20	Bentley, Albert	RB-KR	5-11	214	5	Miami
4	Biasucci, Dean	K	6-0	191	5	Western Carolina
50	Bickett, Duane	LB	6-5	243	5	Southern California
	Bostic, Keith	S	6-1	215	7	Michigan
85	Bouza, Matt	WR	6-3	212	8	California
84	Boyer, Mark	TE	6-4	242	5	Southern California
88	Brandes, John	TE	6-2	255	3	Cameron, Oklahoma
80	Brooks, Bill	WR-PR	6-0	191	4	Boston University
	Brown, Phillip	LB	6-2	230	1	Alabama
52	Bulluck, Brian	LB	6-3	236	1	North Carolina State
71	Call, Kevin	T	6-7	302	6	Colorado State
17	Chandler, Chris	QB	6-4	210	2	Washington
	Clancy, Sam	DE	6-7	275	6	Pittsburgh
38	Daniel, Eugene	CB	5-11	178	6	Louisiana State
48	Dee, Donnie	TE	6-4	247	2	Tulsa
29	Dickerson, Eric	RB	6-3	217	7	Southern Methodist
69	Dixon, Randy	G	6-3	290	3	Pittsburgh
53	Donaldson, Ray	C	6-3	288	10	Georgia
	Eisenhooth, Stan	C	6-5	274	2	Towson State
37	Goode, Chris	CB	6-0	195	3	Alabama
78	Hand, Jon	DE	6-7	298	4	Alabama
54	Herrod, Jeff	LB	6-0	243	2	Mississippi
75	Hinton, Chris	T	6-4	295	7	Northwestern
21	Holt, John	CB	5-10	179	9	West Texas State
	Jackson, Earnest	RB	5-9	222	7	Texas A&M
90	Johnson, Ezra	DE	6-4	250	13	Morris Brown
60	McQuaid, Dan	T	6-7	278	4	Nevada-Las Vegas
28	Miller, Chuckie	CB	5-10	180	2	UCLA
93	Odom, Cliff	LB	6-2	245	9	Texas-Arlington
	Plummer, Bruce	S-CB	6-1	194	3	Mississippi State
39	Prior, Mike	S	6-0	204	4	Illinois State
49	Pruitt, James	WR	6-3	198	4	Cal State-Fullerton
	Puzzuoli, Dave	NT	6-3	260	6	Pittsburgh
47	Robinson, Freddie	S	6-1	190	3	Alabama
3	Stark, Rohn	P	6-3	204	8	Florida State
26	Swoope, Craig	S	6-1	214	4	Illinois
27	Taylor, Keith	DB	5-11	193	2	Illinois
99	Thompson, Donnell	DE	6-4	275	9	North Carolina
10	Trudeau, Jack	QB	6-3	214	4	Illinois
64	Utt, Ben	G	6-6	286	8	Georgia Tech
83	Verdin, Clarence	WR-PR	5-8	163	4	Southwestern Louisiana
	Weathers, Clarence	WR	5-9	170	7	Delaware State
	Willis, Mitch	DE	6-8	280	5	Southern Methodist
34	Wonsley, George	RB	5-10	219	6	Mississippi State
56	Young, Fredd	LB	6-1	233	6	New Mexico State

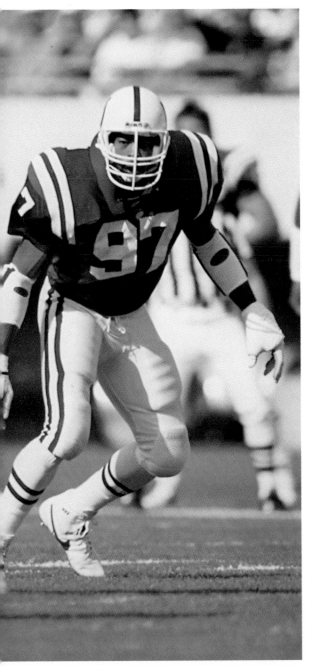

10th-round draftee O'Brien Alston proved to be an excellent acquisition.

MIAMI DOLPHINS

Address Joe Robbie Stadium, 2269 N.W. 199th Street, Miami, Florida 33056.

Stadium Joe Robbie Stadium, Miami.
Capacity 74,930 *Playing Surface* Grass (PAT).

Team Colours Aqua, Coral, and White.

Head Coach Don Shula – 20th year; 27th NFL.

Championships Division 1971,'72,'73,'74,'79,'81,'83,'84,'85; Conference 1971,'72,'73,'82,'84; Super Bowl 1972,'73.

History AFL 1966-69, AFC 1970-

Offense

'This one was tougher than all the others combined,' admitted Miami head coach Don Shula, looking back on a season in which the Dolphins went 6-10 and lost all eight of their games against AFC East rivals. But there are many reasons for thinking that this club, which owned its division for so long, could easily reassert that authority. First, there is quarterback Dan Marino. His reputation may have been dented over the last two years but his appetite for league records is unsatiated and he remains one of the most feared passers in the league. Inevitably, the passing offense had to suffer from the lack of a complementary rushing game. In turn, existing veteran running backs Lorenzo Hampton and Troy Stradford have failed to live up to their initial promise, but it is easy to be optimistic about draftee Sammie Smith. A powerful runner with tremendous speed and moves, the only nagging worry about Smith is that he has had injuries and has never played a full season. Ron Davenport, a genuine performer, will continue as the starting fullback. At wide receiver, Miami has a pair which can match any in the NFL. In 1988, Mark Clayton, a four-time Pro Bowler, set a Dolphins club record with 86 receptions and had the most receiving touchdowns (14) in the NFL. In terms of receiving yardage over the past five years, his total of 5,440 is unsurpassed. Clayton's partner, Mark Duper, is coming back from a league suspension which ended his season after Week Twelve. There is little to choose between these two multi-talented players. In only his first season, tight end Ferrell Edmunds demonstrated that, in just a few strides, he could leave all but the very fastest defenders stumbling in his furrow. His average of 17.4 yards over 33 receptions is better than that of many starting wide receivers. Former starter Bruce Hardy will return after injury but he is unlikely to displace Edmunds. Turning to the offensive line, one marvels yet again at the miracles worked by coach John Sandusky. Year in and year out the Dolphins give up the fewest sacks - the last of seven sacks conceded over the entire 1988 season was against the Colts on Week Four. Former all-pro center Dwight Stephenson has lost his battle with injury, leaving Jeff Dellenbach unchallenged at center, flanked by Roy Foster and the fast-improving Harry Galbreath. Two 11th-year men, Jon Giesler and Ronnie Lee, are immovable in the tackle positions.

Defense

It is only with grinding slowness that the defense is coming around and may now have just enough talent in key positions to go out looking for the opposition. John Bosa is coming off reconstructive knee surgery and is rehabilitating well enough to suggest that he could resume at defensive right end in a line which has Pro Bowl alternate Brian Sochia at nose tackle and the solid T.J. Turner at defensive left end. Jackie Cline, who started nine games in place of the injured Bosa, is a very useful backup. Former Cardinals Pro Bowler E.J. Junior is projected to start at left outside linebacker with Eric Kumerow holding an edge over Hugh Green to start on the right side. Green and the tenacious Rick Graf are the senior reserves for the outside positions. Mark Brown and the excellent John Offerdahl continue to occupy the inside spots but the aggressive Dave Ahrens could play a useful part. Without question, Junior will give the Dolphins a boost, and the same should be true of Louis Oliver, who was Miami's second pick in the first round, and even draftee David Holmes, who came in round four. A superb physical specimen of rare size and speed, Oliver has all the instincts of a tiger and hits like a train. His only problem may be a lack of judgement, but this is countered by the value of his total commitment. Entering training camp, the Dolphins project Oliver to become the starting free safety with Jarvis Williams shifting to strong safety, ahead of Bud Brown and Liffort Hobley. Interestingly, Williams and Oliver were teammates at the University of Florida. The probability is that Paul Lankford and William Judson will continue in the cornerback positions, with Don McNeal the senior backup, just a step behind Lankford. Last year, Williams and Judson shared the team lead, each with four pass interceptions.

1989 SCHEDULE OF GAMES		
September		
10 BUFFALO		4:00
17 at New England		1:00
24 NEW YORK JETS		4:00
October		
1 at Houston		12:00
8 CLEVELAND		1:00
15 at Cincinnati		1:00
22 GREEN BAY		1:00
29 at Buffalo		1:00
November		
5 INDIANAPOLIS		1:00
12 at New York Jets		1:00
19 at Dallas		12:00
26 PITTSBURGH		1:00
December		
3 at Kansas City		12:00
10 NEW ENGLAND (night)		8:00
17 at Indianapolis		1:00
24 KANSAS CITY		1:00

Special Teams

Both punter Reggie Roby and placekicker Fuad Reveiz have been working during the offseason to iron out the flaws which led to some inconsistencies in the 1988 campaign. In all common sense, neither man is threatened. Backup wide receiver Scott Schwedes is a class punt returner. If Sammie Smith performs immediately, Hampton may be required to earn his keep returning kickoffs.

1989 DRAFT

Round	Name	Pos.	Ht.	Wt.	College
1.	Smith, Sammie	RB	6-2	225	Florida State
1.	Oliver, Louis	S	6-2	225	Florida
4.	Holmes, David	CB-S	6-1	191	Syracuse
5.	Uhlenhake, Jeff	C	6-3	270	Ohio State
6.	Pritchett, Wes	LB	6-4	234	Notre Dame
7.	Zdelar, Jim	T	6-4	288	Youngstown State
8.	Stoyanovich, Pete	K	5-10	178	Indiana
9.	Batiste, Dana	LB	6-0	225	Texas A&M
10.	Glover, Deval	WR	5-11	184	Syracuse
10.	Ross, Greg	DT	6-2	272	Memphis State
11.	Weidner, Bert	DT	6-3	261	Kent State
12.	Brown, J.B.	S	6-0	189	Maryland

VETERAN ROSTER

No.	Name	Pos.	Ht.	Wt.	NFL Year	College
50	Ahrens, Dave	LB	6-4	245	9	Wisconsin
86	Banks, Fred	WR	5-10	180	4	Liberty
97	Bosa, John	DE	6-4	273	3	Boston College
43	Brown, Bud	S	6-0	193	6	Southern Mississippi
51	Brown, Mark	LB	6-2	238	7	Purdue
36	Brown, Tom	RB	6-1	220	1	Pittsburgh
59	Brudzinski, Bob	LB	6-4	235	13	Ohio State
77	Cheek, Louis	T	6-6	295	2	Texas A&M
	Clark, Greg	LB	6-0	221	2	Arizona State
83	Clayton, Mark	WR	5-9	184	7	Louisville
98	Cline, Jackie	DE-NT	6-5	280	3	Alabama
67	Conlin, Chris	C-G	6-3	280	2	Penn State
91	Cross, Jeff	DE	6-4	270	2	Missouri
30	Davenport, Ron	RB	6-2	232	5	Louisville
65	Dellenbach, Jeff	C	6-5	280	5	Wisconsin
74	Dennis, Mark	T	6-6	290	3	Illinois
85	Duper, Mark	WR	5-9	190	8	Northwestern State, La.
80	Edmunds, Ferrell	TE	6-6	248	2	Maryland
61	Foster, Roy	G	6-4	275	8	Southern California
53	Frye, David	LB	6-2	227	7	Purdue
58	Furjanic, Tony	LB	6-1	228	4	Notre Dame
48	Gage, Steve	S	6-3	210	3	Tulsa
62	Galbreath, Harry	G	6-1	275	2	Tennessee
42	Gibson, Ernest	CB	5-10	185	6	Furman
79	Giesler, Jon	T	6-5	272	11	Michigan
99	Graf, Rick	LB	6-5	249	3	Wisconsin
55	Green, Hugh	LB	6-2	228	9	Pittsburgh
27	Hampton, Lorenzo	RB-KR	5-11	208	5	Florida
84	Hardy, Bruce	TE	6-4	234	11	Arizona State
92	Hill, Nate	NT	6-4	275	2	Auburn
29	Hobley, Liffort	S	6-0	202	4	Louisiana State
11	Jensen, Jim	WR-QB	6-4	220	9	Boston University
73	Johnson, Greg	G	6-4	295	2	Oklahoma
49	Judson, William	CB	6-1	192	8	South Carolina State
54	Junior, E.J.	LB	6-3	235	9	Alabama
88	Kinchen, Brian	TE	6-2	238	2	Louisiana State
90	Kumerow, Eric	LB	6-7	260	2	Ohio State
44	Lankford, Paul	CB	6-1	190	8	Penn State
72	Lee, Ronnie	T	6-3	275	11	Baylor
20	Logan, Marc	RB	5-11	225	2	Kentucky
13	Marino, Dan	QB	6-4	222	7	Pittsburgh
	Markland, Jeff	TE	6-3	245	1	Illinois
28	McNeal, Don	CB	6-0	193	9	Alabama
56	Offerdahl, John	LB	6-3	237	4	Western Michigan
10	Pease, Brent	QB	6-2	204	3	Montana
7	Reveiz, Fuad	K	5-11	220	5	Tennessee
4	Roby, Reggie	P	6-2	242	7	Iowa
81	Schwedes, Scott	WR-PR	6-0	182	3	Syracuse
70	Sochia, Brian	NT	6-3	275	7	N.W. Oklahoma State
35	Stark, Chad	RB	6-1	226	1	North Dakota State
31	Starr, Eric	RB	5-9	199	1	North Carolina
18	Stoudt, Cliff	QB	6-4	215	11	Youngstown State
23	Stradford, Troy	RB	5-9	192	3	Boston College
82	Teal, Jimmy	WR	5-11	175	5	Texas A&M
24	Thomas, Rodney	CB	5-10	190	2	Brigham Young
96	Thorp, Don	DE	6-4	260	4	Illinois
76	Toth, Tom	G	6-5	282	4	Western Michigan
95	Turner, T.J.	DE	6-4	280	4	Houston
21	Watkins, Bobby	CB	5-10	180	8	Southwest Texas State
26	Williams, Jarvis	S	5-11	196	2	Florida

Mark Clayton led the NFL with 14 touchdown receptions.

NEW ENGLAND PATRIOTS

AFC EASTERN DIVISION

Address Sullivan Stadium, Route 1, Foxboro, Mass. 02035.
Stadium Sullivan Stadium, Foxboro.
Capacity 60,794 *Playing Surface* Super Turf.
Team Colours Red, White, and Blue.
Head Coach Raymond Berry – 6th year.
Championships Division 1978,'86; Conference 1985.
History AFL 1960-69, AFC 1970-
    (Until 1971, they were known as the Boston Patriots.)

Offense

Needing only to beat Denver on the final weekend to reach the playoffs, the Patriots came up short, thus ending one of the more impressive charges of the 1988 season. Coming into 1989, they look very solid, the only problem for head coach Raymond Berry being to sort out the talent at quarterback and wide receiver. The quarterback problem focuses on Doug Flutie and former starter Tony Eason, with veteran Steve Grogan and Marc Wilson on the fringes. With the Patriots featuring the rushing game, the diminutive Flutie fitted the part, but, despite his particular kind of magic, his arm does not have quite the range of a healthy and more-experienced Tony Eason. The chances are that Eason will be standing over center on opening day. It was when right tackle Bruce Armstrong persuaded Berry to use the rushing game more often that rookie John Stephens came into his own. Even for a first-round pick, his contribution was a pleasant surprise as he dominated opponents and seemed to gain strength as the games wore on. His partnership with fullback Robert Perryman, ahead of backups Reggie Dupard and Mosi Tatupu, assures the Patriots of continued productivity. And they can anticipate much greater variety with the strengthening of the wide receiving corps via the draft. Hart Lee Dykes drifts easily into the unmarked spaces before cushioning the ball in his bucket-sized, kid-gloved hands. A potential superstar, he joins Irving Fryar and veteran Stanley Morgan. Fryar may never live up to his billing but, even short of that, he does pose a problem every time he lines up. Morgan is one of the great receivers of all time and it may be that neither of the backups, Cedric Jones and Sammy Martin, sees much action. Veteran tight end Russ Francis may not be back after undergoing knee surgery and it was sensible to draft Marv Cook to join Lin Dawson, Eric Sievers and Steve Johnson in what will be a healthy competition. Completing this fine offensive unit, the line now plays with great cohesion and confidence. Armstrong has emerged as the natural leader and Danny Villa has established ownership of the left tackle position. Left guard Sean Farrell received votes for one or two all-pro squads and right guard Ron Wooten was a solid, 14-game starter. At center, it was on merit that Mike Baab displaced Trevor Matich, the latter who, together with Paul Fairchild, now provides quality depth.

Defense

Despite injuries to key players, at times the Patriots' defense was virtually impenetrable and they ended the season ranked fifth in the entire NFL. The return of defensive end Kenneth Sims, who suffered a ruptured achilles tendon in the opening regular-season game, must help the defensive line which was forced to rely too heavily on Garin Veris and Brent Williams, the latter who led the team with eight sacks. Veris, in particular, is much better when used in short bursts. Rookie nose tackle Tim Goad made a major contribution, starting in all but the first two games. The departure of Toby Williams left a vacancy at reserve nose tackle but the unit was given a boost by the signing of former Rams starter Gary Jeter, who came as a free agent and joins another good defensive end, Milford Hodge, in reserve. Hovering behind the line, Andre Tippett still rates as the best all-purpose outside linebacker in the AFC. The other starters in a fine unit are Ed Reynolds, Johnny Rembert and Lawrence McGrew. Again, they missed the competitiveness of Ed Williams, who had started the final seven games of the 1987 season. Williams has had extensive surgery on a knee injury he sustained in the opening preseason game. The secondary is outstanding, with Raymond Clayborn the leader of a quartet completed by left cornerback Ronnie Lippett, strong safety Roland James and free safety Fred Marion. Clayborn, Marion and James shared the club lead with four interceptions. Following the loss of reserves Eugene Profit and Ernest Gibson in free agent moves, the Patriots used the draft to acquire four players with both Eric Coleman and Maurice Hurst coming in the top four rounds.

1989 SCHEDULE OF GAMES		
September		
10 at New York Jets		4:00
17 MIAMI		1:00
24 SEATTLE		1:00
October		
1 at Buffalo		1:00
8 HOUSTON		1:00
15 at Atlanta		1:00
22 at San Francisco		1:00
29 at Indianapolis		1:00
November		
5 NEW YORK JETS		1:00
12 NEW ORLEANS		1:00
19 BUFFALO		1:00
26 at Los Angeles Raiders		1:00
December		
3 INDIANAPOLIS		1:00
10 at Miami (night)		8:00
17 at Pittsburgh		1:00
24 LOS ANGELES RAMS		1:00

Special Teams

Poor placekicking may have lost the Patriots a couple of crucial games and the chances are that with free agent Teddy Garcia having gone to the Cardinals, former Atlanta kicker Greg Davis may beat out Jason Staurovsky. Punter Jeff Feagles had a modest gross average but to the Patriots his value lay in placing the ball inside the opposing 20-yard line 24 times. Also, only 40.7 per cent of his punts were returned. Irving Fryar continues to make punt returning a thing of grace and beauty. He ranked a respectable sixth in the NFL. Kickoff returner Sammy Martin ranked fifth in the NFL with an average boosted by a 95-yard touchdown return.

1989 DRAFT

Round	Name	Pos.	Ht.	Wt.	College
1.	Dykes, Hart Lee	WR	6-3	222	Oklahoma State
2.	Coleman, Eric	CB	5-11	185	Wyoming
3.	Cook, Marv	TE	6-5	243	Iowa
3.	Gannon, Chris	DE	6-5	260	Southwestern Louisiana
4.	Hurst, Maurice	CB	5-9	185	Southern
4.	Timpson, Michael	WR	5-11	175	Penn State
6.	Mitchel, Eric	RB	5-11	200	Oklahoma
7.	Lindstrom, Eric	LB	6-2	231	Boston College
8.	Rice, Rodney	CB	5-7	175	Brigham Young
8.	Zackery, Tony	S	6-1	200	Washington
9.	Norris, Darron	RB	5-9	192	Texas
9.	Wilson, Curtis	C	6-3	273	Missouri
10.	McNeil, Emanuel	DT	6-2	270	Tennessee-Martin
11.	Hinz, Tony	RB	6-0	210	Harvard
12.	Chubb, Aaron	LB	6-4	220	Georgia

VETERAN ROSTER

No.	Name	Pos.	Ht.	Wt.	NFL Year	College
39	Allen, Marvin	RB	5-10	215	2	Tulane
78	Armstrong, Bruce	T	6-4	284	3	Louisville
68	Baab, Mike	C	6-4	270	8	Texas
28	Bowman, Jim	S	6-2	210	5	Central Michigan
59	Brown, Vincent	LB	6-2	245	2	Mississippi Valley State
26	Clayborn, Raymond	CB	6-1	186	13	Texas
	Davis, Greg	K	5-11	197	3	Citadel
87	Dawson, Lin	TE	6-3	240	8	North Carolina State
	Douglas, David	T	6-4	280	4	Tennessee
21	Dupard, Reggie	RB	5-11	205	4	Southern Methodist
11	Eason, Tony	QB	6-4	212	7	Illinois
66	Fairchild, Paul	G-C	6-4	270	6	Kansas
62	Farrell, Sean	G	6-3	260	8	Penn State
6	Feagles, Jeff	P	6-0	198	2	Miami
2	Flutie, Doug	QB	5-10	175	4	Boston College
81	Francis, Russ	TE	6-6	242	14	Oregon
80	Fryar, Irving	WR-PR	6-0	200	6	Nebraska
48	Gadbois, Dennis	WR	6-1	183	3	Boston University
72	Goad, Tim	NT	6-3	280	2	North Carolina
14	Grogan, Steve	QB	6-4	210	15	Kansas State
35	Hansen, Bruce	RB	6-1	230	2	Brigham Young
97	Hodge, Milford	DE	6-3	278	4	Washington State
41	Holmes, Darryl	S	6-2	190	3	Fort Valley State
32	James, Craig	RB	6-0	215	6	Southern Methodist
38	James, Roland	S	6-2	191	10	Tennessee
	Jeter, Gary	DE	6-4	260	13	Southern California
85	Johnson, Steve	TE	6-6	245	2	Virginia Tech
83	Jones, Cedric	WR	6-1	184	8	Duke
	Jones, Mike	WR	5-11	183	7	Tennessee State
93	Jordan, Tim	LB	6-3	226	3	Wisconsin
42	Lippett, Ronnie	CB	5-11	180	7	Miami
31	Marion, Fred	S	6-2	191	8	Miami
82	Martin, Sammy	WR-KR	5-11	175	2	Louisiana State
64	Matich, Trevor	C-T	6-4	270	5	Brigham Young
50	McGrew, Lawrence	LB	6-5	233	9	Southern California
16	McGuire, Kennard	WR	5-10	170	1	Tennessee
23	McSwain, Rod	CB	6-1	198	6	Clemson
67	Moore, Steve	T	6-5	305	6	Tennessee State
86	Morgan, Stanley	WR	5-11	181	13	Tennessee
34	Perryman, Bob	RB	6-1	233	3	Michigan
76	Rehder, Tom	T	6-7	280	2	Notre Dame
52	Rembert, Johnny	LB	6-3	234	7	Clemson
95	Reynolds, Ed	LB	6-5	242	7	Virginia
88	Scott, Willie	TE	6-4	245	9	South Carolina
	Sievers, Eric	TE	6-3	238	9	Maryland
77	Sims, Ken	DE	6-5	271	7	Texas
4	Staurovsky, Jason	K	5-9	170	3	Tulsa
44	Stephens, John	RB	6-1	220	2	Northwestern State, La.
30	Tatupu, Mosi	RB	6-0	227	12	Southern California
56	Tippett, Andre	LB	6-3	241	8	Iowa
60	Veris, Garin	DE	6-4	255	5	Stanford
	Viaene, Dave	T	6-5	291	1	Minnesota-Duluth
73	Villa, Danny	T	6-5	305	3	Arizona State
94	Ward, David	LB	6-2	232	1	Southern Arkansas
96	Williams, Brent	DE	6-3	278	4	Toledo
54	Williams, Ed	LB	6-4	244	5	Texas
	Wilson, Marc	QB	6-6	205	9	Brigham Young
61	Wooten, Ron	G	6-4	273	8	North Carolina

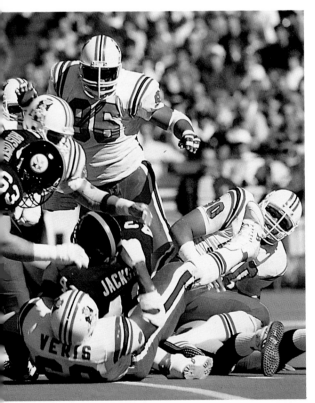

Brent Williams (# 96) led the Patriots with eight sacks.

NEW YORK JETS

Address 598 Madison Avenue, New York, N.Y. 10022.
Stadium Giants Stadium, East Rutherford.
  Capacity 76,891 *Playing Surface* AstroTurf.
Team Colours Kelly Green and White.
Head Coach Joe Walton – 7th year.
Championships AFL 1968; Super Bowl 1968.
History AFL 1960-69, AFC 1970-
  (Until 1963, they were known as the New York Titans.)

Offense

A year in which the Jets were not supposed to trouble anyone ended when they beat the Giants in the final minute to end up with a winning season. A close look at the offense reveals a squad which fits the model almost perfectly. There are three running backs, Freeman McNeil, Johnny Hector and Roger Vick, each of whom averaged better than four yards per carry. Ninth-year veteran McNeil has just had his best season since 1985 and it is good for the club that Hector, who led the team with ten touchdowns, provides a constant challenge. Vick continues to make steady progress though he has yet to take a game by the scruff of the neck. Again, each one plays a significant part in the passing offense. Turning to the specialists in that area, pass receiving, wide receiver Al Toon now is regarded as the AFC's premier possession receiver. And the fact that his average per reception is modest does no more than describe the way he is used by the Jets. Toon can go the distance with the best of them. When the Jets do need to go long, they turn to 13th-year veteran wide receiver Wesley Walker, who defies all logic by maintaining an advantage in speed even over the legions of young fliers who crowd the NFL's defensive secondaries. It is one of pro football's more exciting moments when Walker filters over the middle to make his reception before completing the distance, as surely will happen in the 1989 campaign. Following the retirement of Kurt Sohn, JoJo Townsell remains as the senior backup. As usual, the Jets can expect a good yield from tight end Mickey Shuler, who is coming off his second-best season for the club. Gradually, backup tight end K.D. Dunn is being eased into action. The most important aspect of the Jets' 1988 campaign may be the progress made by the offensive line, and it came despite the lengthy absence of top draftee tackle Dave Cadigan, who went on injured reserve with an ankle problem in mid-October. His return will strengthen a group which features tackles Reggie McElroy and the much improved Jeff Criswell, guards Dan Alexander and former first-rounder Mike Haight, and center Jim Sweeney. At quarterback the Jets may truly have found a pair which can share the role. Ken O'Brien is the classical sort, composed in the pocket and, on his day, a destroyer. When his poise begins to fade, Pat Ryan, the tough competitor, slips into the position with all the ease of a well-engineered component.

Defense

The abrupt loss of defensive end Mark Gastineau, who retired when seeming to be on his way back to top form, turned out not to be a factor for a defense which, though not yet dominating, has developed a belief in itself. Even so, a combination of coaching philosophy, the departures of free agents and the odd retirement dictated that the defense be given priority in a draft which yielded three defensive ends, a defensive tackle, three linebackers and two safeties. All three of draftee defensive ends, Dennis Byrd, Ron Stallworth and Marvin Washington, have the opportunity to make an impact as pass rushers on a defensive line which could use a few more sacks. Paul Frase closed out the season as the starter at defensive left end, with Scott Mersereau at nose tackle and team sack leader Marty Lyons at right end. With the arrival of top pick Jeff Lageman and third-rounder Joe Mott, the latter who played defensive end in college, the quality begins to stack up at linebacker. The probability is that both players will challenge in the outside positions for they could hardly be expected to displace veteran inside linebackers Kyle Clifton and Troy Benson, who, in that order, led the team in tackles. Equally, the current outside linebackers, Alex Gordon and Kevin McArthur, will not step aside without a fight and even backup Robin Cole, whose arrival from Pittsburgh had a catalytic effect, will want to have a say in things. The defensive secondary came together beautifully when the 1988 rookies, free safety Erik McMillan and right cornerback James Hasty, joined strong safety Rich Miano and left cornerback Bobby Humphery. Certainly, the rookies were challenged by opposing quarterbacks, but they responded in like kind with McMillan grabbing an AFC-best eight interceptions and Hasty coming second in the club with five. Miano was the third-leading tackler. There's just the chance that Terry Williams, returning after injury, will challenge Humphery.

1989 SCHEDULE OF GAMES	September	
	10 NEW ENGLAND	4:00
	17 at Cleveland	1:00
	24 at Miami	4:00
	October	
	1 INDIANAPOLIS	1:00
	9 LOS ANGELES RAIDERS (Mon.)	9:00
	15 at New Orleans	3:00
	22 at Buffalo	1:00
	29 SAN FRANCISCO	4:00
	November	
	5 at New England	1:00
	12 MIAMI	1:00
	19 at Indianapolis (night)	8:00
	26 ATLANTA	1:00
	December	
	3 at San Diego	1:00
	10 PITTSBURGH	1:00
	17 at Los Angeles Rams	1:00
	23 BUFFALO (Sat.)	12:30

Fullback Roger Vick has made steady progress.

Special Teams

Humphery and Townsell share the kickoff return duties to good effect. Indeed, Humphery, who ranked fourth in the NFL, could claim to offer the most consistent yield, for his average did not include a big return. Townsell comes into his own on punt returns, in which role he led the AFC. Pat Leahy is a fine placekicker, and although punter Joe Prokop's gross average was modest he planted 26 inside the opposing 20-yard line.

1989 DRAFT

Round	Name	Pos.	Ht.	Wt.	College
1.	Lageman, Jeff	LB	6-5	239	Virginia
2.	Byrd, Dennis	DE	6-4	265	Tulsa
3.	Mott, Joe	LB	6-3	240	Iowa
4.	Stallworth, Ron	DE	6-4	258	Auburn
5.	Martin, Tony	WR	6-0	188	Mesa, Colorado
6.	Washington, Marvin	DE	6-4	245	Idaho
6.	Dixon, Titus	WR-KR	5-6	162	Troy State
7.	Moore, Stevon	S	5-11	202	Mississippi
8.	Brown, Anthony	RB	5-9	210	West Virginia
9.	Marlatt, Pat	DT	6-5	270	West Virginia
10.	Bob, Adam	LB	6-1	242	Texas A&M
11.	Holmes, Artie	S	5-11	200	Washington State
12.	Snead, Willie	WR	5-11	190	Florida

VETERAN ROSTER

No.	Name	Pos.	Ht.	Wt.	NFL Year	College
60	Alexander, Dan	G	6-4	274	13	Louisiana State
31	Barber, Marion	RB	6-3	228	8	Minnesota
54	Benson, Troy	LB	6-2	235	4	Pittsburgh
64	Bingham, Guy	C-G	6-3	260	10	Montana
42	Booty, John	CB-S	6-0	179	2	Texas Christian
66	Cadigan, Dave	T	6-4	285	2	Southern California
59	Clifton, Kyle	LB	6-4	236	6	Texas Christian
	Cofield, Tim	LB	6-2	245	4	Elizabeth City State
90	Cole, Robin	LB	6-2	225	13	New Mexico
	Collier, Steve	T	6-7	342	2	Bethune-Cookman
61	Criswell, Jeff	T	6-7	284	3	Graceland
	Curtis, Bobby	LB	6-3	250	2	Savannah State
80	Dunn, K.D.	TE	6-2	237	5	Clemson
30	Faaola, Nuu	RB	5-11	220	4	Hawaii
91	Frase, Paul	DE	6-5	273	2	Syracuse
55	Gordon, Alex	LB	6-5	246	3	Cincinnati
79	Haight, Mike	G	6-4	281	4	Iowa
84	Harper, Michael	WR	5-10	180	4	Southern California
40	Hasty, James	CB	6-0	200	2	Washington State
34	Hector, Johnny	RB	5-11	202	7	Texas A&M
28	Howard, Carl	CB	6-2	190	6	Rutgers
48	Humphery, Bobby	CB-KR	5-10	180	6	New Mexico State
	Konecny, Mark	RB-PR	6-0	200	3	Alma
	Kurisko, Jamie	TE	6-3	240	2	Southern Connecticut
5	Leahy, Pat	K	6-0	196	16	St Louis
93	Lyons, Marty	DE	6-5	269	11	Alabama
15	Mackey, Kyle	QB	6-3	216	3	East Texas State
57	McArthur, Kevin	LB	6-2	250	4	Lamar
68	McElroy, Reggie	T	6-6	276	7	West Texas State
22	McMillan, Erik	S	6-2	197	2	Missouri
24	McNeil, Freeman	RB	5-11	209	9	UCLA
94	Mersereau, Scott	NT	6-3	273	2	Southern Connecticut
36	Miano, Rich	S	6-0	200	5	Hawaii
46	Mitchell, Michael	CB	5-9	192	2	Howard Payne
86	Neubert, Keith	TE	6-5	250	1	Nebraska
77	Nichols, Gerald	NT	6-2	267	3	Florida State
7	O'Brien, Ken	QB	6-4	200	7	California-Davis
6	Prokop, Joe	P	6-2	224	4	Cal Poly-Pomona
25	Radachowsky, George	S	5-11	190	5	Boston College
	Riley, Bobby	WR	5-8	168	1	Oklahoma State
92	Rose, Ken	LB	6-1	204	3	Nevada-Las Vegas
10	Ryan, Pat	QB	6-3	210	12	Tennessee
75	Schreiber, Adam	C-G	6-4	277	6	Texas
82	Shuler, Mickey	TE	6-3	231	12	Penn State
	Sterling, Rob	S	5-11	195	1	Maine
53	Sweeney, Jim	C	6-4	270	6	Pittsburgh
88	Toon, Al	WR	6-4	205	5	Wisconsin
83	Townsell, JoJo	WR-PR	5-9	180	5	UCLA
43	Vick, Roger	RB	6-3	228	3	Texas A&M
	Walker, Jackie	LB	6-5	245	4	Jackson State
85	Walker, Wesley	WR	6-0	182	13	California
33	Williams, Terry	CB	5-11	191	2	Bethune-Cookman
76	Withycombe, Mike	T-G	6-5	295	2	Fresno State

CINCINNATI BENGALS

Address 200 Riverfront Stadium, Cincinnati, Ohio 45202.
Stadium Riverfront Stadium, Cincinnati.
  Capacity 59,754 *Playing Surface* AstroTurf-8.
Team Colours Black, Orange, and White.
Head Coach Sam Wyche – 6th year.
Championships Division 1970,'73,'81,'88; Conference 1981,'88.
History AFL 1968-69, AFC 1970-

Offense

Everything should be rosy for a Cincinnati squad which has no obvious weaknesses and may look forward to being even stronger in the coming season. If there is a worry, it is over quarterback Boomer Esiason, who, as the NFL leading passer, directed the Bengals' surge to the AFC Central division title but showed little of that form in the playoffs. Subsequently, a sore rotator cuff kept him out of the Pro Bowl. The shoulder was a significant problem but, after treatment in the offseason, he began passing in early June and there is every prospect that he will be back to full form. Even so, and following the loss of third-stringer Mike Norseth, the Bengals used a third-round option to draft Erik Wilhelm. The offensive line will be without injured right tackle Joe Walter, whose influence from mid-season onwards added great impetus to the final push. After reconstructive knee surgery, he could be unavailable for the entire year. However, it is not that the Bengals are short on what, by tradition, is a huge line. Led by the AFC's premier tackle, Anthony Munoz, it is solid in every phase of play. The other starters are tackle Brian Blados, guards Bruce Reimers and Max Montoya, and center Bruce Kozerski, the latter who has made dramatic strides. At running back, last year's rookie, Ickey Woods, quickly has emerged as the leader and forms a first-class, cut-and-thrust partnership with the nippy James Brooks. Woods rushed for 1,066 yards, and while Brooks fell short of the target by 69 yards, both players averaged better than five yards per carry. Stanford Jennings is the senior reserve at halfback but the suspension of Stanley Wilson did leave a gap behind Woods at fullback, and it was with this in mind that Eric Ball was selected with the club's first draft option. Catching passes is not a problem, with Eddie Brown darting down one sideline and either Tim McGee or Cris Collinsworth on the other side. Brown, who had single-game hauls of 143, 127, 103, an NFL-best 216 and 115 yards, can rip any team apart. Reserve Ira Hillary has deep speed. From the tight end position, Rodney Holman makes a fine contribution to the passing offense and throws a decent block. Behind him, Jim Riggs is making steady progress, though he will remain the third-stringer if Eric Kattus returns from injury.

Defense

It is difficult to remember the Bengals ever being tough on defense, but the marshmallow image is a thing of the past and, particularly in the secondary, they are beginning to appear professionally secure. The reappearance of nose tackle Tim Krumrie, whose sickening injury in the Super Bowl was a major factor in the Bengals' inability to harry Joe Montana, is crucial. The breaks in his leg did not have complications and he is expected to be in full training, if not quite ready, by opening day. The usual starting defensive ends are Jim Skow, who led the club with 9.5 sacks, and Jason Buck, who is rapidly adjusting to the pace of the pros. On obvious passing downs, backup tackle David Grant joins the line in what often is a 4-1-6 formation. Grant does have a nose for action and he could be a useful substitute for Krumrie in the early stages. From the linebackers the club does need greater pressure. They are not found wanting on rushing plays - when the opposition comes at them - but they show little by way of imagination in causing a ruckus. The return of inside linebacker Kevin Walker, who was injured for most of his rookie season, could bring extra pressure on the opposing centers. Otherwise, the starting four will have Reggie Williams, the great veteran for whom it will be the final season, and Leon White on the outsides, with Joe Kelly partnering Carl Zander inside. White made good progress to beat out Emanuel King, who has left the club. The secondary was exposed by Joe Montana but it remains true that cornerbacks Lewis Billups and Eric Thomas can cover all but the very best wide receivers one-on-one. Strong safety David Fulcher is developing a league-wide reputation for his blitzing and free safety Solomon Wilcots did a fine job replacing Robert Jackson. Wilcots, however, may be eased aside by the multiple talents of Rickey Dixon, last year's first-round pick, who is ready to make his bid.

1989 SCHEDULE OF GAMES		
September		
10 at Chicago		12:00
17 PITTSBURGH		1:00
25 CLEVELAND (Mon.)		9:00
October		
1 at Kansas City		12:00
8 at Pittsburgh		1:00
15 MIAMI		1:00
22 INDIANAPOLIS		1:00
29 TAMPA BAY		1:00
November		
5 at Los Angeles Raiders		1:00
13 at Houston (Mon.)		8:00
19 DETROIT		1:00
26 at Buffalo		1:00
December		
3 at Cleveland		1:00
10 SEATTLE		1:00
17 HOUSTON		1:00
25 at Minnesota (Mon.)		8:00

Special Teams

Placekicker Jim Breech does not have a powerful leg but his pressure field goals in Super Bowl XXIII confirmed his value to the Bengals. Punter Lee Johnson helps out by kicking off and being on hand for long-range field goals - he landed a 50-yarder in 1988. Ira Hillary may return more punts after averaging 9.8 yards in 1988 while Stanford Jennings now causes more than a few tremors after returning one kickoff 98 yards for a touchdown in the regular season and almost matching that distance in the Super Bowl.

1989 DRAFT

Round	Name	Pos.	Ht.	Wt.	College
2.	Ball, Eric	RB	6-1	216	UCLA
2.	Childress, Freddie	G	6-3	322	Arkansas
3.	Wilhelm, Erik	QB	6-2	215	Oregon State
4.	Owens, Kerry	LB	6-1	233	Arkansas
4.	Woods, Rob	T	6-5	275	Arizona
5.	Tuatagaloa, Natu	DT	6-3	256	California
6.	Taylor, Craig	RB	5-11	224	West Virginia
7.	Smith, Kendal	WR-KR	5-10	182	Utah State
8.	Chenault, Chris	LB	6-1	242	Kentucky
9.	Stephens, Richard	T	6-6	290	Tulsa
10.	Holloway, Cornell	CB	5-9	175	Pittsburgh
10.	Jean, Bob	QB	6-2	210	New Hampshire
11.	Wells, Dana	NT	6-0	269	Arizona
12.	Jones, Scott	T-G	6-4	265	Washington

VETERAN ROSTER

No.	Name	Pos.	Ht.	Wt.	NFL Year	College
35	Barber, Chris	S	6-0	187	2	North Carolina A&T
53	Barker, Leo	LB	6-2	227	6	New Mexico State
24	Billups, Lewis	CB	5-11	190	4	North Alabama
74	Blados, Brian	T-G-C	6-5	295	6	North Carolina
55	Brady, Ed	LB	6-2	235	6	Illinois
3	Breech, Jim	K	5-6	161	11	California
21	Brooks, James	RB	5-10	182	9	Auburn
81	Brown, Eddie	WR	6-0	185	5	Miami
99	Buck, Jason	DE	6-5	264	3	Brigham Young
27	Bussey, Barney	S	6-0	195	4	South Carolina
80	Collinsworth, Cris	WR	6-5	192	9	Florida
29	Dixon, Rickey	CB-S	5-11	181	2	Oklahoma
73	Edwards, Eddie	DE	6-5	256	13	Miami
7	Esiason, Boomer	QB	6-5	225	6	Maryland
33	Fulcher, David	S	6-3	228	4	Arizona State
17	Fulhage, Scott	P	5-11	191	3	Kansas State
98	Grant, David	NT	6-4	277	2	West Virginia
71	Hammerstein, Mike	DE	6-4	270	3	Michigan
89	Hillary, Ira	WR-PR	5-11	190	3	South Carolina
40	Holifield, Jon	RB	6-0	202	1	West Virginia
82	Holman, Rodney	TE	6-3	238	8	Tulane
36	Jennings, Stanford	RB-KR	6-1	205	6	Furman
68	Jetton, Paul	G	6-4	288	1	Texas
11	Johnson, Lee	P	6-2	198	5	Brigham Young
84	Kattus, Eric	TE	6-5	235	4	Michigan
58	Kelly, Joe	LB	6-2	231	4	Washington
64	Kozerski, Bruce	C	6-4	275	6	Holy Cross
69	Krumrie, Tim	NT	6-2	268	7	Wisconsin
88	Martin, Mike	WR-PR	5-10	186	7	Illinois
72	McClendon, Skip	DE	6-7	275	3	Arizona State
85	McGee, Tim	WR	5-10	175	4	Tennessee
65	Montoya, Max	G	6-5	275	11	UCLA
78	Munoz, Anthony	T	6-6	278	10	Southern California
86	Parker, Carl	WR	6-2	201	2	Vanderbilt
75	Reimers, Bruce	G	6-7	280	6	Iowa State
87	Riggs, Jim	TE	6-5	245	3	Clemson
94	Romer, Rich	LB	6-3	214	2	Union College
77	Rourke, Jim	G-T	6-5	263	9	Boston College
15	Schonert, Turk	QB	6-1	196	10	Stanford
70	Skow, Jim	DE	6-3	255	4	Nebraska
22	Thomas, Eric	CB	5-11	181	3	Tulane
59	Walker, Kevin	LB	6-2	238	2	Maryland
63	Walter, Joe	T	6-6	290	5	Texas Tech
51	White, Leon	LB	6-3	245	4	Brigham Young
41	Wilcots, Solomon	S	5-11	185	3	Colorado
57	Williams, Reggie	LB	6-1	232	14	Dartmouth
30	Woods, Ickey	RB	6-2	232	2	Nevada-Las Vegas
91	Zander, Carl	LB	6-2	235	5	Tennessee

Defensive back Rickey Dixon should command a starting spot.

CLEVELAND BROWNS

Address Tower B, Cleveland Stadium, Cleveland, Ohio 44114.

Stadium Cleveland Stadium, Cleveland.
  Capacity 80,098 *Playing Surface* Grass.

Team Colours Seal Brown, Orange, and White.

Head Coach Bud Carson – 1st year.

Championships Division 1971,'80,'85,'86,'87; AAFC 1946,'47,'48,'49; NFL 1950,'54,'55,'64.

History AAFC 1946-49, NFL 1950-69, AFC 1970-

Offense

Despite injuries to key players, the most costly being the loss of quarterback Bernie Kosar for seven full games, the Browns reached the playoffs for the fourth consecutive year and, with the offensive line as the only possible exception, they are expected to be stronger for their 1989 challenge. The problem on the line comes with the departure of free agent left guard Larry Williams, who started in 13 games. It remains to be seen just how valuable he was but it means that backup Rickey Bolden will be given the chance to start in company with guard Dan Fike, tackles Paul Farren and Cody Risien, and center Gregg Rakoczy. Free agent guard Ted Banker started for the Jets in 1988 before sustaining an injury. The loss of backup center Frank Winters has been cushioned by the signing of free agent Tom Baugh, who started the first ten games of last season for Kansas City before injury. Kosar has recovered from his knocks and is ready to re-establish the momentum which saw him win the 1987 AFC passing title. With not the most elegant delivery in pro football, his passes nonetheless fly true and there is not the slightest flaw in his self-confidence. His senior backup still seems likely to be Mike Pagel or Don Strock, the latter whose skills seem immune to the erosive effects of time. The starting receivers, Webster Slaughter and Reginald Langhorne, do not lack for speed, and they are supported by the sure hands of Brian Brennan. The new kid on the block, draftee Lawyer Tillman, can play at either wide receiver or tight end, and, with the speed that fits the Browns' philosophy, almost certainly will be seen as the successor to the great veteran tight end, Ozzie Newsome. Backup Derek Tennell is used in double-tight end slots and on special teams. At running back, where major changes have taken place, the Browns appear to be improved, perhaps even greatly. Earnest Byner has gone to the Redskins in exchange for Mike Oliphant in a move which trades away guaranteed productivity for the prospect of exciting speed. More significantly, the Browns used their premier option in the draft to select Eric Metcalf, an all-purpose back with active feet and super open-field moves. Indeed, the evolving picture throughout the offense is one of speed and elusiveness, and it is as well that the Browns have the hefty Kevin Mack at fullback.

Defense

The loss of both starting nose tackle Bob Golic and pass-rushing defensive end Sam Clancy leaves the Browns wafer thin for the defensive line. Veteran defensive end Carl Hairston and Michael Dean Perry will compete for the right side spot, Darryl Sims will play at nose tackle and either Al Baker or Charles Buchanan will come in at left defensive end. Fourth-round draftee defensive end Andrew Stewart provides some depth. At linebacker, the Browns have come out ahead in moves which saw the departure of the disappointing Mike Junkin to Kansas City and the signing of former Colts starter Barry Krauss, the latter who will compete with Eddie Johnson to start at right inside linebacker. David Grayson's pedigree finally told as he fought his way through to start after being given his big chance in the 1987 replacement games. His rapid emergence countered the slow development of 1988 first-round pick Clifford Charlton. The other starters, Mike Johnson and Clay Matthews, are first class. Johnson led the club with 132 tackles while Matthews, a current Pro Bowler, shared the club lead with six quarterback sacks. The linebacking is very sound and that is also true of the secondary, where tenth-round draftee Brian Washington, elbowed his way in to start 14 games at strong safety. The reputations of cornerbacks Frank Minnifield and Hanford Dixon have reached the level of respectability which comes with having been voted to the Pro Bowl for the last three years. However, the growing feeling is that the key player in the secondary is free safety Felix Wright, who led the club with five interceptions as one measurable aspect of his value. Backups Stephen Braggs and Thane Gash have been joined by two good prospects in draftees Kyle Kramer and Gary Wilkerson.

1989 SCHEDULE OF GAMES		
September		
10	at Pittsburgh	4:00
17	NEW YORK JETS	1:00
25	at Cincinnati (Mon.)	9:00
October		
1	DENVER	1:00
8	at Miami	1:00
15	PITTSBURGH	4:00
23	CHICAGO (Mon.)	9:00
29	HOUSTON	1:00
November		
5	at Tampa Bay	1:00
12	at Seattle	1:00
19	KANSAS CITY	1:00
23	at Detroit (Thanksgiving)	12:30
December		
3	CINCINNATI	1:00
10	at Indianapolis	4:00
17	MINNESOTA	1:00
23	at Houston (Sat. night)	7:00

Special Teams

Bryan Wagner should take over as punter and the Browns will be satisfied if he can match the output of departed free agent Max Runager. Placekicker Matt Bahr will be challenged by draftee Dan Plocki but such a steady veteran is not likely to be troubled. For Gerald (Ice Cube) McNeil it was not a banner year, but he is likely to remain and may even return a few kickoffs following the release of Glen Young.

1989 DRAFT

Round	Name	Pos.	Ht.	Wt.	College
1.	Metcalf, Eric	RB	5-9	178	Texas
2.	Tillman, Lawyer	WR-TE	6-4	223	Auburn
4.	Stewart, Andrew	DE	6-4	255	Cincinnati
5.	Kramer, Kyle	S	6-2	175	Bowling Green
5.	Joines, Vernon	WR	6-1	190	Maryland
6.	Wilkerson, Gary	CB	6-0	183	Penn State
7.	Graybill, Mike	T	6-7	260	Boston University
8.	Aeilts, Rick	TE	6-5	245	Southeast Missouri State
10.	Buddenberg, John	T	6-5	270	Akron
11.	Plocki, Dan	K	5-7	176	Maryland
12.	Brown, Marlon	LB	6-3	221	Memphis State

VETERAN ROSTER

No.	Name	Pos.	Ht.	Wt.	NFL Year	College
9	Bahr, Matt	K	5-10	175	11	Penn State
60	Baker, Al	DE	6-6	280	12	Colorado State
43	Baker, Tony	RB	5-10	180	3	East Carolina
68	Banker, Ted	G-C	6-2	275	6	Southeast Missouri
97	Banks, Robert	DE	6-5	254	2	Notre Dame
64	Baugh, Tom	C	6-3	285	4	Southern Illinois
87	Birden, J.J.	WR	5-9	160	1	Oregon
24	Blaylock, Anthony	CB	5-11	190	2	Winston-Salem State
77	Bolden, Rickey	T-G	6-4	280	6	Southern Methodist
36	Braggs, Stephen	CB	5-10	180	3	Texas
86	Brennan, Brian	WR	5-9	178	6	Boston College
72	Buchanan, Charles	DE	6-3	245	2	Tennessee State

No.	Name	Pos.	Ht.	Wt.	NFL Year	College
85	Butler, Ray	WR	6-3	204	10	Southern California
58	Charlton, Clifford	LB	6-3	240	2	Florida
25	Collins, Patrick	RB	5-9	188	2	Oklahoma
29	Dixon, Hanford	CB	5-11	195	9	Southern Mississippi
74	Farren, Paul	T	6-6	280	7	Boston University
69	Fike, Dan	G	6-7	280	5	Florida
30	Gash, Thane	S	6-0	200	2	East Tennessee State
90	Gibson, Tom	DE	6-7	250	1	Northern Arizona
39	Glenn, Kerry	CB	5-9	175	3	Minnesota
56	Grayson, David	LB	6-2	230	3	Fresno State
78	Hairston, Carl	DE	6-2	280	14	Maryland-Eastern Shore
23	Harper, Mark	CB	5-9	185	4	Alcorn State
35	Hill, Will	S	6-0	200	2	Bishop College
51	Johnson, Eddie	LB	6-1	225	9	Louisville
59	Johnson, Mike	LB	6-1	225	4	Virginia Tech
26	Jones, Keith	RB	5-10	182	1	Nebraska
95	Jones, Marlon	DE	6-4	260	2	Central State, Ohio
66	Jones, Tony	T	6-5	280	2	Western Carolina
19	Kosar, Bernie	QB	6-5	210	5	Miami
55	Krauss, Barry	LB	6-3	255	11	Alabama
88	Langhorne, Reggie	WR	6-2	200	5	Elizabeth City State
34	Mack, Kevin	RB	6-0	235	5	Clemson
42	Manoa, Tim	RB	6-1	227	3	Penn State
57	Matthews, Clay	LB	6-2	245	12	Southern California
89	McNeil, Gerald	WR-PR	5-7	147	4	Baylor
31	Minnifield, Frank	CB	5-9	185	6	Louisville
82	Newsome, Ozzie	TE	6-2	232	12	Alabama
7	Norseth, Mike	QB	6-2	200	3	Kansas
	Oliphant, Mike	RB-KR	5-10	183	2	Puget Sound
10	Pagel, Mike	QB	6-2	211	8	Arizona State
92	Perry, Michael Dean	DE-NT	6-0	285	2	Clemson
75	Pike, Chris	DE	6-7	301	1	Tulsa
73	Rakoczy, Gregg	C-G	6-6	290	3	Miami
63	Risien, Cody	T	6-7	280	10	Texas A&M
99	Sims, Darryl	DE-NT	6-3	290	5	Wisconsin
84	Slaughter, Webster	WR	6-0	170	4	San Diego State
12	Strock, Don	QB	6-5	220	16	Virginia Tech
38	Swarn, George	RB	5-10	220	1	Miami, Ohio
81	Tennell, Derek	TE	6-5	245	3	UCLA
80	Usher, Darryl	WR	5-8	170	1	Illinois
15	Wagner, Bryan	P	6-2	200	3	Cal State-Northridge
50	Waiters, Van	LB	6-4	240	2	Indiana
48	Washington, Brian	S	6-0	210	2	Nebraska
	Woods, Chris	WR-PR	5-11	190	3	Auburn
22	Wright, Felix	S	6-2	190	5	Drake

Defensive end Michael Dean Perry should see more time as a starter.

HOUSTON OILERS

AFC CENTRAL DIVISION

Address 6910 Fannin Street, Houston, Texas 77030.
Stadium Astrodome, Houston.
  Capacity 50,594 *Playing Surface* AstroTurf-8.
Team Colours Columbia Blue, Scarlet, and White.
Head Coach Jerry Glanville – 5th year.
Championships AFL 1960,'61.
History AFL 1960-69, AFC 1970-

Offense

Head coach Jerry Glanville may have his detractors for his outspoken manner and his unorthodox approach to enthusing his team, but he has taken the Oilers to victories in the wild card game in each of the last two years and no one can deny that they enter the 1989 season as unquestioned contenders for a title. Warren Moon has established himself as one of the NFL's most respected quarterbacks. Both the soundness of his judgement and the quality of his passing were reflected in his rank of fifth in the NFL. And it is reassuring that, should Moon be injured, reserve quarterback Cody Carlson can step in and play with confidence. With Carlson starting, over Weeks Two to Six the Oilers went 3-2. At running back the one difficulty is in keeping everyone happy. In Mike Rozier they have a steady, 1,000-yard rusher but Lorenzo White, who, unlike Rozier, has breakaway speed, also has that extra by way of big-game presence. All things being equal, White could make a claim to start ahead of Rozier. However, other players, including the speedy Allen Pinkett and by no means least, Alonzo Highsmith, make the selection difficult. When clubs collect several running backs it is in the likelihood that some will not come through. In Houston's case, every one has been a success. Having said all that, Highsmith may be the key to the future. A multi-purpose fullback, thus far he has been used only sparingly and one wonders what might evolve were Highsmith and White to be designated the permanent starting pair. Between the wide receivers, Drew Hill and Ernest Givins, there is little to choose, with Hill having a slight statistical edge. As a partnership they now rate alongside Miami's Clayton and Duper. The third receiver, Curtis Duncan, does well with his meagre opportunities. Haywood Jeffires, a former first-round pick, is a class player but has to bide his time. The former Tampa Bay starter Calvin Magee has been signed as a free agent and probably will take over in the space vacated by Jamie Williams. He can catch passes but will be used more for his blocking in the Oilers' system. The starting offensive line remained intact for the entire season. With Bruce Davis and Dean Steinkuhler at tackle, Mike Munchak and Bruce Matthews at guard and the much underrated Jay Pennison at center, the line is very powerful. First-round pick David Williams would appear to be the future replacement for Davis.

Defense

On the defensive line there are five excellent players for three starting spots. The senior trio will have Ray Childress and William Fuller at defensive end and Doug Smith at nose tackle. But Richard Byrd gave admirable service when Smith was under suspension and Sean Jones rates as one of the NFL's most consistent pass rushing defensive ends. Jones came third on the team with 7.5 sacks, raising his four-year total to 37.5. The team lead in sacks was shared by Childress and Fuller, each with 8.5. The last two years have seen a gradual firming at linebacker but there still is room for an impact player. Second-round draftee Scott Kozak would not fit that description, with pass defense as his outstanding quality. For the moment, then, there is no obvious challenge to the starting quartet which has John Grimsley and Al Smith on the insides, with Robert Lyles and Johnny Meads on the outsides. Grimsley's team-leading 111 tackles, 15 more than Smith in second place, caught the eye of Buffalo head coach Marv Levy, who made him his personal selection to the Pro Bowl. Of the outside linebackers, Lyles is the run-stuffer whereas Meads plays with a bias towards rushing the passer, in which capacity he had eight sacks. The loss of starting strong safety Keith Bostic might well be a problem for many clubs but the Oilers are knee-deep in talent. Patrick Allen and Steve Brown form an excellent pairing on the corners while Jeff Donaldson is entrenched at free safety. When the Oilers protected Quintin Jones and not Bostic the identity of the future strong safety was made clear. But that was before they selected defensive back Bubba McDowell, who has the speed of a cornerback, the instincts of a safety and the experience of having played on one of college football's pro-style teams.

1989 SCHEDULE OF GAMES	September	
	10 at Minnesota	3:00
	17 at San Diego	1:00
	24 BUFFALO	12:00
	October	
	1 MIAMI	12:00
	8 at New England	1:00
	15 at Chicago	12:00
	22 PITTSBURGH	12:00
	29 at Cleveland	1:00
	November	
	5 DETROIT	12:00
	13 CINCINNATI (Mon.)	8:00
	19 LOS ANGELES RAIDERS	3:00
	26 at Kansas City	12:00
	December	
	3 at Pittsburgh	1:00
	10 TAMPA BAY	12:00
	17 at Cincinnati	1:00
	23 CLEVELAND (Sat. night)	7:00

Special Teams

Houston does have a need for kick returners who can go the distance. They have several adequate players but only Lorenzo White stands out – and his talents probably will be applied at running back. Tony Zendejas misses the odd easy one but is widely regarded as being among the class of the league. Punter Greg Montgomery came through a difficult rookie season and may face a challenger, as yet unidentified, in camp.

1989 DRAFT

Round	Name	Pos.	Ht.	Wt.	College
1.	Williams, David	T	6-4	292	Florida
2.	Kozak, Scott	LB	6-2	221	Oregon
3.	McDowell, Bubba	S-CB	6-0	193	Miami
4.	Harris, Rod	WR-KR	5-10	182	Texas A&M
5.	Montgomery, Glenn	NT	6-0	268	Houston
6.	Orlando, Bo	S	5-9	175	West Virginia
7.	Rogers, Tracy	LB	6-1	243	Fresno State
8.	Mays, Alvoid	CB	5-10	170	West Virginia
9.	Mrosko, Bob	TE-DE	6-5	260	Penn State
10.	Johnson, Tracy	RB	5-11	229	Clemson
11.	Smider, Brian	T	6-3	297	West Virginia
12.	Hartlieb, Chuck	QB	6-1	206	Iowa

If used as a feature running back, Alonzo Highsmith could rank among the NFL's best.

VETERAN ROSTER

No.	Name	Pos.	Ht.	Wt.	NFL Year	College
29	Allen, Patrick	CB	5-10	182	6	Utah State
24	Brown, Steve	CB	5-11	192	7	Oregon
38	Bryant, Domingo	S	6-4	178	3	Texas A&M
71	Byrd, Richard	DE-NT	6-4	267	5	Southern Mississippi
35	Byrum, Carl	RB	6-0	235	4	Mississippi Valley State
14	Carlson, Cody	QB	6-3	199	3	Baylor
79	Childress, Ray	DE	6-6	270	5	Texas A&M
39	Clinton, Charles	CB	5-8	170	1	San Jose State
77	Davis, Bruce	T	6-6	315	11	UCLA
28	Dishman, Cris	CB	6-0	180	2	Purdue
31	Donaldson, Jeff	S	6-0	190	6	Colorado
80	Duncan, Curtis	WR-PR	5-11	185	3	Northwestern
21	Eaton, Tracey	S	6-1	190	2	Portland State
51	Fairs, Eric	LB	6-3	240	4	Memphis State
95	Fuller, William	DE	6-3	269	4	North Carolina
97	Garalczyk, Mark	DT	6-5	272	3	Western Michigan
81	Givins, Ernest	WR	5-9	172	4	Louisville
59	Grimsley, John	LB	6-2	238	6	Kentucky
83	Harris, Leonard	WR-KR	5-8	162	4	Texas Tech
32	Highsmith, Alonzo	RB	6-1	234	3	Miami
85	Hill, Drew	WR	5-9	175	10	Georgia Tech
86	Jackson, Kenny	WR	6-0	180	6	Penn State
84	Jeffires, Haywood	WR	6-2	198	3	North Carolina State
22	Johnson, Kenny	S-PR	5-10	175	10	Mississippi State
23	Johnson, Richard	CB	6-1	190	5	Wisconsin
27	Jones, Quintin	S	5-11	193	2	Pittsburgh
96	Jones, Sean	DE	6-7	273	6	Northeastern
93	Lyles, Robert	LB	6-1	230	6	Texas Christian
73	Maarleveld, J.D.	T	6-6	280	3	Maryland
89	Magee, Calvin	TE	6-3	260	5	Southern
78	Maggs, Don	T-G	6-5	285	3	Tulane
74	Matthews, Bruce	G-C	6-5	293	7	Southern California
91	Meads, Johnny	LB	6-2	235	6	Nicholls State
50	Monger, Matt	LB	6-1	238	4	Oklahoma State
9	Montgomery, Greg	P	6-3	213	2	Michigan State
1	Moon, Warren	QB	6-3	210	6	Washington
63	Munchak, Mike	G	6-3	284	8	Penn State
52	Pennison, Jay	C	6-1	282	4	Nicholls State
20	Pinkett, Allen	RB	5-9	192	4	Notre Dame
30	Rozier, Mike	RB	5-10	213	5	Nebraska
98	Ruth, Mike	NT	6-2	275	2	Boston College
69	Scotts, Colin	DT-DE	6-5	263	3	Hawaii
53	Seale, Eugene	LB	5-10	240	3	Lamar
54	Smith, Al	LB	6-1	236	3	Utah State
99	Smith, Doug	NT	6-5	282	5	Auburn
70	Steinkuhler, Dean	T	6-3	291	6	Nebraska
75	Stroth, Vince	T	6-4	275	3	Brigham Young
88	Verhulst, Chris	TE	6-2	249	1	Chico State
44	White, Lorenzo	RB-KR	5-11	209	2	Michigan State
66	Yarno, George	C	6-2	270	10	Washington State
68	Young, Almon	G	6-3	285	2	Bethune-Cookman
7	Zendejas, Tony	K	5-8	165	5	Nevada-Reno

PITTSBURGH STEELERS

Address Three Rivers Stadium, 300 Stadium Circle, Pittsburgh, Pennsylvania. 15212.

Stadium Three Rivers Stadium, Pittsburgh. *Capacity* 59,000 *Playing Surface* AstroTurf.

Team Colours Black and Gold.

Head Coach Chuck Noll – 21st year.

Championships Division 1972,'74,'75,'76,'77,'78,'79,'83,'84; Conference 1974,'75,'78,'79; Super Bowl 1974,'75,'78,'79.

History NFL 1933-69, AFC 1970- (Until 1940, they were known as the Pittsburgh Pirates.)

Offense

Even before the teams entered camp, the general view was that the Steelers had enjoyed their best draft in more than a decade and that they had every prospect of challenging, even in the difficult AFC Central division. The offense should gather momentum playing behind a line which has quickly developed into a solid force. The final part in the reconstruction process could be draftee Tom Ricketts, who would start at left tackle. This would enable Craig Wolfley to challenge both Brian Blankenship and John Rienstra for the left guard position. Dermontti Dawson, who is regarded as a future all-pro, seems likely to move over to center, replacing the departed Mike Webster. Dawson's spot at right guard would then be returned to former starter Terry Long, with Pro Bowler Tunch Ilkin the only player to stay put. Let's be optimistic and assume that it's all going to happen. If it does, top draftee Tim Worley could have a field day. Said to be almost as fast as Heisman Trophy winner Barry Sanders, he is 20 pounds heavier. In addition he can block and catch passes. Of the current starters, Warren Williams may have to step aside for Worley, with Merril Hoge, who was the leading rusher in 1988 and caught 50 passes, continuing at fullback. Entering his fourth year in the pros, quarterback Bubby Brister has some characteristics of former Steeler Terry Bradshaw. He's all enthusiasm and isn't afraid of failing. 1988 was his first full season as the unchallenged starter and he showed enough style to suggest that he can be a winner although reserve support may be a problem. At wide receiver, Louis Lipps has been struggling for some time as the target player, with no obvious partner emerging. However, the feeling is that draftee Derek Hill could come through to start immediately. The former University of Arizona wide receiver has super hands, power and good speed, criteria which add up to a big-play performer. Charles Lockett and Weegie Thompson, who had 16 starts between them in 1988, are good backups. One of them may even keep out Hill in the early stages. The tight end position continues to have a low priority in the Steelers setup with the tradition being to use a tight end for his blocking. The current starter, Preston Gothard, is a former free agent who has served his apprenticeship with Pittsburgh. Free agent signing Mike Mularkey could quickly establish himself as the senior backup.

Defense

The Steelers are coming off a poor year, with the play of top draftee defensive end Aaron Jones the most disappointing aspect. Only rarely did he show any style and it may be that he needs a great deal more time to learn the ropes. Happily, their top defensive lineman, Keith Willis, will be back after missing an entire season through injury. He and Jones will challenge last year's starting defensive ends, Keith Gary and Tim Johnson, with Gerald Williams continuing to start at nose tackle. The Steelers are better off at linebacker, where Bryan Hinkle will resume after missing the final month of 1988 with an injury. He should displace Darin Jordan, even though the rookie earned many compliments. On the other side, Greg Lloyd was a pleasant surprise, coming through to start after missing his rookie year because of a serious knee injury suffered on the second day of training camp. On the insides, Hardy Nickerson and David Little form a hard-nosed partnership. Little was voted the team's co-MVP after leading the club in tackles. Gregg Carr started five games and rates as the best of the backups, with fourth-round draftee Jerrol Williams offering great promise. The defensive secondary is stocked with brilliant young talent which must soon begin to gel as a unit. Right cornerback Rod Woodson shared the team lead with four interceptions, was third in tackles and defensed 18 passes. It was a package which earned him the co-MVP award. The other corner, Dwayne Woodruff, also stole four passes, the last of which he returned 78 yards for a touchdown. Former second-round draft pick Delton Hall is seen as Woodruff's successor. Also, the projection is that draftee Carnell Lake will eventually replace Cornell Gowdy at strong safety. Thomas Everett, who was slowed by a leg injury, remains unchallenged at free safety.

1989 SCHEDULE OF GAMES		
September		
10 CLEVELAND		4:00
17 at Cincinnati		1:00
24 MINNESOTA		1:00
October		
1 at Detroit		1:00
8 CINCINNATI		1:00
15 at Cleveland		4:00
22 at Houston		12:00
29 KANSAS CITY		1:00
November		
5 at Denver		2:00
12 CHICAGO		1:00
19 SAN DIEGO		1:00
26 at Miami		1:00
December		
3 HOUSTON		1:00
10 at New York Jets		1:00
17 NEW ENGLAND		1:00
24 at Tampa Bay		1:00

Special Teams

Placekicker Gary Anderson broke four team records in 1988 and is always in contention for Pro Bowl selection. Punter Harry Newsome led the NFL with a gross average of 45.4 yards but he had six efforts blocked, and, even allowing for poor snaps, this aspect is a worry. Woodson is a solid punt returner and ranked sixth in the NFL on kick-off returns, including a 92-yard touchdown romp. His kick-off return partner, Dwight Stone, also ran 92 yards for a score.

1989 DRAFT

Round	Name	Pos.	Ht.	Wt.	College
1.	Worley, Tim	RB	6-2	216	Georgia
1.	Ricketts, Tom	T	6-4	295	Pittsburgh
2.	Lake, Carnell	S	6-0	204	UCLA
3.	Hill, Derek	WR	6-1	189	Arizona
4.	Williams, Jerrol	LB	6-4	235	Purdue
5.	Arnold, David	CB-S	6-2	194	Michigan
6.	Stock, Mark	WR	5-11	177	Virginia Military Inst.
7.	Johnson, David	CB	6-0	190	Kentucky
8.	Asbeck, Chris	NT	6-2	264	Cincinnati
9.	Jenkins, A.J.	LB	6-1	237	Cal State-Fullerton
10.	Olsavsky, Jerry	LB	6-0	217	Pittsburgh
11.	Slater, Brian	WR	6-3	199	Washington
12.	Haselrig, Carlton	DE	6-1	273	Pitt-Johnstown

VETERAN ROSTER

No.	Name	Pos.	Ht.	Wt.	NFL Year	College
1	Anderson, Gary	K	5-11	175	8	Syracuse
14	Blackledge, Todd	QB	6-3	227	7	Penn State
60	Blankenship, Brian	G-C	6-1	275	3	Nebraska
6	Brister, Bubby	QB	6-3	205	4	Northeast Louisiana
91	Carr, Gregg	LB	6-2	222	5	Auburn
24	Carter, Rodney	RB	6-0	216	3	Purdue
	Davis, Elgin	RB	5-10	192	3	Central Florida
63	Dawson, Dermontti	G	6-2	271	2	Kentucky
27	Everett, Thomas	S	5-9	179	3	Baylor
68	Freeman, Lorenzo	NT-DT	6-5	298	3	Pittsburgh
92	Gary, Keith	DE	6-3	268	7	Oklahoma
86	Gothard, Preston	TE	6-4	235	5	Alabama
29	Gowdy, Cornell	S	6-1	202	4	Morgan State
22	Griffin, Larry	S	6-0	200	4	North Carolina
35	Hall, Delton	S-CB	6-1	205	3	Clemson
53	Hinkle, Bryan	LB	6-1	222	8	Oregon
81	Hinnant, Mike	TE	6-3	258	2	Temple
33	Hoge, Merril	RB	6-2	226	3	Idaho State
62	Ilkin, Tunch	T	6-3	266	10	Indiana State
65	Jackson, John	T	6-6	282	2	Eastern Kentucky
	Johnson, Jason	WR	5-10	178	2	Illinois State
78	Johnson, Tim	DE	6-3	261	3	Penn State
85	Johnson, Troy	WR	6-1	185	4	Southern
97	Jones, Aaron	DE	6-5	257	2	Eastern Kentucky
55	Jordan, Darin	LB	6-1	235	2	Northeastern
51	Lanza, Chuck	C-G	6-2	263	2	Notre Dame
21	Lee, Greg	CB	6-1	207	2	Arkansas State
83	Lipps, Louis	WR	5-10	190	6	Southern Mississippi
50	Little, David	LB	6-1	230	9	Florida
95	Lloyd, Greg	LB	6-2	224	2	Fort Valley State
89	Lockett, Charles	WR	6-0	181	3	Long Beach State
74	Long, Terry	G	5-11	275	6	East Carolina
	Martin, Tracy	WR	6-3	205	2	North Dakota
	Mularkey, Mike	TE	6-4	238	7	Florida
18	Newsome, Harry	P	6-0	188	5	Wake Forest
54	Nickerson, Hardy	LB	6-2	229	3	California
76	Putzier, Rollin	DT-DE	6-4	281	2	Oregon
64	Reese, Jerry	DE	6-2	267	2	Kentucky
	Richard, Gary	CB	5-9	171	2	Pittsburgh
79	Rienstra, John	G	6-5	268	4	Temple
	Smith, Vinson	LB	6-2	219	2	East Carolina
	Stedman, Troy	LB	6-3	235	2	Washburn
20	Stone, Dwight	RB-KR	6-0	188	3	Middle Tennessee State
90	Stowe, Tyronne	LB	6-1	236	3	Rutgers
87	Thompson, Weegie	WR	6-6	216	6	Florida State
	Wallace, Ray	RB	6-0	220	3	Purdue
98	Williams, Gerald	NT	6-3	262	4	Auburn
42	Williams, Warren	RB	6-0	202	2	Miami
93	Willis, Keith	DE	6-1	263	7	Northeastern
73	Wolfley, Craig	T	6-1	269	10	Syracuse
49	Woodruff, Dwayne	CB	6-0	198	10	Louisville
26	Woodson, Rod	CB-KR	6-0	199	3	Purdue

Right tackle Tunch Ilkin earned his first selection to the AFC-NFC Pro Bowl.

DENVER BRONCOS

Address 5700 Logan Street, Denver, Colorado 80216.
Stadium Denver Mile High Stadium.
   Capacity 76,273 *Playing Surface* Grass (PAT).
Team Colours Orange, Royal Blue, and White.
Head Coach Dan Reeves – 9th year.
Championships Division 1977,'78,'84,'86,'87;
                 Conference 1977, '86,'87.
History AFL 1960-69, AFC 1970-

Offense

Even though only one season has gone by since the Broncos won the second of their consecutive AFC titles, they find themselves in the position of attempting to climb back into contention after a campaign in which not very much went right for them. Of course, whatever happens, quarterback John Elway will be the central focus. After three successive years of improved passer ratings, his numbers took a nose dive and one wonders if the pressures of shouldering the burden are beginning to tell. Enough of this silly talk; Elway can transform any game in a flash. And the Broncos have taken a sensible step to help his cause by drafting a big lad, Doug Widell, who could come in at right guard. Jim Juriga might then compete with Dave Studdard and draftee Darrell Hamilton at left tackle. Elsewhere, left guard Keith Bishop, center Billy Bryan and right tackle Ken Lanier will continue, pressed by the massive, raw talents of Gerald Perry. Free agent acquisitions Paul Blair and Bill Contz bring much-needed veteran presence at tackle. Even though entering his 13th NFL season, running back Tony Dorsett can still show a clean pair of heels and grades out as the most effective running back on the roster. The pairing of Dorsett and his starting fullback partner, Sammy Winder, gives Denver the kind of experience which is not likely to be found wanting when the heat is on. The arrival of draftee Melvin Bratton offers great promise but he still needs time to recover from an extremely serious knee injury suffered in January, 1988. There should be no problems at wide receiver where the 'Three Amigos', Mark Jackson, Vance Johnson and Ricky Nattiel, compete for playing time. The starters are Johnson, who led the team in receptions, and Jackson, who came through with a tremendous burst over the final five games when he caught 29 passes for 533 yards and three touchdowns. Steve Sewell chips in with some useful receptions coming out of the backfield. The tight end position ought not to be a problem with both Clarence Kay and Orson Mobley available. Kay is more consistently enthused than of old but Mobley hasn't quite made the kind of progress expected of a player who was compared with former Denver great Riley Odoms. Spicing the mixture is former Dallas tight end Doug Cosbie, who will not be satisfied with warming the bench.

Defense

There have been significant changes in the defensive coaching staff and it may be an indicator that new defensive coordinator Wade Phillips favours aggression rather than finesse. In short, the Broncos will come out steaming. At least, that's the theory. It seems possible that draftee Warren Powers will step in for departed free agent Walt Bowyer at defensive left end. Of course, veteran backup Freddie Gilbert and free agent signing Alphonso Carreker may have something to say about that. The nose tackle position remains the property of Greg Kragen while Andre Townsend is likely to continue at defensive right end, ahead of Rulon Jones. The pressure against the pass comes from left outside linebacker Simon Fletcher, who recorded a team-high nine sacks. The left side partnership of Fletcher and the versatile Karl Mecklenburg is regarded as the strength of the defense. Right inside linebacker Rick Dennison was second only to club leader Kragen in tackles. Outside Dennison, Michael Brooks is starting to repay the Broncos for their patience during his gradual return to full mobility. The defensive secondary, which went into some decline, did need help and it has arrived in the form of top pick Steve Atwater, whom the Broncos hope will start immediately at free safety. Mike Harden, who was involved in a team-high 1,071 plays in 1988, will return to right cornerback, replacing Jeremiah Castille. Strong safety Dennis Smith may reproduce his previous best form after playing with a series of nagging injuries for much of last season. At right cornerback, the enigmatic Mark Haynes can no longer call up instant speed, though, in the absence of a rapid emergence by Kevin Guidry, he should retain his starting spot. Former Vikings cornerback Wymon Henderson and former Redskin Dennis Woodberry, both of whom have started in the NFL, have arrived as free agents and may have an influence.

1989 SCHEDULE OF GAMES		
September		
10 KANSAS CITY		2:00
18 at Buffalo (Mon.)		9:00
24 LOS ANGELES RAIDERS		2:00
October		
1 at Cleveland		1:00
8 SAN DIEGO		2:00
15 INDIANAPOLIS		2:00
22 at Seattle		1:00
29 PHILADELPHIA		2:00
November		
5 PITTSBURGH		2:00
12 at Kansas City		12:00
20 at Washington (Mon.)		9:00
26 SEATTLE		2:00
December		
3 at Los Angeles Raiders		1:00
10 NEW YORK GIANTS		2:00
16 at Phoenix (Sat.)		2:00
24 at San Diego		1:00

Special Teams

Placekicker Rich Karlis now knows how to use the swirling winds and rarefied atmosphere of Mile High Stadium. In Mike Horan, the Broncos have the current AFC Pro Bowl punter. Horan is coming off one of the best seasons by a punter in recent history. Nattiel keeps in tune as an above-average punt returner. Returning kickoffs, Ken Bell is consistently steady without posing a breakaway threat. The ubiquitous Bell also led the special teams in tackles.

1989 DRAFT

Round	Name	Pos.	Ht.	Wt.	College
1.	Atwater, Steve	S	6-3	216	Arkansas
2.	Widell, Doug	G	6-4	282	Boston College
2.	Powers, Warren	DE	6-6	277	Maryland
3.	Hamilton, Darrell	T	6-5	281	North Carolina
4.	McCullough, Richard	DE	6-4	267	Clemson
5.	Carrington, Darren	CB	6-1	189	Northern Arizona
6.	Stafford, Anthony	RB	5-7	179	Oklahoma
7.	Bratton, Melvin	RB	6-1	225	Miami
8.	Green, Paul	TE	6-2	235	Southern California
9.	Smith, Monte	G	6-4	265	North Dakota
9.	Williams, Wayne	RB	5-10	190	Florida
10.	Butts, Anthony	DT	6-4	273	Mississippi State
11.	Shelton, Richard	CB	5-10	185	Liberty
12.	Javis, John	WR-KR	5-10	181	Howard

VETERAN ROSTER

No.	Name	Pos.	Ht.	Wt.	NFL Year	College
40	Alexander, Jeff	RB	6-0	232	1	Southern
35	Bell, Ken	RB	5-10	190	4	Boston College
54	Bishop, Keith	G	6-3	265	9	Baylor
68	Blair, Paul	T	6-4	280	3	Oklahoma State
34	Braxton, Tyrone	S	5-11	174	2	North Dakota State
56	Brooks, Michael	LB	6-1	235	3	Louisiana State
64	Bryan, Billy	C	6-2	255	13	Duke
95	Bryan, Steve	LB	6-2	256	3	Oklahoma
92	Carreker, Alphonso	DE	6-6	271	6	Florida State
28	Castille, Jeremiah	CB	5-10	175	7	Alabama
63	Contz, Bill	T	6-5	270	7	Penn State
26	Corrington, Kip	S	6-0	175	1	Texas A&M
86	Cosbie, Doug	TE	6-6	238	11	Santa Clara
	Curtis, Scott	LB	6-1	230	2	New Hampshire
55	Dennison, Rick	LB	6-3	220	8	Colorado State
33	Dorsett, Tony	RB	5-11	189	13	Pittsburgh
7	Elway, John	QB	6-3	210	7	Stanford
73	Fletcher, Simon	LB	6-5	240	5	Houston
90	Gilbert, Freddie	DE	6-4	275	4	Georgia
22	Goode, Kerry	RB	5-11	212	2	Alabama
37	Guidry, Kevin	CB	6-0	176	2	Louisiana State
31	Harden, Mike	S	6-1	192	10	Michigan
36	Haynes, Mark	CB	5-11	195	10	Colorado
24	Henderson, Wymon	CB	5-10	186	5	Nevada-Las Vegas
78	Hood, Winford	T	6-3	262	6	Georgia
2	Horan, Mike	P	5-11	190	6	Long Beach State
79	Humphries, Stefan	G	6-3	268	5	Michigan
80	Jackson, Mark	WR	5-10	180	4	Purdue
82	Johnson, Vance	WR	5-11	185	5	Arizona
75	Jones, Rulon	DE	6-6	260	10	Utah State
66	Juriga, Jim	G	6-6	269	2	Illinois
12	Karcher, Ken	QB	6-3	205	3	Tulane
3	Karlis, Rich	K	6-0	180	8	Cincinnati
72	Kartz, Keith	T	6-4	270	3	California
88	Kay, Clarence	TE	6-2	237	6	Georgia
	Kelly, Pat	TE	6-6	252		Syracuse
97	Klostermann, Bruce	LB	6-4	232	3	South Dakota State
99	Knight, Shawn	NT	6-6	288	3	Brigham Young
71	Kragen, Greg	NT	6-3	260	5	Utah State
8	Kubiak, Gary	QB	6-0	192	7	Texas A&M
76	Lanier, Ken	T	6-3	269	9	Florida State
59	Lucas, Tim	LB	6-3	230	3	California
85	Massie, Rick	WR	6-1	190	3	Kentucky
77	Mecklenburg, Karl	LB	6-3	230	7	Minnesota
89	Mobley, Orson	TE	6-5	256	4	Salem College
51	Munford, Marc	LB	6-2	231	3	Nebraska
84	Nattiel, Ricky	WR	5-9	180	3	Florida
60	Perry, Gerald	G-T	6-6	305	2	Southern
53	Peterson, Blake	LB	6-4	245	1	Mesa, Colorado
74	Provence, Andrew	NT	6-3	270	6	South Carolina
48	Robbins, Randy	S	6-2	189	6	Arizona
57	Ruether, Mike	C	6-4	275	4	Texas
50	Ryan, Jim	LB	6-1	225	11	William & Mary
30	Sewell, Steve	RB	6-3	210	5	Oklahoma
49	Smith, Dennis	S	6-3	200	9	Southern California
70	Studdard, Dave	T	6-4	260	11	Texas
94	Thornton, Randy	LB	6-3	220	1	Houston
61	Townsend, Andre	DE	6-3	265	6	Mississippi
32	Ware, Reggie	RB	6-1	249	1	Auburn
81	Watson, Steve	WR	6-4	195	10	Temple
47	Willhite, Gerald	RB	5-10	200	8	San Jose State
23	Winder, Sammy	RB	5-11	203	8	Southern Mississippi
21	Woodberry, Dennis	CB	5-10	183	4	Southern Arkansas
83	Young, Mike	WR	6-1	183	5	UCLA

Wide receiver Mark Jackson led the Broncos in average yards per reception and touchdowns.

KANSAS CITY CHIEFS

Address One Arrowhead Drive, Kansas City, Missouri 64129.

Stadium Arrowhead Stadium, Kansas City.
Capacity 78,067 *Playing Surface* AstroTurf-8.

Team Colours Red, Gold, and White.

Head Coach Marty Schottenheimer – 1st year; 6th NFL.

Championships Division 1971; AFL 1962,'66,'69;
Super Bowl 1969.

History AFL 1960-69, AFC 1970-
(Until 1963, they were known as the Dallas Texans.)

Offense

So much about the Kansas City offense is good that just small changes could bring about a dramatic transformation. Indeed, they have the classic combination at running back in the mercurial Paul Palmer and the thumping, smashing, grinding Christian Okoye. Herman Heard is a valuable third member who can come in and start as he did for the final five games of last season. Rookie James Saxon gained valuable experience as a starter in four games when Okoye was out with hand injuries. New head coach Marty Schottenheimer is impressed with the group as a whole and with Okoye in particular. It is easy to imagine Okoye being the feature back in Schottenheimer's system. Looking at the line, it does show signs of coming together now that the order of seniority has largely been sorted out. Sensibly, the starting quintet will have John Alt and Irv Eatman at tackle, Rich Baldinger and Mark Adickes at guard and Gerry Feehery at center. There is just the possibility that former Pittsburgh starter and nine-time Pro Bowler Mike Webster will depose Feehery. Dave Lutz has emerged as the utility man, a role he underlined last season with two starts at right guard and five at right tackle. Similarly, Byron Ingram was an occasional starter at guard. Former first-round pick Brian Jozwiak is troubled by an arthritic hip and may miss the year. There are no problems at wide receiver, where Carlos Carson and Stephone Paige are the established senior players. In 1988, Carson's productivity fell as Paige, who enjoyed his best pro campaign, played a more prominent part. Behind, but not likely to challenge the starters, the Chiefs have Emile Harry, Lew Barnes and draftee Naz Worthen. At tight end, Jonathan Hayes has been the starter for the last two seasons, but he may be pressed by Alfredo Roberts, who started seven games in 1988. Former Houston starter Chris Dressel was a free agent acquisition. It is at quarterback where the Chiefs are uncertain. Steve DeBerg, a man of wide experience, is unusual, having lost neither the power of his arm nor his enthusiasm after 12 seasons and the frustrations of rejection after giving good service to three clubs. Another much travelled veteran, Ron Jaworski, will be in the shuffle, as will a young man just starting out on the great adventure, second-round draftee Mike Elkins. Your writer would not look beyond DeBerg, who has enough class to bring home a title.

Defense

The worst and the best adequately describes last year when teams ran all over the Chiefs but passed at their peril. Schottenheimer will make significant improvements, we can be sure of that, and he started by signing free agent linebackers Anthony Griggs, Walker Lee Ashley, Greg Gaines and former Cleveland first-round pick Mike Junkin. He continued in the draft with the selection of the best linebacker available, Derrick Thomas, whose acquisition gives the Chiefs another one-man wrecking crew to go with veteran Dino Hackett. In what will be a tough competition, only Hackett, an inside specialist, and Thomas are certain of starting spots. The rest include inside linebackers Jack Del Rio and Aaron Pearson, and outside linebackers Angelo Snipes and Louis Cooper. The three-man defensive line missed the services of nose tackle Bill Maas, who comes back fully fit after missing half the season with a knee injury. Before the injury, Maas, a two-time Pro Bowler, was off to his best start with 52 tackles and four sacks in eight games. He is the class of the line, followed by defensive right end Mike Bell, who was not at his best in a year which saw him suspended for 30 days. Leonard Griffin came into his own on the left side, starting nine games in all and leading the linemen with 96 tackles. But the man Kansas City really wants to come through is 1988 first-round draft pick Neil Smith. Slowed by an ankle injury last season, his emergence would have a major influence. In addition, free agent signings such as nose tackles Greg Meisner and Dan Saleaumua give certain backup support. Without question, Kansas City has the AFC's best secondary. All three of Albert Lewis, Lloyd Burruss and Deron Cherry are Pro Bowlers, with Cherry, who led the Chiefs with seven interceptions, being an automatic selection. The fourth member, Kevin Ross, does not look out of place. Kevin Porter was an excellent replacement when Burruss was injured.

1989 SCHEDULE OF GAMES	September	
	10 at Denver	2:00
	17 LOS ANGELES RAIDERS	12:00
	24 at San Diego	1:00
	October	
	1 CINCINNATI	12:00
	8 at Seattle	1:00
	15 at Los Angeles Raiders	1:00
	22 DALLAS	12:00
	29 at Pittsburgh	1:00
	November	
	5 SEATTLE	12:00
	12 DENVER	12:00
	19 at Cleveland	1:00
	26 HOUSTON	12:00
	December	
	3 MIAMI	12:00
	10 at Green Bay	12:00
	17 SAN DIEGO	12:00
	24 at Miami	1:00

Safety Deron Cherry has been selected to the last six AFC-NFC Pro Bowls.

Special Teams

Given decent field position, Nick Lowery, who begins his tenth NFL season, has the accuracy to tack three points on to any drive. Current punter Kelly Goodburn, who is solid, will be in a competition with ex-Cleveland veteran Max Runager. Returning kicks of both kinds, the quality fell away last year and will be the object of intense activity in training camp.

1989 DRAFT

Round	Name	Pos.	Ht.	Wt.	College
1.	Thomas, Derrick	LB	6-4	230	Alabama
2.	Elkins, Mike	QB	6-2	221	Wake Forest
3.	Worthen, Naz	WR	5-8	172	North Carolina State
4.	Petry, Stanley	CB	5-11	168	Texas Christian
6.	Thomas, Robb	WR	5-11	174	Oregon State
7.	Sancho, Ron	LB	6-2	223	Louisiana State
8.	Tobey, Bryan	RB	6-0	240	Grambling
8.	McNair, Todd	RB	6-0	188	Temple
9.	Phillips, Jack	S	6-0	201	Alcorn State
10.	McGovern, Rob	LB	6-2	225	Holy Cross
11.	Turner, Marcus	CB-S	6-0	189	UCLA
12.	Jones, Bill	RB	6-1	215	Southwest Texas State

VETERAN ROSTER

No.	Name	Pos.	Ht.	Wt.	NFL Year	College
82	Abdur-Ra'oof, Azizuddin	WR	6-0	200	1	Maryland
61	Adickes, Mark	G	6-4	270	4	Baylor
32	Agee, Tommie	RB	6-0	218	2	Auburn
76	Alt, John	T	6-7	290	6	Iowa
54	Ashley, Walker Lee	LB	6-0	230	6	Penn State
77	Baldinger, Rich	G-T	6-4	285	8	Wake Forest
80	Barnes, Lew	WR	5-8	163	3	Oregon
99	Bell, Mike	DE	6-4	260	9	Colorado State
65	Bowyer, Walt	DE	6-4	260	5	Arizona State
34	Burruss, Lloyd	S	6-0	205	9	Maryland
88	Carson, Carlos	WR	5-11	190	10	Louisiana State
20	Cherry, Deron	S	5-11	203	9	Rutgers
62	Chilton, Gene	C	6-3	271	3	Texas
55	Cooper, Louis	LB	6-2	245	5	Western Carolina
25	Copeland, Danny	S	6-2	210	1	Eastern Kentucky
17	DeBerg, Steve	QB	6-3	210	13	San Jose State
50	Del Rio, Jack	LB	6-4	238	5	Southern California
	Dressel, Chris	TE	6-4	245	5	Stanford
75	Eatman, Irv	T	6-7	294	4	UCLA
64	Feehery, Gerry	C	6-2	270	7	Syracuse
91	Gaines, Greg	LB	6-3	229	8	Tennessee
22	Gamble, Kenny	RB	5-10	197	2	Colgate
2	Goodburn, Kelly	P	6-2	198	3	Emporia State
98	Griffin, Leonard	DE	6-4	270	4	Grambling
58	Griggs, Anthony	LB	6-3	230	8	Ohio State
81	Griggs, Billy	TE	6-3	234	5	Virginia
56	Hackett, Dino	LB	6-3	228	4	Appalachian State
86	Harry, Emile	WR-PR	5-11	176	3	Stanford
	Hawkins, Andy	LB	6-2	244	8	Texas A&I
85	Hayes, Jonathan	TE	6-5	239	5	Iowa
44	Heard, Herman	RB	5-10	190	6	Southern Colorado
23	Hill, Greg	CB-S	6-1	202	7	Oklahoma State
60	Ingram, Byron	G	6-2	295	2	Eastern Kentucky
7	Jaworski, Ron	QB	6-1	205	15	Youngstown State
73	Jozwiak, Brian	G	6-5	293	4	West Virginia
	Junkin, Mike	LB	6-3	238	3	Duke
29	Lewis, Albert	CB	6-2	197	7	Grambling
38	Loveall, Calvin	CB	5-9	180	2	Idaho
8	Lowery, Nick	K	6-4	189	10	Dartmouth
59	Lowry, Orlando	LB	6-4	236	5	Ohio State
72	Lutz, David	T	6-6	290	7	Georgia Tech
63	Maas, Bill	NT	6-5	268	6	Pittsburgh
57	Martin, Chris	LB	6-2	234	7	Auburn
92	McCabe, Jerry	LB	6-1	225	4	Holy Cross
14	McManus, Danny	QB	6-0	200	2	Florida State
69	Meisner, Greg	NT	6-3	265	9	Pittsburgh
35	Okoye, Christian	RB	6-1	253	3	Azusa Pacific
83	Paige, Stephone	WR	6-2	185	7	Fresno State
26	Palmer, Paul	RB-KR	5-9	181	3	Temple
96	Pearson, Aaron	LB	6-0	240	4	Mississippi State
24	Pearson, Jayice	CB	5-11	190	4	Washington
27	Porter, Kevin	S	5-10	215	2	Auburn
87	Roberts, Alfredo	TE	6-3	250	2	Miami
31	Ross, Kevin	CB	5-9	182	6	Temple
4	Runager, Max	P	6-1	189	11	South Carolina
97	Saleaumua, Dan	NT	6-0	285	3	Arizona State
70	Sally, Jerome	NT	6-3	270	8	Missouri
21	Saxon, James	RB	5-11	215	2	San Jose State
11	Slayden, Steve	QB	6-1	185	2	Duke
70	Smith, Dave	T	6-7	290	2	Southern Illinois
90	Smith, Neil	DE	6-4	270	2	Nebraska
52	Snipes, Angelo	LB	6-0	227	4	West Georgia
67	Stensrud, Mike	NT	6-5	280	11	Iowa State
53	Webster, Mike	C	6-2	260	16	Wisconsin
67	Wolkow, Troy	G	6-4	280	1	Minnesota

LOS ANGELES RAIDERS

AFC WESTERN DIVISION

Address 332 Center Street, El Segundo, California 90245.

Stadium Los Angeles Memorial Coliseum.
Capacity 92,488 *Playing Surface* Grass.

Team Colours Silver and Black.

Head Coach Mike Shanahan – 2nd year.

Championships Division 1970,'72,'73,'74,'75,'76,'83,'85;
Conference 1976,'80,'83; AFL 1967.
Super Bowl 1976,'80,'83.

History AFL 1960-69, AFC 1970-
(Until 1982, they were known as the Oakland Raiders.)

Offense

The Raiders have spent the last three seasons out of the playoffs and, even though that period has seen many changes, a clear picture of the offense has not emerged. And for progress back up the ladder, more than a few things have to happen. The position at quarterback appears to have been settled, with Jay Schroeder installed as the starter. And he does have all the tangibles - physique, lots of arm and no nerves - to be a true Raider. But it may be the very remnants of the Raiders' traditional long-passing game that are hampering the transition to head coach Mike Shanahan's system, which requires far more than simply dropping back and letting fly. Steve Beuerlein was just shaping up when Schroeder arrived and, if he can live with the disappointment of demotion, he can be an excellent backup. The critical feature of the Raiders' offense is to assemble an offensive line. The starting lineup will include Don Mosebar, Bruce Wilkerson and Bill Lewis as the only certainties, though in positions as yet undetermined. Top second-round draftee Steve Wisniewski looks likely to start, probably at left guard, with Rory Graves perhaps staying on at right tackle. Free agent tackle Dale Hellestrae, whose three-year spell with the Bills was interrupted by a series of nagging injuries, has an excellent opportunity to be a factor. In the new system, tight end Trey Junkin is used as a blocker, leaving pass-receiver supreme, Todd Christensen, redundant and out in the cold. Turning to the more secure aspects of offense, running backs Marcus Allen and Steve Smith can take advantage of every decent opening. Vance Mueller and Steve Strachan are solid backups. The pity is that the best one of all, the fabulous Bo Jackson, will not be available until mid-October. At wide receiver, there is an embarrassment of talent in Tim Brown, Willie Gault, James Lofton and Mervyn Fernandez. Of the four, though, only Brown and, perhaps, Fernandez, can look back at 1988 with fond memories. Brown confirmed the Raiders' judgement in making him their first draft selection by setting a rookie all-purpose yardage record. Again, Fernandez had the best average, 26 yards, of the NFL's front-line receivers. In that respect, Gault wasn't far behind with an average of 24.5, but he wasn't a factor after Week Five. James Lofton, who is one of the NFL's all-time great wide receivers, didn't look quite as secure catching the ball.

Defense

On defense the Raiders are said to be slowing, but that may be a rash conclusion after a season in which injuries played a significant part. In 1989, don't expect them to line up in an orthodox formation. Free-agent signings Bob Golic and Pete Koch are seen as having significant roles, and that could mean using two tackles much more often. Again, defensive ends Scott Davis and Mike Wise showed enough style to suggest that the great Howie Long will need to be at the top of his form if he is to retain his seniority. In some circumstances, then, the Raiders might play 4-3, and the prospects of their using a five-man front, with Greg Townsend pass-rushing from an outside linebacker position, look distinctly good. Last year, Townsend led the AFC with 11.5 sacks. The departure of Reggie McKenzie, whom the Raiders did not protect, and the release of both Milt McColl and Rod Martin cleared the way for new signings Otis Wilson and Emanuel King. Wilson, who was an outside specialist with the Bears, could team up with Matt Millen and Townsend as one permutation. Jerry Robinson may revert to the role of pass coverage, for which his instincts seem best suited. Linden King remains as an excellent squad player and must be given opportunities to exert pressure on the passer. There will be some changes in the secondary where, not long ago, the Raiders used to dominate in one-on-one coverage. Free safety Vann McElroy is the beating heart. Russell Carter, a former Jets first-round pick, and Stacey Toran will compete to start at strong safety. Terry McDaniel returns from injury to resume at left cornerback but, on the right side, it may be that, despite having a solid 1988 campaign, the great Mike Haynes may be displaced by former Chicago starter Mike Richardson, who was a good free agent signing. At the very least, Richardson gives the Raiders top-class depth.

1989 SCHEDULE OF GAMES		
September		
10	SAN DIEGO	1:00
17	at Kansas City	12:00
24	at Denver	2:00
October		
1	SEATTLE	1:00
9	at New York Jets (Mon.)	9:00
15	KANSAS CITY	1:00
22	at Philadelphia	1:00
29	WASHINGTON	1:00
November		
5	CINCINNATI	1:00
12	at San Diego (night)	5:00
19	at Houston	3:00
26	NEW ENGLAND	1:00
December		
3	DENVER	1:00
10	PHOENIX	1:00
17	at Seattle (night)	5:00
24	at New York Giants	1:00

Special Teams

The replacement of Chris Bahr by Jeff Jaeger should not lead to any loss in what is an adequate kicking game. Coincidentally, Jaeger spent last year on injured reserve at Cleveland where the other Bahr, Matt, is the kicker. Punter Jeff Gossett, too, is a former Cleveland player. Last year he led the AFC with 27 of his punts nestling inside the opposing 20-yard line. Tim Brown is a first-class punt returner and, currently, is the NFL's best kickoff returner.

1989 DRAFT

Round	Name	Pos.	Ht.	Wt.	College
2.	Wisniewski, Steve*	G	6-3	266	Penn State
6.	Francis, Jeff	QB	6-3	206	Tennessee
6.	Lloyd, Doug	RB	6-0	217	North Dakota State
8.	Gainer, Derrick	RB	5-11	224	Florida A&M
9.	Gooden, Gary	CB	6-1	180	Indiana
10.	Jackson, Charles	DT	6-4	297	Jackson State

* Drafted by Dallas in round two but obtained in a trade

VETERAN ROSTER

No.	Name	Pos.	Ht.	Wt.	NFL Year	College
44	Adams, Stefon	S-CB	5-10	190	4	East Carolina
89	Alexander, Mike	WR	6-3	215	1	Penn State
32	Allen, Marcus	RB	6-2	205	8	Southern California
33	Anderson, Eddie	S	6-1	195	4	Fort Valley State
	Benson, Thomas	LB	6-2	245	6	Oklahoma
7	Beuerlein, Steve	QB	6-2	205	2	Notre Dame
64	Brown, Ron	DE	6-4	225	3	Southern California
81	Brown, Tim	WR-KR	6-0	195	2	Notre Dame
29	Carter, Russell	S	6-2	200	6	Southern Methodist
46	Christensen, Todd	TE	6-3	230	11	Brigham Young
	Costello, Joe	LB	6-3	244	4	Central Connecticut St.
23	Crudup, Derrick	CB	6-2	210	1	Oklahoma
70	Davis, Scott	DE	6-7	270	2	Illinois
11	Evans, Vince	QB	6-2	200	10	Southern California
86	Fernandez, Mervyn	WR	6-3	195	3	San Jose State
83	Gault, Willie	WR	6-0	180	7	Tennessee
63	Gesek, John	G	6-5	270	3	Cal State-Sacramento
	Golic, Bob	NT	6-3	265	10	Notre Dame
6	Gossett, Jeff	P	6-2	195	8	Eastern Illinois
	Graddy, Sam	WR	5-10	165	2	Tennessee
60	Graves, Rory	T	6-6	285	2	Ohio State
62	Harrell, Newt	G	6-5	295	1	West Texas State
22	Haynes, Mike	CB	6-2	190	14	Arizona State
	Hellestrae, Dale	T	6-5	280	4	Southern Methodist
34	Jackson, Bo	RB	6-1	230	3	Auburn
	Jaeger, Jeff	K	6-0	200	1	Washington
87	Junkin, Trey	TE	6-2	230	7	Louisiana Tech
59	Kimmel, Jamie	LB	6-3	235	3	Syracuse
	King, Emanuel	LB	6-4	251	5	Alabama
52	King, Linden	LB	6-4	245	12	Colorado State
	Koch, Pete	DE	6-6	265	6	Maryland
40	Lee, Zeph	CB	6-3	210	3	Southern California
51	Lewis, Bill	C	6-7	275	4	Nebraska
80	Lofton, James	WR	6-3	190	12	Stanford
75	Long, Howie	DE	6-5	265	9	Villanova
36	McDaniel, Terry	CB	5-10	170	1	Tennessee
26	McElroy, Vann	S	6-2	195	8	Baylor
55	Millen, Matt	LB	6-2	250	10	Penn State
72	Mosebar, Don	T	6-6	280	7	Southern California
42	Mueller, Vance	RB	6-0	215	4	Occidental
71	Pickel, Bill	NT	6-5	265	7	Rutgers
38	Price, Dennis	CB	6-1	175	2	UCLA
	Richardson, Mike	CB	6-0	181	7	Arizona State
77	Riehm, Chris	G	6-6	280	4	Ohio State
57	Robinson, Jerry	LB	6-2	230	11	UCLA
79	Rother, Tim	DT	6-7	265	1	Nebraska
13	Schroeder, Jay	QB	6-4	215	6	UCLA
	Shipp, Jackie	LB	6-2	238	6	Oklahoma
35	Smith, Steve	RB	6-1	230	4	Penn State
39	Strachan, Steve	RB	6-1	220	5	Boston College
96	Taylor, Malcolm	NT	6-6	280	6	Tennessee State
30	Toran, Stacey	S	6-3	200	6	Notre Dame
93	Townsend, Greg	DE	6-3	250	7	Texas Christian
48	Washington, Lionel	CB	6-0	185	7	Tulane
68	Wilkerson, Bruce	G	6-5	280	3	Tennessee
	Wilson, Otis	LB	6-2	227	9	Louisville
90	Wise, Mike	DE	6-7	270	2	California-Davis
66	Wright, Steve	T	6-6	280	7	Northern Iowa

Fullback Steve Smith may have an increasingly important part to play.

SAN DIEGO CHARGERS

AFC WESTERN DIVISION

Address San Diego Jack Murphy Stadium, P.O. Box 20666, San Diego, California 92120.

Stadium San Diego Jack Murphy Stadium.
Capacity 60,750 *Playing Surface* Grass.

Team Colours Navy Blue, White, and Gold.

Head Coach Dan Henning – 1st year; 5th NFL.

Championships Division 1979,'80,'81; AFL 1963.

History AFL 1960-69, AFC 1970-
(For 1960 only, they were known as the Los Angeles Chargers.)

Offense

New head coach Dan Henning has a great deal of sorting out to do in several areas of the squad, not the least important of which is at quarterback, where the situation is complicated further by the rehabilitation facing Mark Vlasic. He had shown himself to be the class of the contenders but suffered a potentially devastating knee injury. Second-round draftee Billy Joe Tolliver joins veterans Mark Malone and David Archer, both of whom have started for other teams in the NFL. What is needed is no more than a reliable mechanic who can deliver the ball with some consistency. An impressive array of strike players can do the rest. Without doubt, at the centre of the offense will be running back Gary Anderson, who, after three years seeking an identity, emerged with explosive force. In 1988, despite missing two games, he gained 1,119 yards at a super average of five, including the NFL-best single-game total of that campaign, 217 yards. The Chargers use a one-back system and that is unlikely to change under Henning. It means that Anderson's talents are maximised and allows for others to come in on spot duty. The shock troops include Tim Spencer, Lionel James, Curtis Adams, Barry Redden and newcomers Timmy Smith and Napoleon McCallum. Obviously, somebody is going to be disappointed. There probably will be significant changes on the offensive line, with not one player certain of starting in any one position. At tackle, John Clay and Brett Miller may hold an advantage over Joel Patten and Gary Kowalski. At guard, the front runners would appear to be ex-Cleveland starter Larry Williams and David Richards, ahead of James FitzPatrick and Broderick Thompson. Two veterans, Dennis McKnight and Don Macek, and draftee Courtney Hall compete for the center spot. Despite the uncertainty there is a good deal of talent available. This definitely is true at wide receiver, where there is speed in abundance. All three of Anthony Miller, Quinn Early and Jamie Holland can burn grass and catch passes, with the versatile Lionel James and Darren Flutie more conservative but valued none the less. Looking at the H-back position, Rod Bernstine, a former first-round pick, needs to recover from a knee injury. As a blocking tight end, Henning can select from Arthur Cox, Joe Caravello and ex-Raider Andy Parker.

Defense

The prospects for the four-man defensive line are good, with Leslie O'Neal gradually returning to full speed after his severe knee injury and with the arrival of draftee Burt Grossman. Starting defensive left end Lee Williams went to his first Pro Bowl as the club leader with 11 sacks. Grossman entered his senior year well fancied and ended it with rave reviews. He is too good to leave warming the bench but he could not expect to displace the current starters, O'Neal and Williams. One solution would be to play Grossman at defensive tackle - he is said to be sufficiently versatile to make the adjustment. Otherwise, the probability is that the Chargers will persevere with Joe Phillips and George Hinkle. It goes without saying that reserve strength is modest. 1988 saw some improvement at linebacker, where the show centres around Billy Ray Smith, who has thrived following his conversion from inside linebacker. Keith Browner and the incumbent, Gary Plummer, will compete to start at right linebacker, and it is probable that former Rams starter Jim Collins will step in at middle linebacker. Collins is a former Pro Bowler. Sensibly, the summary is that the Chargers are some way short of being overwhelming at linebacker. That's true also in the defensive secondary, though not overlooking the unquestioned talents of left cornerback Gill Byrd, who led the Chargers with seven interceptions. The starting free safety, Vencie Glenn, was treated with respect after returning an interception 103 yards for a touchdown in 1987. His starting partner will emerge from a three-way competition involving Pat Miller, Martin Bayless and Lester Lyles, who was signed as a free agent after having started for both the Jets and Phoenix. Unless Sam Seale can find a little more, there is a need for someone to come through to start at right cornerback, an area in which the Chargers do look exposed.

1989 SCHEDULE OF GAMES		
September		
10 at Los Angeles Raiders		1:00
17 HOUSTON		1:00
24 KANSAS CITY		1:00
October		
1 at Phoenix		1:00
8 at Denver		2:00
15 SEATTLE		1:00
22 NEW YORK GIANTS		1:00
29 at Seattle		1:00
November		
5 PHILADELPHIA		1:00
12 LOS ANGELES RAIDERS (night)		5:00
19 at Pittsburgh		1:00
26 at Indianapolis		1:00
December		
3 NEW YORK JETS		1:00
10 at Washington		1:00
17 at Kansas City		12:00
24 DENVER		1:00

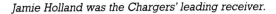

Jamie Holland was the Chargers' leading receiver.

Special Teams

Chris Bahr, who has an advantage in quality over Vince Abbott and Steve DeLine, will be itching to prove the Raiders wrong in not protecting him. The punting is first class with Ralf Mojsiejenko ranking second in the NFL last season in gross average and dropping 22 inside the opposing 20-yard line. Punt returner Lionel James is excellent but, even so, he was overshadowed by the sensational pairing of Holland and Miller, each of whom scored 90-plus-yard touchdowns on kickoff returns.

1989 DRAFT

Round	Name	Pos.	Ht.	Wt.	College
1.	Grossman, Burt	DE	6-6	265	Pittsburgh
2.	Hall, Courtney	C	6-1	269	Rice
2.	Tolliver, Billy Joe	QB	6-1	218	Texas Tech
5.	Smith, Elliot	S	6-2	190	Alcorn State
7.	Butts, Marion	RB	6-1	245	Florida State
7.	Jones, Terrence	QB	6-1	208	Tulane
8.	Brinson, Dana	WR-KR	5-9	167	Nebraska
9.	Davis, Pat	TE	6-3	257	Syracuse
10.	Andrews, Ricky	LB	6-2	236	Washington
11.	Floyd, Victor	RB	6-1	201	Florida State

VETERAN ROSTER

No.	Name	Pos.	Ht.	Wt.	NFL Year	College
10	Abbott, Vince	K	6-0	208	3	Cal State-Fullerton
42	Adams, Curtis	RB	6-0	207	4	Central Michigan
40	Anderson, Gary	RB	6-0	184	5	Arkansas
15	Archer, David	QB	6-2	208	5	Iowa State
3	Bahr, Chris	K	5-10	170	14	Penn State
56	Banks, Chip	LB	6-4	236	7	Southern California
44	Bayless, Martin	S	6-2	212	6	Bowling Green
23	Bennett, Roy	CB	6-2	195	2	Jackson State
82	Bernstine, Rod	TE	6-3	238	3	Texas A&M
58	Brandon, David	LB	6-4	230	3	Memphis State
73	Brilz, Darrick	C	6-3	270	3	Oregon State
57	Browner, Keith	LB	6-6	266	5	Southern California
22	Byrd, Gill	CB	5-11	198	7	San Jose State
95	Campbell, Joe	LB	6-4	245	2	New Mexico State
	Caravello, Joe	TE	6-3	270	3	Tulane
71	Charles, Mike	NT	6-4	296	7	Syracuse
77	Clay, John	T	6-5	305	3	Missouri
31	Coleman, Leonard	CB-S	6-2	202	5	Vanderbilt
96	Collins, Jim	LB	6-2	233	8	Syracuse
88	Cox, Arthur	TE	6-2	277	7	Texas Southern
6	DeLine, Steve	K	5-11	185	2	Colorado State
87	Early, Quinn	WR	6-0	188	2	Iowa
53	Faucette, Chuck	LB	6-3	242	2	Maryland
51	Figaro, Cedric	LB	6-2	250	2	Notre Dame
70	FitzPatrick, James	G	6-7	310	4	Southern California
89	Flutie, Darren	WR	5-10	184	2	Boston College
25	Glenn, Vencie	S	6-0	192	4	Indiana State
97	Hinkle, George	DT-DE	6-5	269	2	Arizona
86	Holland, Jamie	WR	6-2	195	3	Ohio State
79	Howard, Joey	T	6-5	305	1	Tennessee
52	Jackson, Jeff	LB	6-1	242	5	Auburn
26	James, Lionel	RB-WR	5-6	170	6	Auburn
29	Johnson, Demetrious	S	6-0	196	6	Missouri
93	Keys, Tyrone	DE	6-7	291	7	Mississippi State
68	Kowalski, Gary	T	6-6	288	6	Boston College
24	Lyles, Lester	S	6-3	205	5	Virginia
62	Macek, Don	C	6-2	278	14	Boston College
16	Malone, Mark	QB	6-4	222	10	Arizona State
	McCallum, Napoleon	RB	6-2	215	2	Navy
60	McKnight, Dennis	G	6-4	280	8	Drake
83	Miller, Anthony	WR-KR	5-11	185	2	Tennessee
74	Miller, Brett	T	6-7	300	7	Iowa
69	Miller, Les	DT	6-7	293	3	Fort Hays State
48	Miller, Patrick	S	6-1	206	2	Florida
2	Mojsiejenko, Ralf	P	6-3	213	5	Michigan State
91	O'Neal, Leslie	DE	6-4	255	3	Oklahoma State
85	Parker, Andy	TE	6-5	250	6	Utah
78	Patten, Joel	T	6-7	307	4	Duke
34	Patterson, Elvis	CB	5-11	198	6	Kansas
75	Phillips, Joe	DT	6-5	275	4	Southern Methodist
50	Plummer, Gary	LB	6-2	240	4	California
20	Redden, Barry	RB	5-10	219	8	Richmond
65	Richards, David	T	6-5	310	2	UCLA
66	Rosado, Dan	C	6-3	280	3	Northern Illinois
30	Seale, Sam	CB	5-9	185	6	Western State, Colo.
63	Searels, Stacy	G-C	6-5	281	1	Auburn
54	Smith, Billy Ray	LB	6-3	236	7	Arkansas
36	Smith, Timmy	RB	5-11	222	3	Texas Tech
43	Spencer, Tim	RB	6-1	223	5	Ohio State
47	Thomas, Johnny	CB	5-9	190	2	Baylor
76	Thompson, Broderick	G	6-5	295	4	Kansas
13	Vlasic, Mark	QB	6-3	203	3	Iowa
67	Williams, Larry	G	6-5	290	4	Notre Dame
99	Williams, Lee	DE	6-6	271	6	Bethune-Cookman
72	Wilson, Karl	DE	6-4	275	3	Louisiana State
59	Woodard, Ken	LB	6-1	220	8	Tuskegee Institute
80	Yarber, Eric	WR-KR	5-8	156	2	Idaho

SEATTLE SEAHAWKS

Address 11220 N.E. 53rd Street, Kirkland, Washington 98033.
Stadium Kingdome, Seattle.
  Capacity 64,984 *Playing Surface* AstroTurf.
Team Colours Blue, Green, and Silver.
Head Coach Chuck Knox – 7th year; 17th NFL.
Championships Division 1988.
History NFC 1976, AFC 1977-

Offense

A tremendous finish which saw Dave Krieg rate better than 100 in three of the last four games, and an NFL second-best final rating of 94.6 ought to have clinched the starting spot. But experience tells us that he needs only to slip a little to be taken out in favour of Kelly Stouffer, in exchange for whom the Seahawks sent an expensive package of draft options to the Cardinals. With his opportunities in 1988, Stouffer did make encouraging progress and, at the very least, secures the Seahawks' future. Behind Krieg and Stouffer, Seattle has the services of the reliable veteran Jeff Kemp, who has started for the Rams and San Francisco. Once again, the bread-and-butter offense will come from the running back pairing of Curt Warner and John L. Williams. Just how much Warner could have achieved had it not been for that knee injury long ago, we'll never know. We have to settle for a good, occasionally great, 1,000-yard runner. It may even be that Williams takes over. As the 1988 season wore on, Williams really came into it both as a rusher and as a pass receiver. In the final game which brought Seattle the AFC West title, he caught seven passes for 180 yards and a touchdown, and against Cincinnati in the playoffs he caught a further 11 passes for 137 yards and a touchdown. Furthermore, unlike Warner, he seems to be indestructible. The one problem, and it will be a major difficulty, will come if either man goes down with an injury, for behind them there is no one with a record of achievement. Looking at wide receiver, everyone breathed a sigh of relief when future Hall of Famer Steve Largent agreed to come back for one more time around. The NFL all-time leader needs only three more receiving touchdowns to surpass the NFL-record total of 99 set by the legendary Don Hutson. Largent will start in partnership with Brian Blades, who did well as a rookie, ahead of Paul Skansi and free agent Mark Pattison, the latter who is a former University of Washington Huskie and brings good speed. It seems that draftee Travis McNeal is expected to start right away at tight end. The offensive line is solid but has a glaring deficiency at center following the departure of starter Blair Bush. Second-round pick Joe Tofflemire may have to shoulder a heavy burden. Otherwise, top draftee tackle Andy Heck can be brought along steadily while veterans Ron Mattes, Edwin Bailey, Bryan Millard and Mike Wilson take care of things.

Defense

Against all expectations, the Seahawks did not go looking for defensive linemen, either in the free agent pool or the draft. It means that the three-man line of Jacob Green, Joe Nash and Jeff Bryant will remain intact. As usual, Green led the team in sacks with a total of nine which keeps him in third position behind the Giants' Lawrence Taylor and Washington's Dexter Manley in the NFL all-time list. Bryant is steady enough, but Nash has had difficulty exerting his presence in the melee and the feeling is that he represents a vulnerable spot. For trivia fans, all three linemen blocked one kick last year and Nash is the Seahawks' career leader with six. At linebacker the big question mark concerns Brian Bosworth, who appeared lacklustre before going on injured reserve in early December. Bearing in mind that his appearance led to the departure of a disgruntled Fredd Young, Bosworth has a lot of making up to do. Otherwise, the Seahawks are quite well stocked at linebacker with Bruce Scholtz, Dave Wyman and Tony Woods looking the part if, perhaps, Bosworth's replacement, Darren Comeaux, was found wanting on occasion. Wyman, in particular, was extremely impressive and the Seahawks must be glad that his 'trade' to San Francisco of a couple of years ago fell through because of his alleged shoulder problems. The defensive secondary makes a point of picking off lots of passes and last year was no exception with strong safety Paul Moyer intercepting six to lead the team. Second was left cornerback Terry Taylor with five, one of which he returned 27 yards for a touchdown. Overall, though, the quartet has not lived up to the good old days of Kenny Easley, John Harris and Dave Brown. Johnnie Johnson, the former Rams starting free safety, is regarded as one of the league's great run-forcers, though it is not certain that he can displace Eugene Robinson. Patrick Hunter will start at right cornerback with Melvin Jenkins as the senior backup.

1989 SCHEDULE OF GAMES		
September		
10 at Philadelphia		4:00
17 PHOENIX		1:00
24 at New England		1:00
October		
1 at Los Angeles Raiders		1:00
8 KANSAS CITY		1:00
15 at San Diego		1:00
22 DENVER		1:00
29 SAN DIEGO		1:00
November		
5 at Kansas City		12:00
12 CLEVELAND		1:00
19 at New York Giants		4:00
26 at Denver		2:00
December		
4 BUFFALO (Mon.)		6:00
10 at Cincinnati		1:00
17 LOS ANGELES RAIDERS		
(night)		5:00
23 WASHINGTON (Sat.)		1:00

Special Teams

Good special teams play is a Seahawks trademark and, looking at the kicking game, Norm Johnson and Ruben Rodriguez remain unchallenged. Seattle has the NFL's premier punt coverage team. Returning kickoffs and punts may be a problem following the departure of Bobby Joe Edmonds, but it would be no surprise for the Seahawks to whistle up a good one, and fourth-round draftee cornerback James Henry might be that person. Over his last two years in college, Henry returned eight punts for touchdowns.

1989 DRAFT

Round	Name	Pos.	Ht.	Wt.	College
1.	Heck, Andy	T	6-7	262	Notre Dame
2.	Tofflemire, Joe	C	6-2	265	Arizona
3.	Harris, Elroy	RB	5-9	218	Eastern Kentucky
4.	McNeal, Travis	TE	6-3	239	Tennessee-Chattanooga
4.	Henry, James	CB	5-9	190	Southern Mississippi
7.	Nettles, Mike	CB	5-10	188	Memphis State
8.	Williams, Marlin	DE	6-3	260	Western Illinois
9.	Franks, David	G	6-4	300	Connecticut
10.	Fenner, Derrick	RB	6-3	220	North Carolina
11.	Baum, Mike	DE-T	6-5	260	Northwestern
12.	Kors, R.J.	S	6-0	195	Long Beach State

VETERAN ROSTER

No.	Name	Pos.	Ht.	Wt.	NFL Year	College
65	Bailey, Edwin	G	6-4	270	9	South Carolina State
62	Barbay, Roland	NT	6-4	260	2	Louisiana State
89	Blades, Brian	WR	5-11	182	2	Miami
55	Bosworth, Brian	LB	6-2	248	3	Oklahoma
77	Bryant, Jeff	DE	6-5	268	8	Clemson
	Burse, Tony	RB	6-0	220	2	Middle Tennessee State
84	Clark, Louis	WR	6-1	193	2	Mississippi State
67	Clarke, Ken	NT	6-1	271	12	Syracuse
53	Comeaux, Darren	LB	6-1	227	8	Arizona State
69	DesRochers, Dave	T	6-7	290	1	San Diego State
	Embree, Jon	TE	6-2	237	2	Colorado
54	Feasel, Grant	C	6-7	277	5	Abilene Christian
22	Glasgow, Nesby	S	5-10	187	11	Washington
60	Godfrey, Chris	G	6-3	265	7	Michigan
79	Green, Jacob	DE	6-3	254	10	Texas A&M
34	Harmon, Kevin	RB-KR	6-0	190	2	Iowa
29	Harper, Dwayne	CB	5-11	165	2	South Carolina State
63	Hart, Roy	NT	6-1	280	1	South Carolina
	Henton, Anthony	LB	6-1	234	3	Troy State
25	Hollis, David	S	5-11	180	3	Nevada-Las Vegas
23	Hunter, Patrick	CB	5-11	185	4	Nevada-Reno
24	Jenkins, Melvin	CB	5-10	173	3	Cincinnati
	Johnson, Johnnie	S	6-1	183	10	Texas
52	Johnson, M.L.	LB	6-3	229	3	Hawaii
9	Johnson, Norm	K	6-2	197	8	UCLA
26	Justin, Kerry	CB	5-11	185	9	Oregon State
81	Kane, Tommy	WR	5-11	180	2	Syracuse
15	Kemp, Jeff	QB	6-0	198	9	Dartmouth
17	Krieg, Dave	QB	6-1	192	10	Milton
80	Largent, Steve	WR	5-11	191	14	Tulsa
11	Mathison, Bruce	QB	6-3	205	6	Nebraska
70	Mattes, Ron	T	6-6	302	4	Virginia
	McLemore, Chris	RB	6-1	230	3	Arizona
51	Merriman, Sam	LB	6-3	232	6	Idaho
71	Millard, Bryan	G-T	6-5	281	6	Texas
91	Miller, Darrin	LB	6-1	227	2	Tennessee
61	Mitz, Alonzo	DE	6-3	271	4	Florida
21	Moyer, Paul	S	6-1	196	7	Arizona State
72	Nash, Joe	NT	6-2	269	8	Boston College
	Pattison, Mark	WR	6-2	198	4	Washington
97	Porter, Rufus	LB	6-1	207	2	Southern
73	Powell, Alvin	G	6-5	296	3	Winston-Salem State
41	Robinson, Eugene	S	6-0	183	5	Colgate
5	Rodriguez, Ruben	P	6-2	214	3	Arizona
58	Scholtz, Bruce	LB	6-6	241	8	Texas
82	Skansi, Paul	WR-PR	5-11	184	7	Washington
11	Stouffer, Kelly	QB	6-3	210	2	Colorado State
20	Taylor, Terry	CB	5-10	181	6	Southern Illinois
	Thomas, Kevin	C	6-2	265	2	Arizona State
	Traynowicz, Mark	G	6-5	280	5	Nebraska
	Tyler, Robert	TE	6-5	259	1	South Carolina State
28	Warner, Curt	RB	5-11	205	6	Penn State
	Williams, Doug	T-G	6-5	288	3	Texas A&M
32	Williams, John L.	RB	5-11	226	4	Florida
75	Wilson, Mike	T	6-5	274	12	Georgia
57	Woods, Tony	LB	6-4	244	3	Pittsburgh
92	Wyman, David	LB	6-2	234	3	Stanford

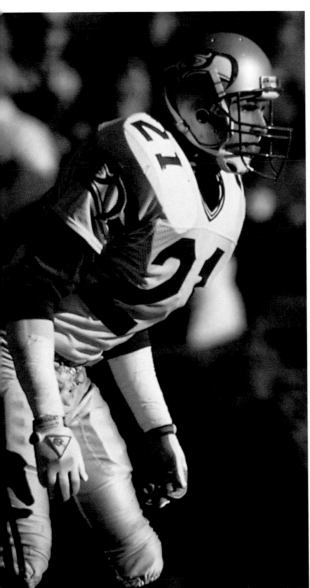

Paul Moyer has emerged from the shadow cast by the retired Kenny Easley.

CHAPTER SEVEN

NATIONAL FOOTBALL CONFERENCE

TEAM RANKINGS

	OFFENSE						DEFENSE					
	Total Yds.	Rushing	Passing	Points For	No. Intercepted	No. Sacked	Total Yds.	Rushing	Passing	Points Against	Interceptions	Sacks
Atlanta	13	5	13	12	9 =	7	13	14	10	8 =	4	12 =
Chicago	8	2	12	8 =	3	1 =	2	1	4	1	3	5 =
Dallas	6	7	5	10	13	6	12	10	12	12	14	4
Detroit	14	14	14	14	6 =	11	11	12	6	7	11 =	3
Green Bay	12	13	9	13	11	10	4	13	2	8 =	8	12 =
L.A. Rams	2	6	2	1	6 =	4	5	6	7	4	5 =	1
Minnesota	5	9	3	2	6 =	8 =	1	4	1	2	1	10
New Orleans	9	3	11	8 =	4	1 =	7	9	8 =	3	9	11
N.Y. Giants	11	11	10	5	1 =	13 =	6	8	8 =	6	11 =	2
Philadelphia	7	8	6	3	5	12	14	5	14	10	2	7 =
Phoenix	3	4	4	7	9 =	8 =	9	11	5	14	10	9
San Francisco	1	1	7	4	1 =	8 =	3	3	3	5	5 =	7 =
Tampa Bay	10	10	8	11	14	5	8	2	13	11	7	14
Washington	4	12	1	6	12	1 =	10	7	11	13	13	5 =

NFC PASSERS

	Att	Comp	% Comp	Yards	Ave Gain	TD	% TD	Long	Int	% Int	Rating Points
Wilson, Wade, *Minn.*	332	204	61.4	2746	8.27	15	4.5	t68	9	2.7	91.5
Everett, Jim, *Rams*	517	308	59.6	3964	7.67	31	6.0	t69	18	3.5	89.2
Montana, Joe, *S.F.*	397	238	59.9	2981	7.51	18	4.5	t96	10	2.5	87.9
Lomax, Neil, *Phoe.*	443	255	57.6	3395	7.66	20	4.5	t93	11	2.5	86.7
Simms, Phil, *Giants*	479	263	54.9	3359	7.01	21	4.4	t62	11	2.3	82.1
Hebert, Bobby, *N.O.*	478	280	58.6	3156	6.60	20	4.2	t40	15	3.1	79.3
Cunningham, Randall, *Phil.*	560	301	53.8	3808	6.80	24	4.3	t80	16	2.9	77.6
Williams, Doug, *Wash.*	380	213	56.1	2609	6.87	15	3.9	58	12	3.2	77.4
Pelluer, Steve, *Dall.*	435	245	56.3	3139	7.22	17	3.9	t61	19	4.4	73.9
Majkowski, Don, *G.B.*	336	178	53.0	2119	6.31	9	2.7	56	11	3.3	67.8
Miller, Chris, *Atl.*	351	184	52.4	2133	6.08	11	3.1	t68	12	3.4	67.3
Wright, Randy, *G.B.*	244	141	57.8	1490	6.11	4	1.6	51	13	5.3	58.9
Hilger, Rusty, *Det.*	306	126	41.2	1558	5.09	7	2.3	56	12	3.9	48.9
Testaverde, Vinny, *T.B.*	466	222	47.6	3240	6.95	13	2.8	t59	35	7.5	48.8
Non-qualifiers											
Rypien, Mark, *Wash.*	208	114	54.8	1730	8.32	18	8.7	t60	13	6.3	85.2
McMahon, Jim, *Chi.*	192	114	59.4	1346	7.01	6	3.1	t63	7	3.6	76.0
Tomczak, Mike, *Chi.*	170	86	50.6	1310	7.71	7	4.1	t76	6	3.5	75.4
Young, Steve, *S.F.*	101	54	53.5	680	6.73	3	3.0	t73	3	3.0	72.2
Long, Chuck, *Det.*	141	75	53.2	856	6.07	6	4.3	40	6	4.3	68.2
Stoudt, Cliff, *Phoe.*	113	63	55.8	747	6.61	6	5.3	t52	8	7.1	64.3
Kramer, Tommy, *Minn.*	173	83	48.0	1264	7.31	5	2.9	47	9	5.2	60.5
Harbaugh, Jim, *Chi.*	97	47	48.5	514	5.30	0	0.0	56	2	2.1	55.9
Dils, Steve, *Atl.*	99	49	49.5	566	5.72	2	2.0	50	5	5.1	52.8
Sweeney, Kevin, *Dall.*	78	33	42.3	314	4.03	3	3.8	28	5	6.4	40.2

t = Touchdown
Leader based on rating points, minimum 224 attempts

NFC RECEIVERS – Most Receptions

	No	Yards	Ave	Long	TD
Ellard, Henry, *Rams*	86	1414	16.4	68	10
Martin, Eric, *N.O.*	85	1083	12.7	t40	7
Smith, J.T., *Phoe.*	83	986	11.9	29	5
Jackson, Keith, *Phil.*	81	869	10.7	41	6
Craig, Roger, *S.F.*	76	534	7.0	22	1
Sanders, Ricky, *Wash.*	73	1148	15.7	t55	12
Carter, Anthony, *Minn.*	72	1225	17.0	t67	6
Monk, Art, *Wash.*	72	946	13.1	t46	5
Byars, Keith, *Phil.*	72	705	9.8	t37	4
Green, Roy, *Phoe.*	68	1097	16.1	52	7
Settle, John, *Atl.*	68	570	8.4	27	1
Hill, Lonzell, *N.O.*	66	703	10.7	35	7
Manuel, Lionel, *Giants*	65	1029	15.8	46	4
Rice, Jerry, *S.F.*	64	1306	20.4	t96	9
Clark, Gary, *Wash.*	59	892	15.1	t60	7
Holohan, Pete, *Rams*	59	640	10.8	29	3
Hill, Bruce, *T.B.*	58	1040	17.9	t42	9
Carrier, Mark, *T.B.*	57	970	17.0	t59	5
Jordan, Steve, *Minn.*	57	756	13.3	38	5
Sharpe, Sterling, *G.B.*	55	791	14.4	51	1
Alexander, Ray, *Dall.*	54	788	14.6	t50	6
Bavaro, Mark, *Giants*	53	672	12.7	36	4
Walker, Herschel, *Dall.*	53	505	9.5	50	2
Martin, Kelvin, *Dall.*	49	622	12.7	t35	3
Kemp, Perry, *G.B.*	48	620	12.9	36	0
McKinnon, Dennis, *Chi.*	45	704	15.6	t76	3
Mandley, Pete, *Det.*	44	617	14.0	56	4
Bryant, Kelvin, *Wash.*	42	447	10.6	47	5
Rathman, Tom, *S.F.*	42	382	9.1	24	0
Johnson, Damone, *Rams*	42	350	8.3	23	6
Jones, Hassan, *Minn.*	40	778	19.5	t68	5
Baker, Stephen, *Giants*	40	656	16.4	t85	7
Carter, Cris, *Phil.*	39	761	19.5	t80	6
Hall, Ron, *T.B.*	39	555	14.2	37	0
Awalt, Robert, *Phoe.*	39	454	11.6	t52	4
James, Garry, *Det.*	39	382	9.8	t39	2
Anderson, Neal, *Chi.*	39	371	9.5	36	0
Woodside, Keith, *G.B.*	39	352	9.0	t49	2

t = Touchdown

NFC RECEIVERS – Most Yards

	Yards	No	Ave	Long	TD
Ellard, Henry, *Rams*	1414	86	16.4	68	10
Rice, Jerry, *S.F.*	1306	64	20.4	t96	9
Carter, Anthony, *Minn.*	1225	72	17.0	t67	6
Sanders, Ricky, *Wash.*	1148	73	15.7	t55	12
Green, Roy, *Phoe.*	1097	68	16.1	52	7
Martin, Eric, *N.O.*	1083	85	12.7	t40	7
Hill, Bruce, *T.B.*	1040	58	17.9	t42	9
Manuel, Lionel, *Giants*	1029	65	15.8	46	4
Smith, J.T., *Phoe.*	986	83	11.9	29	5
Carrier, Mark, *T.B.*	970	57	17.0	t59	5
Monk, Art, *Wash.*	946	72	13.1	t46	5
Clark, Gary, *Wash.*	892	59	15.1	t60	7
Jackson, Keith, *Phil.*	869	81	10.7	41	6
Sharpe, Sterling, *G.B.*	791	55	14.4	51	1
Alexander, Ray, *Dall.*	788	54	14.6	t50	6
Jones, Hassan, *Minn.*	778	40	19.5	t68	5
Carter, Cris, *Phil.*	761	39	19.5	t80	6
Jordan, Steve, *Minn.*	756	57	13.3	38	5
Byars, Keith, *Phil.*	705	72	9.8	t37	4
McKinnon, Dennis, *Chi.*	704	45	15.6	t76	3
Hill, Lonzell, *N.O.*	703	66	10.7	35	7
Bavaro, Mark, *Giants*	672	53	12.7	36	4
Baker, Stephen, *Giants*	656	40	16.4	t85	7
Irvin, Michael, *Dall.*	654	32	20.4	t61	5
Holohan, Pete, *Rams*	640	59	10.8	29	3
Martin, Kelvin, *Dall.*	622	49	12.7	t35	3
Kemp, Perry, *G.B.*	620	48	12.9	36	0
Mandley, Pete, *Det.*	617	44	14.0	56	4

t = Touchdown

Henry Ellard was the NFL leader in yards receiving and led the NFC in receptions.

NFC RUSHERS

	Att	Yards	Ave	Long	TD
Walker, Herschel, *Dall.*	361	1514	4.2	38	5
Craig, Roger, *S.F.*	310	1502	4.8	t46	9
Bell, Greg, *Rams*	288	1212	4.2	44	16
Anderson, Neal, *Chi.*	249	1106	4.4	t80	12
Morris, Joe, *Giants*	307	1083	3.5	27	5
Settle, John, *Atl.*	232	1024	4.4	62	7
Ferrell, Earl, *Phoe.*	202	924	4.6	47	7
Hilliard, Dalton, *N.O.*	204	823	4.0	36	5
Mitchell, Stump, *Phoe.*	164	726	4.4	47	4
Mayes, Rueben, *N.O.*	170	628	3.7	21	3
Cunningham, Randall, *Phil.*	93	624	6.7	t33	6
James, Garry, *Det.*	182	552	3.0	35	5
Byars, Keith, *Phil.*	152	517	3.4	52	6
Toney, Anthony, *Phil.*	139	502	3.6	20	4
Bryant, Kelvin, *Wash.*	108	498	4.6	25	1
Riggs, Gerald, *Atl.*	113	488	4.3	34	1
Fullwood, Brent, *G.B.*	101	483	4.8	t33	7
Smith, Timmy, *Wash.*	155	470	3.0	29	3
Tate, Lars, *T.B.*	122	467	3.8	t47	7
Howard, William, *T.B.*	115	452	3.9	t29	1
Morris, Jamie, *Wash.*	126	437	3.5	t27	2
Rathman, Tom, *S.F.*	102	427	4.2	26	2
Nelson, Darrin, *Minn.*	112	380	3.4	27	1
Heyward, Craig, *N.O.*	74	355	4.8	t73	1
Wilder, James, *T.B.*	86	343	4.0	19	1
Sanders, Thomas, *Chi.*	95	332	3.5	t20	3
White, Charles, *Rams*	88	323	3.7	13	0
Rice, Allen, *Minn.*	110	322	2.9	24	6
Jones, James, *Det.*	96	314	3.3	13	0
Pelluer, Steve, *Dall.*	51	314	6.2	27	2
Anderson, Alfred, *Minn.*	87	300	3.4	18	7
Fenney, Rick, *Minn.*	55	271	4.9	28	3
Suhey, Matt, *Chi.*	87	253	2.9	19	2
Goode, Kerry, *T.B.*	63	231	3.7	22	0
Majkowski, Don, *G.B.*	47	225	4.8	24	1
Anderson, Ottis, *Giants*	65	208	3.2	11	8
Paige, Tony, *Det.*	52	207	4.0	20	0
Muster, Brad, *Chi.*	44	197	4.5	15	0
Woodside, Keith, *G.B.*	83	195	2.3	10	3
Mason, Larry, *G.B.*	48	194	4.0	17	0
Lang, Gene, *Atl.*	53	191	3.6	19	0
Haddix, Michael, *Phil.*	57	185	3.2	15	0
Young, Steve, *S.F.*	27	184	6.8	t49	1
Dozier, D.J., *Minn.*	42	167	4.0	t19	2
Jordan, Tony, *Phoe.*	61	160	2.6	12	3
Simms, Phil, *Giants*	33	152	4.6	17	0
Harris, Darryl, *Minn.*	34	151	4.4	34	1
Delpino, Robert, *Rams*	34	147	4.3	13	0
Carthon, Maurice, *Giants*	46	146	3.2	8	2
Miller, Chris, *Atl.*	31	138	4.5	29	1
Testaverde, Vinny, *T.B.*	28	138	4.9	24	1
Wilson, Wade, *Minn.*	36	136	3.8	15	2
Montana, Joe, *S.F.*	38	132	3.5	15	3
Davis, Kenneth, *G.B.*	39	121	3.1	27	1
Green, Gaston, *Rams*	35	117	3.3	13	0
DuBose, Doug, *S.F.*	24	116	4.8	t37	2
Jordan, Buford, *N.O.*	19	115	6.1	44	0
Carruth, Paul Ott, *G.B.*	49	114	2.3	14	0
Harbaugh, Jim, *Chi.*	19	110	5.8	19	1
Rice, Jerry, *S.F.*	13	107	8.2	29	1
Everett, Jim, *Rams*	34	104	3.1	19	0
McMahon, Jim, *Chi.*	26	104	4.0	16	4
Primus, James, *Atl.*	35	95	2.7	t29	1
Smith, Jeff, *T.B.*	20	87	4.4	23	0
Gentry, Dennis, *Chi.*	7	86	12.3	t58	1
Hebert, Bobby, *N.O.*	37	79	2.1	16	0
Adams, George, *Giants*	29	76	2.6	15	0
Newsome, Tim, *Dall.*	32	75	2.3	8	3

t = Touchdown

NFC SCORING – Kickers

	XP	XPA	FG	FGA	PTS
Cofer, Mike, *S.F.*	40	41	27	38	121
Lansford, Mike, *Rams*	45	48	24	32	117
Andersen, Morten, *N.O.*	32	33	26	36	110
Nelson, Chuck, *Minn.*	48	49	20	25	108
Lohmiller, Chip, *Wash.*	40	41	19	26	97
Zendejas, Luis, *Dall.-Phil.*	35	36	20	27	95
Butler, Kevin, *Chi.*	37	38	15	19	82
Davis, Greg, *Atl.*	25	27	19	30	82
Murray, Ed, *Det.*	22	23	20	21	82
Del Greco, Al, *Phoe.*	42	44	12	21	78
Igwebuike, Donald, *T.B.*	21	21	19	25	78
McFadden, Paul, *Giants*	25	27	14	19	67
Ruzek, Roger, *Dall.*	27	27	12	22	63
Allegre, Raul, *Giants*	14	14	10	11	44
Zendejas, Max, *G.B.*	17	19	9	16	44

NFC SCORING – Touchdowns

	TD	TDR	TDP	TDM	PTS
Bell, Greg, *Rams*	18	16	2	0	108
Anderson, Neal, *Chi.*	12	12	0	0	72
Sanders, Ricky, *Wash.*	12	0	12	0	72
Byars, Keith, *Phil.*	10	6	4	0	60
Craig, Roger, *S.F.*	10	9	1	0	60
Ellard, Henry, *Rams*	10	0	10	0	60
Rice, Jerry, *S.F.*	10	1	9	0	60
Ferrell, Earl, *Phoe.*	9	7	2	0	54
Hill, Bruce, *T.B.*	9	0	9	0	54
Anderson, Alfred, *Minn.*	8	7	1	0	48
Anderson, Ottis, *Giants*	8	8	0	0	48
Fullwood, Brent, *G.B.*	8	7	1	0	48
Settle, John, *Atl.*	8	7	1	0	48
Tate, Lars, *T.B.*	8	7	1	0	48
Baker, Stephen, *Giants*	7	0	7	0	42
Carter, Cris, *Phil.*	7	0	6	1	42
Clark, Gary, *Wash.*	7	0	7	0	42
Green, Roy, *Phoe.*	7	0	7	0	42
Hill, Lonzell, *N.O.*	7	0	7	0	42
James, Garry, *Det.*	7	5	2	0	42
Martin, Eric, *N.O.*	7	0	7	0	42
Walker, Herschel, *Dall.*	7	5	2	0	42

NFC KICKOFF RETURNERS

	No	Yards	Ave	Long	TD
Elder, Donnie, *T.B.*	34	772	22.7	51	0
Burbage, Cornell, *Dall.*	20	448	22.4	53	0
Clack, Darryl, *Dall.*	32	690	21.6	40	0
Gentry, Dennis, *Chi.*	27	578	21.4	51	0
Harris, Darryl, *Minn.*	39	833	21.4	30	0
Atkins, Gene, *N.O.*	20	424	21.2	57	0
Brown, Ron, *Rams*	19	401	21.1	73	0
Gray, Mel, *N.O.*	32	670	20.9	39	0
Sikahema, Vai, *Phoe.*	23	475	20.7	39	0
Fullwood, Brent, *G.B.*	21	421	20.0	31	0
Morris, Jamie, *Wash.*	21	413	19.7	35	0
Lee, Gary, *Det.*	18	355	19.7	39	0
Sanders, Ricky, *Wash.*	19	362	19.1	31	0
DuBose, Doug, *S.F.*	32	608	19.0	44	0
Beals, Shawn, *Phil.*	34	625	18.4	32	0
Woodside, Keith, *G.B.*	19	343	18.1	29	0

t = Touchdown
Leader based on average return, minimum 18 returns

Herschel Walker has the talents to challenge every single-season rushing record.

NFC PUNTERS

	No	Yards	Long	Ave	Total Punts	TB	Blk	Opp Ret	Ret Yds	In 20	Net Ave
Arnold, Jim, *Det.*	97	4110	69	42.4	97	7	0	57	483	22	35.9
Wagner, Bryan, *Chi.*	79	3282	70	41.5	79	10	0	40	447	18	33.4
Buford, Maury, *Giants*	73	3012	66	41.3	75	10	2	36	296	13	33.5
Saxon, Mike, *Dall.*	80	3271	55	40.9	80	15	0	37	239	24	34.2
Horne, Greg, *Phoe.*	79	3228	66	40.9	80	9	1	41	416	16	32.9
Hansen, Brian, *N.O.*	72	2913	64	40.5	73	8	1	39	248	19	34.3
Teltschik, John, *Phil.*	98	3958	70	40.4	101	8	3	45	375	28	33.9
Scribner, Bucky, *Minn.*	84	3387	55	40.3	86	9	2	39	405	23	32.6
Donnelly, Rick, *Atl.*	98	3920	61	40.0	98	6	0	51	297	27	35.7
Camarillo, Rich, *Rams*	40	1579	57	39.5	40	2	0	26	145	11	34.8
Hatcher, Dale, *Rams*	36	1424	54	39.6	36	1	0	17	202	13	33.4
Helton, Barry, *S.F.*	78	3069	53	39.3	79	5	1	47	426	22	32.2
Bracken, Don, *G.B.*	85	3287	62	38.7	86	12	1	39	314	20	31.8
Criswell, Ray, *T.B.*	68	2477	62	36.4	68	0	0	38	273	20	32.4
Coleman, Greg, *Wash.*	39	1505	53	38.6	39	3	0	24	305	8	29.2

Leader based on gross average, minimum 36 punts

NFC SACKERS

	No
White, Reggie, *Phil.*	18.0
Greene, Kevin, *Rams*	16.5
Taylor, Lawrence, *Giants*	15.5
Nunn, Freddie Joe, *Phoe.*	14.0
Harris, Timothy, *G.B.*	13.5
Cofer, Mike, *Det.*	12.0
Haley, Charles, *S.F.*	11.5
Jeter, Gary, *Rams*	11.5
McMichael, Steve, *Chi.*	11.5
Dent, Richard, *Chi.*	10.5
Hampton, Dan, *Chi.*	9.5
Manley, Dexter, *Wash.*	9.0
Ferguson, Keith, *Det.*	8.5
Doleman, Chris, *Minn.*	8.0
Marshall, Leonard, *Giants*	8.0
Millard, Keith, *Minn.*	8.0
Simmons, Clyde, *Phil.*	8.0
Cobb, Garry, *Dall.*	7.5
Martin, George, *Giants*	7.5
Noonan, Danny, *Dall.*	7.5
Wilcher, Mike, *Rams*	7.5
Jackson, Rickey, *N.O.*	7.0
Jones, Ed, *Dall.*	7.0
Swilling, Pat, *N.O.*	7.0
Carter, Michael, *S.F.*	6.5
Jeffcoat, Jim, *Dall.*	6.5
Williams, Eric, *Det.*	6.5
Bruce, Aundray, *Atl.*	6.0
Harvey, Ken, *Phoe.*	6.0
Roberts, Larry, *S.F.*	6.0
Stubbs, Danny, *S.F.*	6.0
Thomas, Henry, *Minn.*	6.0
Baker, Al, *Minn.*	5.5
Jamison, George, *Det.*	5.5
Mann, Charles, *Wash.*	5.5
Brooks, Kevin, *Dall.*	5.0
Brown, Jerome, *Phil.*	5.0
Bryan, Rick, *Atl.*	5.0
Clasby, Bob, *Phoe.*	5.0
Cotton, Marcus, *Atl.*	5.0
Holt, Pierce, *S.F.*	5.0
Owens, Mel, *Rams*	5.0
Winter, Blaise, *G.B.*	5.0
Caldwell, Ravin, *Wash.*	4.0
Gann, Mike, *Atl.*	4.0
Grant, Darryl, *Wash.*	4.0
Green, Tim, *Atl.*	4.0
Holmes, Ron, *T.B.*	4.0
Johnson, Pepper, *Giants*	4.0
Marshall, Wilber, *Wash.*	4.0
Miller, Shawn, *Rams*	4.0
Patterson, Shawn, *G.B.*	4.0
Strickland, Fred, *Rams*	4.0
Walen, Mark, *Dall.*	4.0

NFC PUNT RETURNERS

	No	FC	Yards	Ave	Long	TD
Taylor, John, *S.F.*	44	7	556	12.6	t95	2
Gray, Mel, *N.O.*	25	8	305	12.2	t66	1
Futrell, Bobby, *T.B.*	27	10	283	10.5	40	0
Sikahema, Vai, *Phoe.*	33	8	341	10.3	28	0
Lewis, Leo, *Minn.*	58	19	550	9.5	64	0
Barnes, Lew, *Atl.*	34	8	307	9.0	68	0
Martin, Kelvin, *Dall.*	44	15	360	8.2	21	0
McKinnon, Dennis, *Chi.*	34	8	277	8.1	23	0
McConkey, Phil, *Giants*	40	25	313	7.8	35	0
Mandley, Pete, *Det.*	37	7	287	7.8	25	0
Konecny, Mark, *Phil.*	33	25	233	7.1	24	0
ELlard, Henry, *Rams*	17	3	119	7.0	34	0
Smith, J.T., *Phoe.*	17	2	119	7.0	15	0
Hicks, Cliff, *Rams*	25	0	144	5.8	13	0

t = Touchdown
Leader based on average return, minimum 16 returns

NFC INTERCEPTORS

	No	Yards	Ave	Long	TD
Case, Scott, *Atl.*	10	47	4.7	12	0
Lee, Carl, *Minn.*	8	118	14.8	t58	2
Hoage, Terry, *Phil.*	8	116	14.5	38	0
Jackson, Vestee, *Chi.*	8	94	11.8	46	0
McKyer, Tim, *S.F.*	7	11	1.6	7	0
Hamilton, Harry, *T.B.*	6	123	20.5	58	0
Allen, Eric, *Phil.*	5	76	15.2	21	0
Lott, Ronnie, *S.F.*	5	59	11.8	44	0
Moore, Robert, *Atl.*	5	56	11.2	t47	1
Browner, Joey, *Minn.*	5	29	5.8	18	0
Hopkins, Wes, *Phil.*	5	21	4.2	11	0
Murphy, Mark, *G.B.*	5	19	3.8	9	0
Joyner, Seth, *Phil.*	4	96	24.0	30	0
Solomon, Jesse, *Minn.*	4	84	21.0	t78	1
White, Sheldon, *Giants*	4	70	17.5	39	0
Cecil, Chuck, *G.B.*	4	56	14.0	33	0
Atkins, Gene, *N.O.*	4	42	10.5	40	0
Clark, Bret, *Atl.*	4	40	10.0	21	0
Tate, David, *Chi.*	4	35	8.8	17	0
Wilburn, Barry, *Wash.*	4	24	6.0	14	0
Fuller, Jeff, *S.F.*	4	18	4.5	10	0
Johnson, Johnnie, *Rams*	4	18	4.5	11	0
Reynolds, Ricky, *T.B.*	4	7	1.8	7	0
Mitchell, Devon, *Det.*	3	107	35.7	t90	1
Waymer, Dave, *N.O.*	3	91	30.3	44	0
Gray, Jerry, *Rams*	3	83	27.7	t47	1
Rutland, Reggie, *Minn.*	3	63	21.0	36	0
Jakes, Van, *N.O.*	3	61	20.3	39	0
Marshall, Wilber, *Wash.*	3	61	20.3	43	0
Fullington, Darrell, *Minn.*	3	57	19.0	40	0
Jamison, George, *Det.*	3	56	18.7	t52	1
Walton, Alvin, *Wash.*	3	54	18.0	29	0
Harris, John, *Minn.*	3	46	15.3	27	0
Kinard, Terry, *Giants*	3	46	15.3	39	0

t = Touchdown

Left: Freddie Joe Nunn joined the NFL's elite group of quarterback sackers.

Below: Atlanta cornerback Scott Case won his first NFL interception title.

DALLAS COWBOYS

Address Cowboys Center, One Cowboys Parkway, Irving, Texas 75063.

Stadium Texas Stadium, Irving.
Capacity 63,855 *Playing Surface* Texas Turf.

Team Colours Royal Blue, Metallic Silver Blue, and White.

Head Coach Jimmy Johnson – 1st year.

Championships Division 1970,'71,'73,'76,'77,'78,'79,'81,'85; Conference 1970,'71,'75,'77,'78; Super Bowl 1971,'77.

History NFL 1960-69, NFC 1970-

Offense

In attempting to rally the Cowboys after their worst season since 1960, the year of their NFL debut, new head coach Jimmy Johnson has staked his faith in the quarterback whom, twice before, he had tried but failed to sign. That player, Troy Aikman, eluded him on leaving high school and, subsequently, when transferring from Oklahoma to UCLA. The scouts are in agreement that Aikman has all the mental and physical requirements to become a top professional. In addition, his work habits and discipline fit him perfectly for the traditions of this great club. It would, however, be quite wrong to overlook the claims of incumbent Steve Pelluer, who had four games in which his passer rating was over 100 and came close to winning a couple. Indeed, that may be a more sensible assessment of the club overall, rather than the one which sees it in serious decline. Looking beyond Aikman, the draft may have helped out in more than a few areas, starting at running back, where the hefty Daryl Johnston may be much more than just a blocker for the franchise running back, the great Herschel Walker. Last year, Walker accounted for more than one third of the Cowboys' total yards from scrimmage. The backups include Darryl Clack, who has had little opportunity to express his varied talents waiting in Walker's shadow both as a runner and a receiver. A young group of wide receivers, led by Ray Alexander and Michael Irvin, now rates as a real strength. Alexander, who honed his skills in the CFL after his rejection by Denver in 1984, cost the Cowboys nothing when he signed as a free agent in 1987. Irvin's class was well known and he confirmed it as a 1988 rookie, averaging 20.4 yards on 32 receptions. Third receiver Kelvin Martin was equally productive. Interestingly, Kelvin Edwards' five receptions came on Week One before his injury. The departure of Doug Cosbie leaves Thornton Chandler in charge at tight end. A big offensive line hasn't quite managed to turn mass into momentum. The strength lies at guard in Nate Newton (who ought to know a bit about momentum) and Crawford Ker. Draftee Mark Stepnoski may be seen as ripe for conversion to center, eventually replacing Tom Rafferty. Tackles Dave Widell and Kevin Gogan are expected to continue the learning process.

Defense

In terms of pedigree, the four-man defensive line is unique in consisting of first-round picks, all by the same club. Those selections span the 13 years which separate the arrivals of defensive left end Ed (Too Tall) Jones and defensive right tackle Danny Noonan. The other starters are tackle Kevin Brooks, whose early progress was slowed by injury, and Jim Jeffcoat. The draft brought Rhondy Weston, Tony Tolbert and Jeff Roth to join Mark Walen as the depth. The talent at linebacker looks better than in recent years. No one disputes that Garry Cobb, who shared the team lead with 7.5 sacks, was a windfall following a training camp injury to Jeff Rohrer. Across from Cobb, Ron Burton holds up well despite his preference for the inside. The hope must be that last year's second-round pick, Ken Norton, comes through after making a late contribution on special teams. The inside belongs to Eugene Lockhart, whose role in a modified defensive system may be to go out looking for trouble. Nicknamed 'The Hitting Machine', he is suited to the job. At cornerback, both Everson Walls and Robert Williams, who share a common origin in having joined the team as free agents, have reserved their places. The story of Walls, who turned up at camp with just a pair of boots is well known. He went on to lead the NFL in interceptions two years running. Williams was given his chance to start following an injury to Ron Francis and, later, won it on merit. Williams has the rare ability to mark man-on-man. There will be one certain change at free safety, a position left vacant by the release of Michael Downs. Again, there is no question over the commitment of strong safety Bill Bates, but he is not the fastest player around. Backup Vince Albritton has made a good impression with coach Johnson and Francis is too good a prospect to be left languishing on the bench. In addition, former Cincinnati reserve Ray Horton has been signed. The names will find their places on the teamsheet during the preseason.

1989 SCHEDULE OF GAMES		
September		
10	at New Orleans	12:00
17	at Atlanta	1:00
24	WASHINGTON	12:00
October		
1	NEW YORK GIANTS	3:00
8	at Green Bay	12:00
15	SAN FRANCISCO	12:00
22	at Kansas City	12:00
29	PHOENIX	12:00
November		
5	at Washington (night)	8:00
12	at Phoenix	2:00
19	MIAMI	12:00
23	PHILADELPHIA (Thanksgiving)	3:00
December		
3	LOS ANGELES RAMS	12:00
10	at Philadelphia	1:00
16	at New York Giants (Sat.)	12:30
24	GREEN BAY	12:00

Special Teams

Placekicker Roger Ruzek will hope to bounce back after a season which got off to a bad start because of a contractual dispute. Mike Saxon, the NFL leader in punts inside the 20 for two consecutive years, narrowly failed to make it three. His place on the roster is secure. Respectable and consistent are the words which describe the kick return specialists, Kelvin Martin, Darryl Clack and Cornell Burbage.

1989 DRAFT

Round	Name	Pos.	Ht.	Wt.	College
1.	Aikman, Troy	QB	6-4	223	UCLA
2.	Johnston, Daryl	RB	6-1	238	Syracuse
3.	Stepnoski, Mark	G	6-2	269	Pittsburgh
3.	Weston, Rhondy	DT	6-4	274	Florida
4.	Tolbert, Tony	LB-DE	6-5	230	Texas-El Paso
5.	Jennings, Keith	TE	6-3	241	Clemson
5.	Crockett, Willis	LB	6-2	221	Georgia Tech
5.	Roth, Jeff	DT	6-2	255	Florida
7.	Peterson, Kevin	LB	6-4	227	Northwestern
8.	Foger, Charvez	RB	5-10	211	Nevada-Reno
9.	Jackson, Tim	S	5-11	192	Nebraska
10.	Carter, Rod	LB	6-0	233	Miami
11.	Shannon, Randy	LB	6-0	224	Miami
12.	Ankrom, Scott	WR	6-0	200	Texas Christian

VETERAN ROSTER

No.	Name	Pos.	Ht.	Wt.	NFL Year	College
36	Albritton, Vince	S	6-2	210	6	Washington
87	Alexander, Ray	WR	6-4	193	3	Florida A&M
86	Barksdale, Rod	WR	6-1	192	3	Arizona
40	Bates, Bill	S	6-1	200	7	Tennessee
99	Brooks, Kevin	DT	6-6	273	5	Michigan
82	Burbage, Cornell	WR	5-10	189	3	Kentucky
57	Burton, Ron	LB	6-1	245	3	North Carolina
89	Chandler, Thornton	TE	6-5	240	4	Alabama
42	Clack, Darryl	RB-KR	5-10	220	4	Arizona State
59	Cobb, Garry	LB	6-2	233	11	Southern California
	Coyle, Eric	C	6-3	260	3	Colorado
55	DeOssie, Steve	LB	6-2	246	6	Boston College
81	Edwards, Kelvin	WR	6-2	204	4	Liberty
85	Folsom, Steve	TE	6-5	240	4	Utah
46	Fowler, Todd	RB	6-3	226	5	Stephen F. Austin
38	Francis, Ron	CB	5-9	201	3	Baylor
80	Gay, Everett	WR	6-2	209	2	Texas
66	Gogan, Kevin	T	6-7	306	3	Washington
45	Hendrix, Manny	CB	5-10	181	4	Utah
20	Horton, Ray	CB	5-11	190	7	Washington
52	Hurd, Jeff	LB	6-2	245	2	Kansas State
88	Irvin, Michael	WR	6-2	202	2	Miami
77	Jeffcoat, Jim	DE	6-5	262	7	Arizona State
	Jones, Anthony	TE	6-3	248	5	Wichita State
72	Jones, Ed	DE	6-9	278	15	Tennessee State
68	Ker, Crawford	G	6-3	290	5	Florida
56	Lockhart, Eugene	LB	6-2	235	6	Houston
83	Martin, Kelvin	WR-PR	5-9	163	3	Boston College
58	Naposki, Eric	LB	6-2	230	1	Connecticut
30	Newsome, Timmy	RB	6-1	236	10	Winston-Salem State
61	Newton, Nate	G	6-3	314	4	Florida A&M
73	Noonan, Danny	DT	6-4	266	3	Nebraska
51	Norton, Ken	LB	6-2	236	2	UCLA
31	Owens, Billy	S	6-1	207	2	Pittsburgh
16	Pelluer, Steve	QB	6-4	212	6	Washington
64	Rafferty, Tom	C	6-3	264	14	Penn State
50	Rohrer, Jeff	LB	6-2	222	7	Yale
9	Ruzek, Roger	K	6-1	195	3	Weber State
4	Saxon, Mike	P	6-3	188	5	San Diego State
35	Scott, Kevin	RB	5-9	181	1	Stanford
22	Scott, Victor	S	6-0	214	6	Colorado
10	Secules, Scott	QB	6-3	219	2	Virginia
79	Smith, Daryle	T	6-5	276	3	Tennessee
71	Tuinei, Mark	T	6-5	282	7	Hawaii
95	Walen, Mark	DT	6-5	267	3	UCLA
34	Walker, Herschel	RB	6-1	226	4	Georgia
24	Walls, Everson	CB	6-1	193	9	Grambling
65	White, Bob	G-C	6-5	273	3	Rhode Island
11	White, Danny	QB	6-3	200	14	Arizona State
78	Widell, Dave	T	6-6	300	2	Boston College
23	Williams, Robert	CB	5-10	186	3	Baylor
76	Zimmerman, Jeff	G	6-3	313	3	Florida

Second-year pro Ray Alexander was the Cowboys' leading receiver.

NEW YORK GIANTS

Address Giants Stadium, East Rutherford, New Jersey 07073.

Stadium Giants Stadium, East Rutherford.
Capacity 76,891 *Playing Surface* AstroTurf.

Team Colours Blue, Red, and White.

Head Coach Bill Parcells – 7th year.

Championships Division 1986; Conference 1986.
NFL 1927,'34,'38,'56.
Super Bowl 1986.

History NFL 1925-69, NFC 1970-

Offense

Just 37 seconds separated the Giants from the NFC Eastern division title which seemed theirs before the Jets' Al Toon caught a five-yard touchdown pass. There are many reasons for feeling that the Giants will remain in contention, not least in the prospects for the offensive line which saw two rookies, Eric Moore and John Elliott, and a second-year player, Doug Riesenberg, come through to start. Center Bart Oates is well established though even he is entering only his fifth NFL season. The Giants erred in not protecting veteran starting guard Bill Ard, who was quickly snapped up by Green Bay, and backup center Joe Fields has been released. However, excellent prospects Brian Williams and Bob Kratch were drafted with the club's first two options and Damian Johnson, who has started several games at right guard, is expected to be back from injured reserve to join William Roberts in the pool of good young players. Helping out with the blocking, tight end Mark Bavaro has lost none of his impetus while, in his capacity as a pass receiver, he has just had his third straight year with 50-or-more catches. Zeke Mowatt probably is the best backup tight end in the conference. Looking at the wide receivers, the club's top player, Lionel Manuel, had his first injury-free campaign and gained career-highs with both 65 receptions and 1,029 yards. He led the team, ahead of Bavaro and wide receiver Stephen (Touchdown Maker) Baker, who topped the club with seven touchdown receptions and emphasised his status as the best of a group of three young receivers in which he is joined by Mark Ingram and Odessa Turner. At running back, it was only late in the season that Joe Morris raised a head of steam, and while it was enough to propel him over 1,000 yards his was the best of a team effort which, by comparison with expectations, was mediocre. It may be that the arrival of fourth-round draftee Lewis Tillman will spark the veterans to their best. One man who doesn't need any stimulus is quarterback Phil Simms, whose wisdom, poise and talent brought him his second-best performance as a pro and kept alive the momentum of the offense.

Defense

On defense the Giants were just a little out of tune and slipped four notches down the NFL scale. However, despite missing four games on suspension, the peerless Lawrence Taylor logged 15.5 sacks, just 2.5 behind the NFL leader, Reggie White, and one adrift of the Rams' Kevin Greene. This remarkable man remains as one of the most destructive players in pro football. His outside partner, Carl Banks, fell away a little, coming seventh on the team in tackles and logging only 1.5 sacks. It was Pepper Johnson who made the great improvement. Playing the left inside linebacker position, Johnson was the team leader in tackles with 93, including 77 solos, and he'll continue, probably with Gary Reasons on his right. Reasons started in six games and is the heir apparent to the retired Harry Carson. Another old veteran, defensive end George Martin, also has retired and the experience of a man who can log 7.5 sacks as an occasional pass rusher may be missed if the Giants run into injury problems. As it is, they have an outstanding three-man line with Leonard Marshall and Eric Dorsey flanking nose tackle Jim Burt. Awaiting his chance behind Burt, the immensely powerful Erik Howard could start at nose tackle for many clubs around the NFL. In terms of measurable mayhem, Marshall had eight sacks to rank second in the club. Burt is as hard as a nose tackle needs to be while Dorsey has confirmed the collegiate promise which encouraged the Giants to make him their first-round pick in 1986. Age, wear and tear may be showing in safeties Terry Kinard and Kenny Hill, and yet they came second and fourth on the team in tackles, starting in all 16 games. Perry Williams, who went through the campaign at right cornerback, is entering only his sixth NFL year and should be approaching his prime. In addition, it was a real bonus that rookie Sheldon White came through to start when Mark Collins was unavailable. Collins is expected to re-establish his authority following a hernia problem, and White could challenge Williams to start on the right. The club can always count on the unquenchable aggression of safety Adrian White, who'll be attempting to stay ahead of draftee Greg Jackson.

Lionel Manuel had his best year as a pro.

Special Teams

The probability is that both placekicker Raul Allegre and former Pro Bowl punter Sean Landeta will return from injured reserve to reclaim their roster spots. When it comes to returning kicks, the club is well down the list in both categories but they don't give up much yardage either and didn't concede a touchdown in 1988. Wide receiver Phil McConkey should continue returning punts while draftee Dave Meggett has returned kickoffs and punts successfully in college.

1989 DRAFT

Round	Name	Pos.	Ht.	Wt.	College
1.	Williams, Brian	G-C	6-4	295	Minnesota
3.	Kratch, Bob	G-T	6-3	286	Iowa
3.	Jackson, Greg	S	6-0	202	Louisiana State
4.	Tillman, Lewis	RB	5-11	192	Jackson State
4.	Henke, Brad	NT	6-3	273	Arizona
5.	Meggett, Dave	RB	5-7	179	Towson State
6.	Cross, Howard	TE	6-4	244	Alabama
7.	Popp, David	T	6-5	280	Eastern Illinois
8.	Guyton, Myron	S	6-0	200	Eastern Kentucky
9.	Greene, A.J.	CB	5-7	160	Wake Forest
10.	Lowe, Rodney	DE	6-4	258	Mississippi
11.	Rinehart, Jerome	LB	6-4	245	Tennessee-Martin
12.	Smith, Eric	LB	6-2	229	UCLA

VETERAN ROSTER

No.	Name	Pos.	Ht.	Wt.	NFL Year	College
33	Adams, George	RB	6-1	225	4	Kentucky
2	Allegre, Raul	K	5-10	167	7	Texas
85	Baker, Stephen	WR	5-8	160	3	Fresno State
58	Banks, Carl	LB	6-4	235	6	Michigan State
89	Bavaro, Mark	TE	6-4	245	5	Notre Dame
64	Burt, Jim	NT	6-1	260	9	Miami
78	Carter, Jon	DE	6-4	260	1	Pittsburgh
44	Carthon, Maurice	RB	6-1	225	5	Arkansas State
25	Collins, Mark	CB	5-10	190	4	Cal State-Fullerton
98	Cooks, Johnie	LB	6-4	251	8	Mississippi State
	Cox, Greg	S	6-0	223	2	San Jose State

No.	Name	Pos.	Ht.	Wt.	NFL Year	College
77	Dorsey, Eric	DE	6-5	280	4	Notre Dame
76	Elliott, John	T	6-7	305	2	Michigan
28	Flynn, Tom	S	6-0	195	6	Pittsburgh
37	Haddix, Wayne	CB	6-1	203	3	Liberty
54	Headen, Andy	LB	6-5	242	7	Clemson
48	Hill, Kenny	S	6-0	195	9	Yale
15	Hostetler, Jeff	QB	6-3	212	5	West Virginia
74	Howard, Erik	NT	6-4	268	4	Washington State
82	Ingram, Mark	WR	5-10	188	3	Michigan State
68	Johnson, Damian	G	6-5	290	4	Kansas State
52	Johnson, Pepper	LB	6-3	248	4	Ohio State
43	Kinard, Terry	S	6-1	200	7	Clemson
	Lambrecht, Mike	NT	6-1	271	3	St Cloud State
5	Landeta, Sean	P	6-0	200	4	Towson State
86	Manuel, Lionel	WR	5-11	180	6	Pacific
70	Marshall, Leonard	DE	6-3	285	7	Louisiana State
80	McConkey, Phil	WR-PR	5-10	170	6	Navy
60	Moore, Eric	G-T	6-5	290	2	Indiana
20	Morris, Joe	RB	5-7	195	8	Syracuse
84	Mowatt, Zeke	TE	6-3	240	6	Florida State
65	Oates, Bart	C	6-3	265	5	Brigham Young
12	Perez, Mike	QB	6-1	210	1	San Jose State
55	Reasons, Gary	LB	6-4	234	6	Northwestern State, La.
26	Richardson, Tim	RB	6-0	215	1	Pacific
72	Riesenberg, Doug	T-G	6-5	275	3	California
66	Roberts, William	T	6-5	280	5	Ohio State
81	Robinson, Stacy	WR	5-11	186	5	North Dakota State
22	Rouson, Lee	RB	6-1	222	5	Colorado
	Schippang, Gary	T	6-4	275	1	West Chester
51	Shaw, Ricky	LB	6-4	240	2	Oklahoma State
11	Simms, Phil	QB	6-3	214	10	Morehead State
56	Taylor, Lawrence	LB	6-3	243	9	North Carolina
	Thompson, Reyna	CB	6-0	193	4	Baylor
83	Turner, Odessa	WR	6-3	205	3	Northwestern State, La.
73	Washington, John	DE	6-4	275	4	Oklahoma State
27	Welch, Herb	CB	5-11	180	4	UCLA
36	White, Adrian	S	6-0	200	3	Florida
71	White, Robb	DE	6-4	270	2	South Dakota
39	White, Sheldon	CB	5-11	188	2	Miami, Ohio
23	Williams, Perry	CB	6-2	203	6	North Carolina State
	Winters, Frank	C	6-3	280	3	Western Illinois

PHILADELPHIA EAGLES

Address Veterans Stadium, Broad St. and Pattison Ave.,
Philadelphia, Pennsylvania 19148.
Stadium Veterans Stadium, Philadelphia.
Capacity 65,356 *Playing Surface* AstroTurf-8.
Team Colours Kelly Green, Silver, and White.
Head Coach Buddy Ryan – 4th year.
Championships Division 1980,'88; Conference 1980;
NFL 1948,'49,'60.
History NFL 1933-69, NFC 1970-

Offense

Well coached and playing with lots of heart, the Eagles hung on until the Giants cracked and gained their first divisional title since 1980. It will not be easier in 1989 but the team will be just that bit stronger, not simply because of new players but more for the fact the coaches now know how to use the strengths of the players they already have. Running back Keith Byars probably will never be the game-breaker he was in college but he has become a really productive dual-purpose player, last year clocking up 1,222 yards on 152 carries and 72 receptions and leading the team with ten touchdowns. Anthony Toney had some problems with injuries but he now looks the part as a starting fullback. In what was the smallest draft by a team in NFL history, two more running backs arrived and, of these, Robert Drummond has a distinct chance of making a contribution. Powerful and speedy, he is the perfect multi-purpose kind who could play either at halfback or fullback. For the last two years the major contribution to the rushing offense has come from Randall Cunningham, who became the first quarterback since Tobin Rote of Green Bay (1951 and 1952) to lead his team in rushing in two consecutive seasons. At 77.6 his passer rating isn't that impressive but it is just a part of an outstanding package which was the single most important reason for the Eagles' success. Also helping out was a pass receiving corps in which rookie tight end Keith Jackson was sensational, falling short of the rookie receiving record by only two catches. All three wide receivers Cris Carter, Mike Quick and Ron Johnson are the kind who love to go downtown. They averaged 19.5, 23.1 and 21.9 yards respectively. Quick's season was marred by a broken leg but he was back in time for the playoffs. That much maligned offensive line continued to improve, not by much but at least they gave up fewer sacks than both the Giants and the Cardinals. There will be changes in 1989, with former Rams first-round draftee Mike Schad projected to start at left guard, with David Alexander displacing Dave Rimington at center. Former Colts Pro Bowler Ron Solt is recovering well from knee surgery and is seen as the successor to Ron Baker at right guard. Matt Darwin and Ron Heller should remain in the tackle positions, with Reggie Singletary, Ken Reeves and Ben Tamburello snapping at the heels of the starters.

Defense

Statistically, the defense is poor but try telling that to the Eagles' opponents, who repeatedly saw field position taken away with big plays. The defense gave up a league-worst 4,443 passing yards and yet had an NFL second-best 32 interceptions. Cleverly, Buddy Ryan rotated his lads to disguise weaknesses and enhance strengths. There are no problems on the defensive line where Reggie White, Mike Pitts, Jerome Brown and Clyde Simmons impose a reign of terror. White led the NFL with 18 sacks. And when the opportunity arose to grab defensive end Al Harris, whom the Bears had left as an unprotected free agent, he was quickly snapped up by Buddy Ryan, who had coached Harris at Chicago. Harris is going to start at right linebacker, that much is certain, with Seth Joyner continuing on the left side. The fast-improving Byron Evans is set to take over from Mike Reichenbach at middle linebacker. Last year, Dwayne Jiles came in against the run and Ty Allert was used in the nickel defense. Draftees Jessie Small and Britt Hager are typical, all-action Ryan players and Small, certainly, has a contribution to make right away. In an inspired move, the Eagles converted Todd Bell to outside linebacker, but in 1989 he will challenge for one of the safety positions. That is where the weight of tackling falls, with starters Andre Waters and Wes Hopkins leading the team with 154 and 146 tackles respectively. It was a brilliant idea to bring in Terry Hoage at free safety on passing downs. It meant that Hopkins would not be overexposed to a flood of deep receivers while Hoage, who was able to apply a fresh pair of legs, picked off eight enemy passes to lead the team. Shifting to a nickel-linebacker role on those occasions, Hopkins grabbed five interceptions. Veteran Roynell Young will not be with the Eagles for a tenth year, leaving the left cornerback position open to a competition involving Izel Jenkins and Eric Everett. Rookie Eric Allen started in all 16 games at right cornerback and had five interceptions. William Frizzell is the senior backup.

Special Teams

The club is satisfied with Luis Zendejas, who failed only occasionally from kickable distance. Punter John Teltschik has settled in, and though he had three efforts blocked he did place an NFL-best 28 punts inside the opposing 20-yard line. Ex-CFL player Henry (Gizmo) Williams brings his dazzling speed to the kick return department. Draftee Britt Hager may make a name for himself as a special-teams tackler.

1989 DRAFT

Round	Name	Pos.	Ht.	Wt.	College
2.	Small, Jessie	LB	6-3	240	Eastern Kentucky
3.	Drummond, Robert	RB	6-1	205	Syracuse
3.	Hager, Britt	LB	6-0	222	Texas
6.	Sherman, Heath	RB	5-11	200	Texas A&I

VETERAN ROSTER

No.	Name	Pos.	Ht.	Wt.	NFL Year	College
32	Abercrombie, Walter	RB	6-0	210	8	Baylor
72	Alexander, David	G-C	6-3	282	3	Tulsa
21	Allen, Eric	CB	5-10	188	2	Arizona State
58	Allert, Ty	LB	6-2	233	4	Texas
87	Bailey, Eric	TE	6-5	240	2	Kansas State
63	Baker, Ron	G	6-4	274	12	Oklahoma State
49	Bell, Todd	S	6-1	212	8	Ohio State
99	Brown, Jerome	DT	6-2	288	3	Miami
51	Butcher, Paul	LB	6-0	230	4	Wayne State
41	Byars, Keith	RB	6-1	238	4	Ohio State
80	Carter, Cris	WR	6-3	194	3	Ohio State
6	Cavanaugh, Matt	QB	6-2	210	12	Pittsburgh
12	Cunningham, Randall	QB	6-4	203	5	Nevada-Las Vegas
78	Darwin, Matt	T	6-4	275	4	Texas A&M
56	Evans, Byron	LB	6-2	235	3	Arizona
77	Evans, Donald	DE	6-2	258	2	Winston-Salem State
42	Everett, Eric	CB	5-10	170	2	Texas Tech

No.	Name	Pos.	Ht.	Wt.	Year	College
33	Frizzell, William	S	6-3	205	6	North Carolina Central
86	Garrity, Gregg	WR	5-10	169	7	Penn State
90	Golic, Mike	DT	6-5	275	4	Notre Dame
95	Harris, Al	LB	6-5	265	10	Arizona State
73	Heller, Ron	T	6-6	280	6	Penn State
22	Higgs, Mark	RB	5-7	196	2	Kentucky
34	Hoage, Terry	S	6-3	201	6	Georgia
48	Hopkins, Wes	S	6-1	212	6	Southern Methodist
88	Jackson, Keith	TE	6-2	250	2	Oklahoma
46	Jenkins, Izel	CB	5-10	191	2	North Carolina State
53	Jiles, Dwayne	LB	6-4	250	5	Texas Tech
85	Johnson, Ron	WR	6-3	186	5	Long Beach State
59	Joyner, Seth	LB	6-2	248	4	Texas-El Paso
94	Kaufusi, Steve	DE	6-4	260	1	Brigham Young
97	Klingel, John	DE	6-3	267	3	Eastern Kentucky
37	Lilly, Sammy	DB	5-9	172	1	Georgia Tech
89	Little, Dave	TE	6-2	226	6	Middle Tennessee State
9	McPherson, Don	QB	6-1	183	1	Syracuse
57	Moten, Ron	LB	6-1	230	1	Florida
71	Patchan, Matt	T	6-4	275	1	Miami
74	Pitts, Mike	DT	6-5	277	7	Alabama
82	Quick, Mike	WR	6-2	190	8	North Carolina State
66	Reeves, Ken	T-G	6-5	270	5	Texas A&M
55	Reichenbach, Mike	LB	6-2	230	6	East Stroudsburg
50	Rimington, Dave	C	6-3	288	7	Nebraska
79	Schad, Mike	G	6-5	290	2	Queen's, Canada
98	Schuster, Joe	DT	6-4	260	1	Iowa
96	Simmons, Clyde	DE	6-6	276	4	Western Carolina
68	Singletary, Reggie	G	6-3	280	4	North Carolina State
65	Solt, Ron	G	6-3	288	5	Maryland
61	Tamburello, Ben	G-C	6-3	278	2	Auburn
10	Teltschik, John	P	6-2	209	4	Texas
25	Toney, Anthony	RB	6-0	227	4	Texas A&M
20	Waters, Andre	S	5-11	199	6	Cheyney
92	White, Reggie	DE	6-5	285	5	Tennessee
	Williams, Henry	WR-KR	5-6	180	1	East Carolina
8	Zendejas, Luis	K	5-9	170	3	Arizona State

Wide receiver Cris Carter is a long-ball threat.

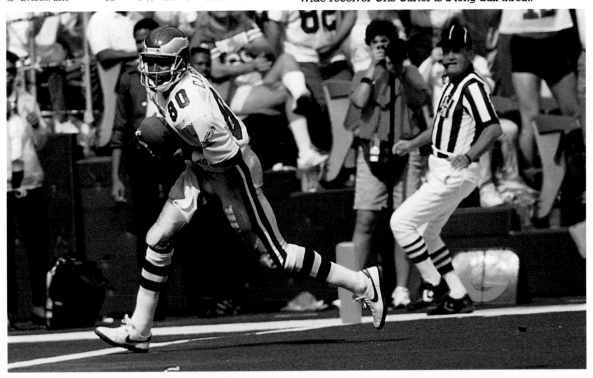

PHOENIX CARDINALS

NFC EASTERN DIVISION

Address P.O. Box 888, Phoenix, Arizona 85001-0888.
Stadium Sun Devil Stadium, Tempe, Arizona.
 Capacity 74,000 *Playing Surface* Grass.
Team Colours Cardinal Red, Black, and White.
Head Coach Gene Stallings – 4th year.
Championships Division 1974,'75; NFL 1925,'47.
History NFL 1920-69, NFC 1970-
 (They were known as the Chicago Cardinals until 1960, when they moved to St Louis. In 1988, the franchise, still under the same ownership, was transferred to Phoenix.)

Offense

'Just a little lacking in one or two areas' may be the best description of a Cardinals team which had fought its way to the top of the NFC East over a nine-week period, in one game mounting an astonishing, 24-point comeback to beat San Francisco, only to suffer losses in the final five games. At times, the rushing game flourished, with Earl Ferrell having his best year as a pro and taking over the team leadership from the reliable Stump Mitchell. Ron Wolfley is a safe short-yardage specialist and there is more than a little untapped potential in last year's rookies, Tony Jordan and Tony Jeffery. Without being likely to run an opponent ragged, neither can the rushing offense be taken lightly. The passing offense, however, presents a more exciting picture. Indeed, the Cardinals have several ways to break a game open, starting at tight end where both Jay Novacek and Robert Awalt are excellent receivers. Novacek also can play as a third wide receiver and perhaps the Cardinals had that in mind when they used their second-round option to select Auburn tight end Walter Reeves. The senior wide receivers, J.T. Smith and Roy Green, combined for more catches, 151, than any other starting pair in the NFL at a time when both men should be slowing. For some reason, the Pro Bowl voters continue to overlook Smith, who has the most pass receptions (254) in the league over the last three seasons. Green is coming off his best campaign since 1984. Ernie Jones made a useful contribution, nipping in for the odd big gain to raise his average per reception to 21.6 yards. The one worry over the passing game concerns the fitness of starting quarterback Neil Lomax, a two-time Pro Bowler, who is bothered by chronic inflammation of his left hip. Class performer though he is, the club was obliged to take steps to find a quality backup, and that player came in the shape of former Cowboys and Colts starter Gary Hogeboom. Tom Tupa occupies the insurance spot. The offensive line gradually is losing its anonymity as left tackle Luis Sharpe cements his position in the Pro Bowl squad. Right tackle Tootie Robbins turned in his best showing since his all-rookie campaign of 1982. Center Derek Kennard answered the bell in 16 games and developed a fine partnership with starting guards Todd Peat and Lance Smith. Joe Bostic and Mark MacDonald are sound back-

ups, but the Cardinals wisely used the draft to build for the future in selecting Joe Wolf and Mike Zandofsky with high options.

Defense

Defensively, the Cardinals made great strides, from 25th overall in 1987 to 14th. Making a major contribution was defensive left end Freddie Joe Nunn, who kept up the momentum he gathered in 1987 with an overpowering display which produced a team-leading 14 sacks. His is the kind of presence which brings out the best in others, and that was true of Rod Saddler, who started the first nine games at defensive right end before shifting to defensive right tackle to make way for David Galloway, who was returning after injury. Consistency and perseverance mark the play of defensive left tackle Bob Clasby. The departure of free agent Curtis Greer leaves Steve Alvord and Sean McNanie as the senior reserves. It is at linebacker where the Cardinals have been building, and that process continued in the draft with the selection of Eric Hill in the first round and Richard Tardits in the fifth. Last year's first-round pick, Ken Harvey, showed super form - he had six sacks - and is set to take over at right outside linebacker from E.J. Junior, who has gone to the Dolphins. The left side currently belongs to 1986 first-rounder Anthony Bell but Hill must have a chance to take over. Niko Noga plugs the middle. At strong safety, Tim McDonald etched his message in black and blue, leading the team with almost twice as many tackles as the next best. McDonald, who also forced four fumbles, could be destined for greatness. The hard-hitting Lonnie Young, who was injured after starting 12 games, is fit to resume at free safety. Two much-maligned cornerbacks, Cedric Mack and Carl Carter, started in partnership for all but the two games in which Mack was displaced by Young. Both Carter and Mack came through the bad times and, beyond the halfway point, they rebounded in fine style. Reggie Phillips and Roland Mitchell are the senior backups.

1989 SCHEDULE OF GAMES		
September		
10 at Detroit		1:00
17 at Seattle		1:00
24 at New York Giants		1:00
October		
1 SAN DIEGO		1:00
8 at Washington		4:00
15 PHILADELPHIA		1:00
22 ATLANTA		1:00
29 at Dallas		12:00
November		
5 NEW YORK GIANTS		2:00
12 DALLAS		2:00
19 at Los Angeles Rams		1:00
26 TAMPA BAY		2:00
December		
3 WASHINGTON		2:00
10 at Los Angeles Raiders		1:00
16 DENVER (Sat.)		2:00
24 at Philadelphia		1:00

Special Teams

For some time the Cardinals have sought consistency in their kicking games and they have had more than their share of disappointments. Competing for the job of place-kicker are incumbent Al Del Greco, Teddy Garcia, and draftee Kendall Trainor. The punting situation is less competitive, with only draftee Chris Becker and, perhaps, veteran Tom Tupa involved. Vai Sikahema is among the NFL's elite dual-purpose returners while special-teamer Ron Wolfley is an uncompromising wedge-buster.

1989 DRAFT

Round	Name	Pos.	Ht.	Wt.	College
1.	Hill, Eric	LB	6-1	248	Louisiana State
1.	Wolf, Joe	G-T	6-5	279	Boston College
2.	Reeves, Walter	TE	6-3	251	Auburn
3.	Zandofsky, Mike	G	6-2	297	Washington
4.	Wahler, Jim	DT	6-3	259	UCLA
5.	Tardits, Richard	LB	6-2	220	Georgia
5.	Edeen, David	DE	6-3	260	Wyoming
6.	Taylor, Jay	CB	5-9	174	San Jose State
7.	Royal, Rickey	CB	5-9	183	Sam Houston State
8.	Burch, John	RB	5-10	200	Tennessee-Martin
9.	Trainor, Kendall	K	6-1	202	Arkansas
10.	Becker, Chris	P	6-2	192	Texas Christian
11.	Hunter, Jeff	DE	6-4	267	Albany State, Ga.
12.	Nelson, Todd	G	6-5	289	Wisconsin

VETERAN ROSTER

No.	Name	Pos.	Ht.	Wt.	NFL Year	College
	Adams, Michael	CB	5-10	195	3	Arkansas State
60	Alvord, Steve	DT	6-4	272	3	Washington
80	Awalt, Robert	TE	6-5	248	3	San Diego State
55	Bell, Anthony	LB	6-3	231	4	Michigan State
	Bellini, Mark	WR	5-11	185	3	Brigham Young
71	Bostic, Joe	G	6-3	268	11	Clemson
44	Brim, Michael	CB-S	6-0	186	2	Virginia Union
	Carr, Lydell	RB	6-0	226	1	Oklahoma
41	Carter, Carl	CB	5-11	180	4	Texas Tech
34	Clark, Jessie	RB	6-0	233	7	Arkansas
79	Clasby, Bob	DT	6-5	260	4	Notre Dame
17	Del Greco, Al	K	5-10	191	6	Auburn
74	Dill, Scott	T-G	6-5	272	2	Memphis State
31	Ferrell, Earl	RB	6-0	240	8	East Tennessee State
65	Galloway, David	DE	6-3	279	8	Florida
	Garcia, Teddy	K	5-10	190	2	Northeast Louisiana
81	Green, Roy	WR	6-0	195	11	Henderson, Ark.
	Hadd, Gary	DT	6-4	270	2	Minnesota
56	Harvey, Ken	LB	6-2	225	2	California
	Hogeboom, Gary	QB	6-4	208	10	Central Michigan
83	Holmes, Don	WR	5-10	180	4	Mesa, Colorado
51	Hunley, Ricky	LB	6-2	250	6	Arizona
	Jax, Garth	LB	6-2	230	4	Florida State
28	Jeffery, Tony	RB	5-11	208	2	Texas Christian
86	Jones, Ernie	WR	5-11	186	2	Indiana
59	Jones, Tyrone	LB	6-0	220	1	Southern
32	Jordan, Tony	RB	6-2	220	2	Kansas State
	Kauahi, Kani	C	6-2	271	8	Hawaii
70	Kennard, Derek	C	6-3	285	4	Nevada-Reno
	Kirk, Randy	LB	6-2	227	3	San Diego State
15	Lomax, Neil	QB	6-3	215	9	Portland State
76	MacDonald, Mark	G-C	6-4	265	5	Boston College
47	Mack, Cedric	CB	6-0	194	7	Baylor
46	McDonald, Tim	S	6-2	207	3	Southern California
	McKenzie, Reggie	LB	6-1	235	5	Tennessee
95	McNanie, Sean	DE	6-5	270	7	San Diego State
35	Mimbs, Robert	RB	5-10	197	1	Kansas
25	Mitchell, Roland*	CB	5-11	180	3	Texas Tech
30	Mitchell, Stump	RB	5-9	188	9	Citadel
57	Noga, Niko	LB	6-1	235	6	Hawaii
85	Novacek, Jay	TE	6-4	235	5	Wyoming
78	Nunn, Freddie Joe	DE	6-4	255	5	Mississippi
64	Peat, Todd	G	6-2	294	3	Northern Illinois
48	Phillips, Reggie	CB	5-10	175	5	Southern Methodist
63	Robbins, Tootie	T	6-5	302	8	East Carolina
72	Saddler, Rod	DT-DE	6-5	276	3	Texas A&M
87	Schillinger, Andy	WR	5-11	179	2	Miami, Ohio
67	Sharpe, Luis	T	6-4	260	8	UCLA
36	Sikahema, Vai	RB-KR	5-9	191	4	Brigham Young
84	Smith, J.T.	WR	6-2	185	12	North Texas State
61	Smith, Lance	G	6-2	262	5	Louisiana State
97	Spachman, Chris	DE	6-5	275	1	Nebraska
19	Tupa, Tom	QB-P	6-4	220	2	Ohio State
89	Walczak, Mark	TE	6-6	246	3	Arizona
24	Wolfley, Ron	RB	6-0	222	5	West Virginia
43	Young, Lonnie	S	6-1	182	5	Michigan State
	Zordich, Mike	S	5-11	199	3	Penn State

So much depends on the fitness of quarterback Neil Lomax.

WASHINGTON REDSKINS

Address Redskin Park, P.O. Box 17247, Dulles
International Airport, Washington, D.C. 20041.
Stadium Robert F. Kennedy Stadium, Washington.
Capacity 55,670 *Playing Surface* Grass (PAT).
Team Colours Burgundy and Gold.
Head Coach Joe Gibbs – 9th year.
Championships Division 1972,'83,'84,'87;
Conference 1972,'82,'83,'87;
NFL 1937,'42; Super Bowl 1982,'87.
History NFL 1932-69, NFC 1970-
(Originally named the Boston Braves for the 1932
season only, they were renamed the Boston Redskins
until, in 1937, they moved to Washington.)

Offense

Perhaps, after all, the so-called Super Bowl jinx has some influence. For there is no rational explanation for the Redskins' stall and subsequent tailspin which saw them lose five of their final six games. Even now, supporting evidence is elusive and it is only a feeling that, somewhere along the way, they lost their sense of direction. Certainly, at running back, there was the absence of a dominant personality. Kelvin Bryant was easing into that role before his season ended with a Week Ten injury. Timmy Smith could not reproduce his 1987 playoff form and it was asking rather a lot of rookie Jamie Morris to come through when others could not come close. In the offseason, the Redskins took drastic action by trading for starters Earnest Byner (ex-Cleveland) and Gerald Riggs (ex-Atlanta). With two strokes, they have acquired a pairing which can exploit to the full those huge holes created by one of pro football's finest power-blocking offensive lines. During the 1988 campaign, the order and composition of the line changed seven times, but, with the retirement of R.C. Thielemann, the picture clears a little. The names of the formidable personnel available have the sound of a pro football 'Who's Who?'. All of Jim Lachey, Russ Grimm, Raleigh McKenzie, Jeff Bostic, Mark May and Joe Jacoby could slot into almost any NFL line. The serious competition for playing time is at left guard and center, and involves McKenzie, Grimm and Bostic, the latter who may be the odd man out. Should the line need blocking assistance it comes from tight end Don Warren, who has been joined by Mike Tice. The H-back in the one-back set is Craig McEwen, who is a decent receiver. When comes the need to air the ball, the Redskins have two strong-armed rocket-launchers in starter Doug Williams and backup Mark Rypien. The Redskins underlined their confidence in Rypien by readily trading away Jay Schroeder to the Raiders. Williams does lack consistency but, on his day, he can murder the opposition. Of course, he is helped by a trio of wide receivers from which any two could start. Last year, Ricky Sanders came out on top in every respect - receptions, yards and touchdowns - with the more

sedate Art Monk one shy of Sanders' reception total and the turf-burning Gary Clark not far behind. With each man capable of winning a game by his own efforts, they form an excellent trio.

Defense

Though not looking quite the fearsome force which closed down on Denver in the Super Bowl, the Redskins defense did improve two notches in the NFL list. Once again the charge was led by a four-man defensive line on which the venerable Dave Butz enjoyed his 15th pro year. Butz has retired, leaving Dean Hamel the favourite to pair up with right tackle Darryl Grant. They'll hold the fort waiting for the arrival of the cavalry in the form of defensive ends Dexter Manley and Charles Mann. Manley, who missed part of training camp on suspension, led the club with nine sacks, 3.5 ahead of Mann. This line was expected to peak in 1989, however, it remains to be seen just how important a contribution Butz made. At linebacker, there is a wall of vast experience hingeing on the youngest of the three starters, right linebacker Wilber Marshall. Both Monte Coleman and middle linebacker Neal Olkewicz are now 11th-year pros but still would be fancied to hold off the challenges of backups Kurt Gouveia and sometime starter Mel Kaufman. With Marshall pressuring the passer, Olkewicz stuffs the middle while Coleman often drops back into pass coverage. It is not likely that the starting quartet in the defensive secondary will be disturbed. Strong safety Alvin Walton's 16-game campaign produced a club-leading 189 tackles and free safety Todd Bowles solidified his reputation patrolling the open acres. Injuries were a factor at cornerback, where Barry Wilburn missed six games and his replacement, Brian Davis, spent the last month on the reserve list. Right cornerback Darrell Green missed most of the final two games but he confirmed his fitness by winning the NFL's Fastest Man competition in May. With Davis giving the club quality depth

1989 SCHEDULE OF GAMES		
September		
11 NEW YORK GIANTS (Mon.)		9:00
17 PHILADELPHIA		1:00
24 at Dallas		12:00
October		
1 at New Orleans		12:00
8 PHOENIX		4:00
15 at New York Giants		1:00
22 TAMPA BAY		1:00
29 at Los Angeles Raiders		1:00
November		
5 DALLAS (night)		8:00
12 at Philadelphia		1:00
20 DENVER (Mon.)		9:00
26 CHICAGO		4:00
December		
3 at Phoenix		2:00
10 SAN DIEGO		1:00
17 at Atlanta		4:00
23 at Seattle (Sat.)		1:00

Quarterback Doug Williams may have to fight off a challenge.

on the corners, Clarence Vaughn has emerged as the senior reserve at safety. The departure of Steve Gage and Travis Curtis probably encouraged the drafting of safety Tim Smiley in round five.

Special Teams

Rookie placekicker Chip Lohmiller took time to find his accuracy but he showed great determination, and, by the end of the campaign, a 29-yard miss notwithstanding, he was looking the part. Several punters, including Greg Coleman, Tommy Barnhardt and Greg Horne will vie for the job in 1989. Darrell Green could be a Pro Bowl punt returner if the Redskins would turn him loose. As it is, the opportunity is wide open. Sixth-round draftee Anthony Johnson returned kickoffs in college and may be the new partner for Jamie Morris.

1989 DRAFT

Round	Name	Pos.	Ht.	Wt.	College
3.	Rocker, Tracy	DT	6-2	270	Auburn
4.	Graham, Jeff*	QB	6-3	196	Long Beach State
5.	Smiley, Tim	S	6-0	190	Arkansas State
5.	Robinson, Lybrant	DE	6-5	230	Delaware State
6.	Johnson, Anthony	CB	5-8	176	Southwest Texas State
7.	Hendrix, Kevin	LB	6-2	266	South Carolina
9.	Darrington, Charles	TE	6-3	225	Kentucky
10.	Schlereth, Mark	G	6-3	250	Idaho
12.	Johnson, Jimmie	TE	6-3	240	Howard
12.	Mickles, Joe	RB	5-9	220	Mississippi

* Drafted by Green Bay in round four but obtained in a trade

VETERAN ROSTER

No.	Name	Pos.	Ht.	Wt.	NFL Year	College
14	Barnhardt, Tom	P	6-3	205	3	North Carolina
95	Benish, Dan	DT	6-5	275	6	Clemson
	Bonner, Brian	LB	6-1	225	1	Minnesota
53	Bostic, Jeff	C	6-2	260	10	Clemson
23	Bowles, Todd	S	6-2	203	4	Temple
29	Branch, Reggie	RB	5-11	235	4	East Carolina
	Brown, Ray	G-T	6-5	280	4	Arkansas State
24	Bryant, Kelvin	RB	6-2	195	4	North Carolina
	Byner, Earnest	RB	5-10	215	6	East Carolina
50	Caldwell, Ravin	LB	6-3	229	3	Arkansas
	Chipps, Dale	WR	6-0	186	1	Towson State
84	Clark, Gary	WR	5-9	173	5	James Madison
15	Coleman, Greg	P	6-0	184	13	Florida A&M
51	Coleman, Monte	LB	6-2	230	11	Central Arkansas
34	Davis, Brian	CB	6-2	190	3	Nebraska
	Dillahunt, Ellis	S	5-11	190	2	East Carolina
	Duckens, Mark	DT	6-4	270	1	Arizona State
	Elam, Onzy	LB	6-2	225	2	Tennessee State
54	Gouveia, Kurt	LB	6-1	227	3	Brigham Young
	Graham, Don	LB	6-2	244	2	Penn State
77	Grant, Darryl	DT	6-1	275	9	Rice
28	Green, Darrell	CB	5-8	170	7	Texas A&I
68	Grimm, Russ	G	6-3	275	9	Pittsburgh
78	Hamel, Dean	DT	6-3	280	5	Tulsa
59	Harbour, Dave	C	6-4	265	2	Illinois
62	Hitchcock, Ray	C	6-2	289	2	Minnesota
	Hobbs, Stephen	WR	5-11	190	1	North Alabama
	Horne, Greg	P	6-0	188	3	Arkansas
16	Humphries, Stan	QB	6-2	223	1	Northeast Louisiana
66	Jacoby, Joe	T	6-7	305	9	Louisville
55	Kaufman, Mel	LB	6-2	230	8	Cal Poly-SLO
61	Kehr, Rick	G	6-3	285	2	Carthage
74	Koch, Markus	DE	6-5	275	4	Boise State
79	Lachey, Jim	T	6-6	290	5	Ohio State
8	Lohmiller, Chip	K	6-3	213	2	Minnesota
	Mandeville, Chris	S	6-1	213	3	California-Davis
72	Manley, Dexter	DE	6-3	257	9	Oklahoma State
71	Mann, Charles	DE	6-6	270	7	Nevada-Reno
91	Manusky, Greg	LB	6-1	242	2	Colgate
58	Marshall, Wilber	LB	6-1	230	6	Florida
	Maxey, Curtis	DT	6-3	298	2	Grambling
73	May, Mark	G-T	6-6	295	9	Pittsburgh
	Mayhew, Martin	CB	5-8	172	1	Florida State
32	McEwen, Craig	H-B	6-1	220	3	Utah
37	McGill, Darryl	RB	5-10	210	1	Wake Forest
63	McKenzie, Raleigh	C-G	6-2	270	5	Tennessee
86	Middleton, Ron	TE	6-2	252	4	Auburn
	Mims, Carl	CB	5-10	180	1	Sam Houston State
81	Monk, Art	WR	6-3	209	10	Syracuse
22	Morris, Jamie	RB	5-7	188	2	Michigan
	Morris, Mike	C-G	6-5	275	3	Northeast Missouri State
52	Olkewicz, Neal	LB	6-0	230	11	Maryland
87	Orr, Terry	TE	6-3	227	4	Texas
	Profit, Eugene	CB	5-10	175	3	Yale
38	Reaves, Willard	RB	5-11	200	1	Northern Arizona
	Riggs, Gerald	RB	6-1	232	8	Arizona State
11	Rypien, Mark	QB	6-4	234	3	Washington State
83	Sanders, Ricky	WR	5-11	180	4	Southwest Texas State
76	Simmons, Ed	T	6-5	280	3	Eastern Washington
	Stokes, Fred	DE	6-3	262	3	Georgia Southern
	Tamm, Ralph	G	6-3	285	1	West Chester
	Tice, Mike	TE	6-7	244	9	Maryland
31	Vaughn, Clarence	S	6-0	202	3	Northern Illinois
40	Walton, Alvin	S	6-0	180	4	Kansas
85	Warren, Don	TE	6-4	242	11	San Diego State
	Whisenhunt, Ken	H-B	6-3	240	5	Georgia Tech
45	Wilburn, Barry	CB	6-3	186	5	Mississippi
17	Williams, Doug	QB	6-4	220	9	Grambling

CHICAGO BEARS

Address Halas Hall, 250 N. Washington, Lake Forest, Illinois 60045.

Stadium Soldier Field, Chicago.
Capacity 66,030 *Playing Surface* Grass.

Team Colours Navy Blue, Orange, and White.

Head Coach Mike Ditka – 8th year.

Championships Division 1984,'85,'86,'87,'88; Conference 1985; NFL 1921,'32,'33,'40,'41,'43,'46,'63. Super Bowl 1985.

History NFL 1920-69, NFC 1970-
(Before 1922, they were known as firstly the Decatur Staleys and then the Chicago Staleys.)

Offense

It says a great deal for the quality of the Bears' organization that the team remains competitive at the very highest level, even though several areas were in transition and despite the loss of top players to injury. It may be most significant of all that the offensive line still is a potent force. The starting quintet will have Jim Covert and Keith Van Horne at tackle, Mark Bortz and Tom Thayer at guards and Jay Hilgenberg at center. Hilgenberg's domination of San Francisco's Michael Carter in the Bears' regular-season victory was one of the features of the campaign. Both he and Covert are Pro Bowlers. In the playoffs, Van Horne did the unthinkable by closing down on Philadelphia's Reggie White. Thayer keeps out a first-class backup in Kurt Becker while Mark Bortz may just be the best active guard not to attain Pro Bowl status. A step back from the line, there are changes afoot, perhaps even at quarterback where Mike Tomczak has shown that he can run the team. Of course, Jim McMahon is his superior in most aspects, including that of inspiring those around him, but it must now be accepted that he'll miss games because of knocks. Leading up to the draft, there even were trade rumours linking McMahon with San Diego. Behind these two seniors, Jim Harbaugh is a well-disciplined pro capable of respectable emergency duty. With the need to use more than one quarterback and the loss of star wide receiver Willie Gault, who was traded to the Raiders, the passing offense fell away a little. Encouragingly, though, Dennis McKinnon's most productive year as a pro cushioned the loss of Gault and both Dennis Gentry and Ron Morris chipped in with valuable contributions. Gentry, in particular, took advantage of his opportunities to play. Rookie Wendell Davis, meanwhile, came along steadily. With veteran Emery Moorehead retiring, the expressive James Thornton appears to have a lead over Cap Boso to start at tight end. Running back is one area in which the Bears are secure. Neal Anderson is coming off his first 1,000-yard campaign and he looks good for many more. Going into camp, the veteran Matt Suhey has the seniority at fullback but the time is fast approaching when Brad Muster is installed, a step which will complete the regeneration and launch the Bears into a new era.

Defense

On defense, the Bears slipped just slightly but not by enough to offer any encouragement to their opponents. And this area was given priority in the top half of the draft. Interestingly, in the Bears' 1988 system, all the leading sackers played on the line of scrimmage in the order, Steve McMichael (11.5), Richard Dent (10.5), Dan Hampton (9.5) and Al Harris (3.5). Harris, whose involvement increased because of injuries to William Perry and Dent, has left to join his old coach, Buddy Ryan, at Philadelphia. While Harris will be missed, his loss is cushioned by the news that Perry has decided that the time is right to lose a few pounds. At anything less than 290 pounds, Perry could be tremendous. In addition, draftee defensive end Trace Armstrong came in round one. There have been changes at linebacker, though the departure of Otis Wilson, who sat out the whole of 1988 with an injury, is not felt to be a factor. Ron Rivera and Jim Morrissey have come through to start either side of the indomitable Mike Singletary, the latter whom many coaches see as exerting an influence equal to that of the Giants' Lawrence Taylor. Inevitably, he led the Bears with 170 tackles, a huge 65 more than the next best, strong safety Dave Duerson. Backups Dante Jones and Troy Johnson are joined by second-round pick John Roper. There will be one definite change in the secondary, with top draftee Donnell Woolford taking over from the departed Mike Richardson at left cornerback. On the other corner, Vestee Jackson is now well established and led the club with eight interceptions. Four-time Pro Bowler Duerson continues to receive the utmost respect and Maurice Douglass did well at free safety after taking over for the injured Shaun Gayle. Gayle would start but it is not certain that he will recover fully from his neck injury. As a further backup beyond David Tate, who had four interceptions, and Todd Krumm, safety Markus Paul was drafted in round four.

1989 SCHEDULE OF GAMES	September	
	10 CINCINNATI	12:00
	17 MINNESOTA	3:00
	24 at Detroit	1:00
	October	
	2 PHILADELPHIA (Mon.)	8:00
	8 at Tampa Bay	1:00
	15 HOUSTON	12:00
	23 at Cleveland (Mon.)	9:00
	29 LOS ANGELES RAMS	12:00
	November	
	5 at Green Bay	12:00
	12 at Pittsburgh	1:00
	19 TAMPA BAY	12:00
	26 at Washington	4:00
	December	
	3 at Minnesota (night)	7:00
	10 DETROIT	12:00
	17 GREEN BAY	12:00
	24 at San Francisco	1:00

Special Teams

Placekicker Kevin Butler is woven into the fabric of the Bears' scene and looks set for a long engagement. He rarely misses the pressure kicks and now ranks fifth in the club's all-time scoring list. Of the free agents and hopefuls competing for the job of punter, Ray Criswell would appear to have the best credentials. The chances are that draftee Woolford will take over the punt returns from McKinnon, but Gentry, who is a threat every time he touches the ball, should continue as the senior kickoff returner.

VETERAN ROSTER

No.	Name	Pos.	Ht.	Wt.	NFL Year	College
54	Adickes, John	C	6-3	264	3	Baylor
35	Anderson, Neal	RB	5-11	210	4	Florida
79	Becker, Kurt	G	6-5	269	8	Michigan
62	Bortz, Mark	G	6-6	272	7	Iowa
86	Boso, Cap	TE	6-3	240	3	Illinois
6	Butler, Kevin	K	6-1	204	5	Georgia
94	Chapura, Dick	DT	6-3	275	2	Missouri
74	Covert, Jim	T	6-4	278	7	Pittsburgh
11	Criswell, Ray	P	6-0	195	3	Florida
82	Davis, Wendell	WR	5-11	188	2	Louisiana State
95	Dent, Richard	DE	6-5	268	7	Tennessee State
37	Douglass, Maurice	S	5-11	200	4	Kentucky
22	Duerson, Dave	S	6-1	212	7	Notre Dame
23	Gayle, Shaun	S	5-11	194	6	Ohio State
29	Gentry, Dennis	WR-KR	5-8	180	8	Baylor
99	Hampton, Dan	DT-DE	6-5	274	11	Arkansas
4	Harbaugh, Jim	QB	6-3	204	3	Michigan
63	Hilgenberg, Jay	C	6-3	260	9	Iowa
24	Jackson, Vestee	CB	6-0	186	4	Washington
92	Johnson, Troy	LB	6-0	236	2	Oklahoma
53	Jones, Dante	LB	6-1	236	2	Oklahoma
88	Kozlowski, Glen	WR	6-1	205	3	Brigham Young
44	Krumm, Todd	S	6-0	189	2	Michigan State
43	Lynch, Lorenzo	S	5-9	199	3	Cal State-Sacramento
85	McKinnon, Dennis	WR-PR	6-1	177	6	Florida State
9	McMahon, Jim	QB	6-1	198	8	Brigham Young
76	McMichael, Steve	DT	6-2	268	10	Texas
84	Morris, Ron	WR	6-1	195	3	Southern Methodist
51	Morrissey, Jim	LB	6-3	227	5	Michigan State
25	Muster, Brad	RB	6-3	231	2	Stanford
72	Perry, William	DT	6-2	320	5	Clemson
52	Pruitt, Mickey	LB-S	6-1	206	2	Colorado
59	Rivera, Ron	LB	6-3	240	6	California
20	Sanders, Thomas	RB-KR	5-11	203	5	Texas A&M
75	Shannon, John	DT	6-3	269	2	Kentucky
50	Singletary, Mike	LB	6-0	230	9	Baylor
97	Smith, Sean	DE	6-4	290	3	Grambling
39	Stewart, Curtis	RB	5-11	208	1	Auburn
32	Stinson, Lemuel	CB	5-9	159	2	Texas Tech
26	Suhey, Matt	RB	5-11	213	10	Penn State
49	Tate, David	S	6-0	177	2	Colorado
57	Thayer, Tom	G	6-4	270	5	Notre Dame
80	Thornton, James	TE	6-2	242	2	Cal State-Fullerton
18	Tomczak, Mike	QB	6-1	198	5	Ohio State
78	Van Horne, Keith	T	6-6	283	9	Southern California
73	Wojciechowski, John	T-G	6-4	270	3	Michigan State

1989 DRAFT

Round	Name	Pos.	Ht.	Wt.	College
1.	Woolford, Donnell	CB	5-9	188	Clemson
1.	Armstrong, Trace	DE	6-4	268	Florida
2.	Roper, John	LB	6-1	228	Texas A&M
2.	Zawatson, Dave	T-G	6-4	265	California
3.	Fontenot, Jerry	G	6-3	259	Texas A&M
4.	Paul, Markus	S	6-0	203	Syracuse
5.	Green, Mark	RB	5-11	181	Notre Dame
5.	Gilbert, Greg	LB	6-2	217	Alabama
7.	Brothers, Richard	S	6-0	200	Arkansas
7.	Snyder, Brent	QB	6-3	230	Utah State
8.	Woods, Tony	DT	6-5	265	Oklahoma
8.	Dyko, Chris	T	6-6	271	Washington State
9.	Harper, LaSalle	LB	6-1	235	Arkansas
9.	Sanders, Byron	RB	5-9	187	Northwestern
10.	Millikan, Todd	TE	6-2	238	Nebraska
10.	Simpson, John	WR	6-0	170	Baylor
11.	Nelms, Joe	DT	6-4	264	California
11.	Streeter, George	S	6-1	210	Notre Dame
12.	Weygand, Freddy	WR	6-0	192	Auburn
12.	Phillips, Anthony	G	6-2	286	Oklahoma

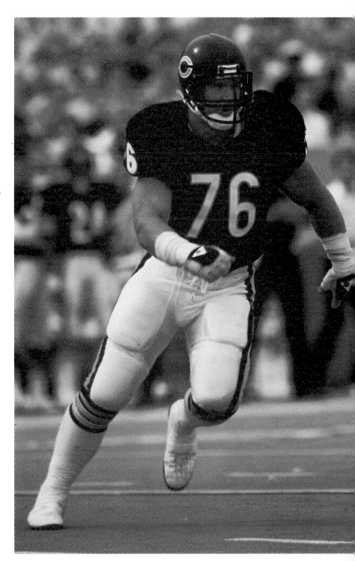

Undersized defensive tackle Steve McMichael is a tower of strength.

DETROIT LIONS

NFC CENTRAL DIVISION

Address Pontiac Silverdome, 1200 Featherstone Road – Box 4200, Pontiac, Michigan 48057.

Stadium Pontiac Silverdome.
Capacity 80,638 *Playing Surface* AstroTurf.

Team Colours Honolulu Blue and Silver.

Head Coach Wayne Fontes – 2nd year.

Championships Division 1983; NFL 1935,'52,'53,'57.

History NFL 1930-69, NFC 1970-
(Until 1934, they were known as the Portsmouth (Ohio) Spartans.)

Offense

There is a settled look about the offensive line of tackles Lomas Brown and Harvey Salem, guards Kevin Glover and Joe Milinichik, and center Steve Mott, which started in every game except for the Week Ten absence of Milinichik. It is a group which has come through difficult, learning years and may now be ready to begin repaying some of that experience. Draftee Mike Utley was the most honoured player in Washington State history and will press for playing time at guard. In 1988, the line gave up 52 sacks and didn't open up that many holes. But there was uncertainty at quarterback and often, because of a predictable coaching philosophy, defenses were able to plan their ambushes some way ahead of time. The problem at quarterback will be solved only by the emergence of Chuck Long, who was considered to be a franchise player when he was drafted in the 1986 first round. Last year, both Long and his backup, Eric Hipple, spent time on injured reserve, meaning that emergency replacement Rusty Hilger started in nine games. Is it out of the question that draftee Rodney Peete could direct the Lions' new-style offense? Peete has a decent arm and all the coolness of a supremely confident athlete. Furthermore, he is mobile, and that could be a major factor in a novel offensive system which could drive everyone back to the drawing board. The plan is to use three or four receivers and one running back on most downs. And in line with this, wide receiver John Ford was selected in round two to join existing veterans Pete Mandley, Jeff Chadwick, Gary Lee and Stephen Starring. Each one has had his good days but they have been few and far between. Ford's value is deep speed combined with toughness, a trait which may best describe tight end Pat Carter. In the opinion of your writer, the key to the Lions' future lies at running back, a position which should be galvanised into a frenzy of activity by the arrival of top draftee Barry Sanders. With statistics resembling the US budget deficit, Sanders ran away with the Heisman Trophy and has made history as the first true junior to enter the NFL draft. James Jones is a tough nut and Garry James shows flashes of open-field speed, but Sanders is lightning in a bottle.

Defense

The three-man defensive line was another area which remained intact for all but a couple of games - defensive right end Keith Ferguson was out for two weeks early in the season. But the departure of almost every backup left a weakness which made the signing of free agents Steve Hamilton (ex-Redskins) and Tom Baldwin (ex-Jets) crucial. Curtis Green is returning from injury and there was some help from the draft, with defensive tackle Lawrence Pete the best-looking prospect. It is very likely that the starters, nose tackle Jerry Ball and defensive left end Eric Williams, will not be ousted. The immediate impact made by Chris Spielman gave an extra shove to the progress of 1987 which had been catalysed by the arrival of Dennis Gibson. Spielman, who partnered Gibson at inside linebacker, established a Lions club record with 153 tackles, beating the mark of 148 set by Ken Fantetti in 1981. Gibson, too, raised his personal best to 116 tackles. At right outside linebacker, Michael Cofer had a superb year, logging 12 sacks, a total which was the highest by any linebacker in Lions history, and earning a starting berth in his first Pro Bowl appearance. Not to be left out, the fourth member of the unit, George Jamison, made excellent progress with 77 tackles, including 14 in one game against the Vikings, 5.5 sacks and three interceptions. Remarkably, the total playing experience at linebacker adds up to only 11 years, with Cofer accounting for six. Former starter Jimmy Williams is regarded with the greatest respect but, after missing the last 11 games because of injury, it is not certain that he can displace Jamison. The defensive secondary, in which rookie strong safety Bennie Blades had a significant influence in partnership with free safety Devon Mitchell, is another area of growing strength. Jerry Holmes and Bruce McNorton held up, starting all year in the cornerback positions. Reassuringly, James Griffin, William White, Raphel Cherry, free agent Willie Tullis and draftee Ray Crockett provide good depth.

1989 SCHEDULE OF GAMES		
September		
10 PHOENIX		1:00
17 at New York Giants		4:00
24 CHICAGO		1:00
October		
1 PITTSBURGH		1:00
8 at Minnesota		12:00
15 at Tampa Bay		1:00
22 MINNESOTA		1:00
29 vs Green Bay at Milwaukee		12:00
November		
5 at Houston		12:00
12 GREEN BAY		1:00
19 at Cincinnati		1:00
23 CLEVELAND (Thanksgiving)		12:30
December		
3 NEW ORLEANS		1:00
10 at Chicago		12:00
17 TAMPA BAY		1:00
24 at Atlanta		1:00

Special Teams

It is an understatement that the kicking game is first class. Placekicker Eddie Murray was successful on 20 of 21 field goal attempts to tie the NFL single-season record for accuracy. Punter Jim Arnold earned a repeat trip to the Pro Bowl. With the arrival of specialists Mel Gray (ex-Saints) and Bobby Joe Edmonds (ex-Seattle), Detroit could have the best kick return game in the NFL next season.

1989 DRAFT

Round	Name	Pos.	Ht.	Wt.	College
1.	Sanders, Barry	RB	5-8	197	Oklahoma State
2.	Ford, John	WR	6-2	200	Virginia
3.	Utley, Mike	G	6-6	286	Washington State
4.	Crockett, Ray	CB	5-9	181	Baylor
5.	Pete, Lawrence	DT	6-1	270	Nebraska
6.	Peete, Rodney	QB	6-0	197	Southern California
7.	Woods, Jerry	DB	5-9	183	Northern Michigan
8.	Parker, Chris	DT	6-4	287	West Virginia
9.	MacCready, Derek	DE	6-4	266	Ohio State
10.	Phillips, Jason	WR	5-9	175	Houston
11.	Karpinski, Keith	LB	6-3	221	Penn State
12.	Cribbs, James	DT	6-3	269	Memphis State

VETERAN ROSTER

No.	Name	Pos.	Ht.	Wt.	NFL Year	College
65	Andolsek, Eric	G	6-2	277	2	Louisiana State
6	Arnold, Jim	P	6-3	211	7	Vanderbilt
68	Baack, Steve	G	6-4	265	5	Oregon
	Baldwin, Tom	DE	6-4	275	5	Tulsa
93	Ball, Jerry	NT	6-1	292	3	Southern Methodist
61	Barrows, Scott	C-G	6-3	280	4	West Virginia
	Beaty, Doug	RB	6-1	221	1	Appalachian State
36	Blades, Bennie	S	6-1	221	2	Miami
75	Brown, Lomas	T	6-4	275	5	Florida
87	Carter, Pat	TE	6-4	250	2	Florida State
	Caston, Toby	LB	6-1	240	3	Louisiana State
89	Chadwick, Jeff	WR	6-3	190	7	Grand Valley State
45	Cherry, Raphel	S	6-0	190	4	Hawaii
	Clark, Robert	WR	5-11	175	2	North Carolina Central
55	Cofer, Michael	LB	6-5	245	7	Tennessee
	Dallafior, Ken	G	6-4	278	5	Minnesota
	Edmonds, Bobby Joe	RB-KR	5-11	186	4	Arkansas
77	Ferguson, Keith	DE	6-5	260	9	Ohio State
	Gambol, Chris	T	6-6	303	2	Iowa
98	Gibson, Dennis	LB	6-2	240	3	Iowa State
53	Glover, Kevin	G-C	6-2	275	5	Maryland
	Gray, Mel	RB-KR	5-9	166	4	Purdue
62	Green, Curtis	NT-DE	6-3	270	9	Alabama State
34	Griffin, James	S	6-2	203	7	Middle Tennessee State
	Hamilton, Steve	DE	6-4	270	5	East Carolina
12	Hilger, Rusty	QB	6-4	205	5	Oklahoma State
17	Hipple, Eric	QB	6-2	211	9	Utah State
43	Holmes, Jerry	CB	6-2	175	8	West Virginia
33	James, Garry	RB	5-10	214	4	Louisiana State
58	Jamison, George	LB	6-1	226	3	Cincinnati
30	Jones, James	RB	6-2	230	7	Florida
	Jones, Victor	LB	6-2	250	2	Virginia Tech
83	Lee, Gary	WR	6-1	202	3	Georgia Tech
50	Lockett, Danny	LB	6-2	250	3	Arizona
16	Long, Chuck	QB	6-4	221	4	Iowa
82	Mandley, Pete	WR-PR	5-10	195	6	Northern Arizona
14	McCoin, Danny	QB	6-3	206	1	Cincinnati
29	McNorton, Bruce	CB	5-11	175	8	Georgetown, Kentucky
74	Milinichik, Joe	G	6-5	275	3	North Carolina State
31	Mitchell, Devon	S	6-1	194	3	Iowa
42	Morris, Randall	RB	6-0	200	6	Tennessee
52	Mott, Steve	C	6-3	265	7	Alabama
3	Murray, Ed	K	5-10	180	10	Tulane
49	Paige, Tony	RB	5-10	235	6	Virginia Tech
26	Painter, Carl	RB	5-9	195	2	Hampton Institute
51	Robinson, Shelton	LB	6-2	236	8	North Carolina
60	Rogers, Reggie	DE	6-6	280	3	Washington
86	Roundtree, Ray	WR	6-0	182	2	Penn State
84	Rubick, Rob	TE	6-3	234	8	Grand Valley State
73	Salem, Harvey	T-G	6-6	285	7	California
64	Sanders, Eric	T-G	6-7	280	9	Nevada-Reno
72	Singer, Curt	T	6-5	279	3	Tennessee
54	Spielman, Chris	LB	6-0	247	2	Ohio State
81	Starring, Stephen	WR	5-10	172	7	McNeese State
	Tullis, Willie	CB	5-11	195	9	Troy State
35	White, William	CB	5-10	191	2	Ohio State
76	Williams, Eric	DE	6-4	286	6	Washington State
59	Williams, Jimmy	LB	6-3	230	8	Nebraska
38	Williams, Scott	RB	6-2	234	4	Georgia

Linebacker Chris Spielman has had an inspirational effect.

GREEN BAY PACKERS

Address 1265 Lombardi Avenue, P.O. Box 10628, Green Bay, Wisconsin 54307-0628.

Stadia Lambeau Field, Green Bay, and Milwaukee County Stadium, Milwaukee.
Capacity (Lambeau Field) 57,093, (Milwaukee County Stadium) 56,051. *Playing Surfaces* Grass, both stadia.

Team Colours Dark Green, Gold, and White.

Head Coach Lindy Infante – 2nd year.

Championships Division 1972.
NFL 1929,'30,'31,'36,'39,'44,'61,'62,'65,'66,'67.
Super Bowl 1966,'67.

History NFL 1921-69, NFC 1970-

Offense

An ample draft and an NFL-leading 20 free-agent signings, strongly suggest that there will be many changes to the roster. It means that the shape of a Packers team in the process of major redesign will not crystallise until the pre-season is underway. For certain, there will be the immense, dominating figure of top draftee Tony Mandarich on the offensive line, probably at right tackle. Mandarich is rated as the best offensive lineman to enter the NFL since Anthony Munoz and, even before he has thrown a block in anger, his name is written into some all-pro teams. Of the many possible permutations, one would see Ken Ruettgers continuing at left tackle, Keith Uecker and Ron Hallstrom battling for the right guard spot and free agent signings Blair Bush at center and Billy Ard at left guard. An army of veterans, including the talented Dave Croston and Darryl Haley, will be involved in the scramble for backup spots. There also is uncertainty at quarterback, but at least the serious competition involves only the current veterans, Randy Wright and Don Majkowski, with draftee Anthony Dilweg in the background. Wright is the calm, careful, accurate passer, whereas the strong-armed Majkowski has all the style and panache. The latter are qualities which may just be enough to give Majkowski the first crack at the job. The feeling is that the steady shift of emphasis towards the passing game, which was given priority with the selection of Sterling Sharpe in 1988, will continue. With the return of former starting wide receivers Walter Stanley and Phillip Epps to full fitness, emergency starter Perry Kemp and backup Aubrey Matthews will be involved in a struggle with free agent Carl Bland (ex-Lions) and draftees Erik Affholter and Jeff Query. Even at tight end, the situation is not resolved, with Ed West and Clint Didier attempting to hold off John Spagnola, Gary Wilkins and Brent Novoselsky. At running back, with the departure of Kenneth Davis went what little speed there was. The remaining veterans form a group which has power rather than elusiveness as its overall description. That aspect did not change with the arrival of free agent Michael Haddix, who joins incumbent starters Brent Fullwood and Larry Mason, and backups Keith Woodside and Paul Ott Carruth.

Defense

The picture on defense is somewhat clearer, the only major departure having been that of starting defensive left end Alphonso Carreker. The feeling was that Shawn Patterson was ready to displace Carreker anyway. Without much fuss, with a blend of youth and experience, the Packers have begun to tighten the screw and, last year, ranked seventh in the NFL. Nose tackles Toby Williams and Jerry Boyarsky, who is expected to return from injured reserve, and defensive right end Robert Brown are solid run-stuffers. In Boyarsky's absence, Blaise Winter did well, even coming second on the team with five sacks. Draftee defensive end Matt Brock may add a little sparkle. The real explosion comes from a mean set of linebackers, starting with the ferocious Tim Harris who led the team in both tackles (97) and sacks (13.5). Brian Noble put a little extra into his run defense after ending his early-season holdout. Again, Johnny Holland does not look out of place and veteran left outside linebacker John Anderson shows no signs of slowing. Behind them, though, the quality falls off rather too quickly for comfort and one has the feeling that there will be some anxious pacing on the side-line every time one of the starters takes a little longer than usual to stand up after a tackle. The secondary contains the vast experience of cornerbacks Dave Brown and Mark Lee, and safety Mark Murphy, who, between them, can look back on 30 campaigns in the NFL. The secret of their longevity lies in excellent work habits. The fourth starter, rookie free safety Chuck Cecil, soon had quarterbacks looking the other way and, by the end of the campaign, had banked four interceptions. Free agent cornerback Van Jakes, who started for the Saints in 1988, was an excellent acquisition and should demand playing time. The other prominent reserves, safeties Ken Stills and Tiger Greene, come into their own as nickel backs.

1989 SCHEDULE OF GAMES	September	
	10 TAMPA BAY	12:00
	17 NEW ORLEANS	12:00
	24 at Los Angeles Rams	1:00
	October	
	1 ATLANTA at Milwaukee	12:00
	8 DALLAS	12:00
	15 at Minnesota	12:00
	22 at Miami	1:00
	29 DETROIT at Milwaukee	12:00
	November	
	5 CHICAGO	12:00
	12 at Detroit	1:00
	19 at San Francisco	1:00
	26 MINNESOTA at Milwaukee	12:00
	December	
	3 at Tampa Bay	1:00
	10 KANSAS CITY	12:00
	17 at Chicago	12:00
	24 at Dallas	12:00

Green Bay needs a big year from running back Brent Fullwood.

Special Teams

After a season in which four placekickers were tried, the Packers have introduced other candidates in the shape of free agent Kirk Roach and draftee Chris Jacke. Punter Don Bracken will face a stiff challenge from draftee Brian Shulman and Maury Buford, the latter who certainly can handle the job. As for the punt returns, Ron Pitts ran 63 yards for a touchdown, but that was the only shaft of sunlight to penetrate the grey clouds. Free agent Darryl Harris looks the most likely kickoff returner.

1989 DRAFT

Round	Name	Pos.	Ht.	Wt.	College
1.	Mandarich, Tony	T	6-5	315	Michigan State
3.	Brock, Matt	DE	6-4	267	Oregon
3.	Dilweg, Anthony	QB	6-3	215	Duke
4.	Affholter, Erik*	WR	5-11	180	Southern California
5.	Query, Jeff	WR	5-11	165	Millikin
5.	Workman, Vince	RB	5-10	193	Ohio State
6.	Jacke, Chris	K	5-10	182	Texas-El Paso
7.	Hall, Mark	DT-DE	6-4	285	Southwestern Louisiana
8.	King, Thomas	S	6-1	190	Southwestern Louisiana
8.	Shulman, Brian	P	5-10	189	Auburn
9.	Kirby, Scott	T	6-5	290	Arizona State
10.	Jessie, Ben	S	6-0	205	Southwest Texas State
11.	Stallworth, Cedric	CB	5-11	180	Georgia Tech
12.	Shiver, Stan	S	6-2	210	Florida State

* Drafted by Washington in round four but obtained in a trade

VETERAN ROSTER

No.	Name	Pos.	Ht.	Wt.	NFL Year	College
47	Ambrose, J.R.	WR	6-0	185	1	Mississippi
59	Anderson, John	LB	6-3	229	12	Michigan
67	Ard, Bill	G	6-3	270	9	Wake Forest
76	Ariey, Mike	T	6-6	285	1	San Diego State
31	Armentrout, Joe	RB	6-0	225	1	Wisconsin
69	Bartlett, Doug	DE-DT	6-2	257	2	Northern Illinois
	Bland, Carl	WR	5-11	182	6	Virginia Union
82	Bolton, Scott	WR	6-0	188	2	Auburn
61	Boyarsky, Jerry	NT	6-3	290	8	Pittsburgh
17	Bracken, Don	P	6-1	211	5	Michigan
32	Brown, Dave	CB	6-1	197	15	Michigan
93	Brown, Robert	DE	6-2	267	8	Virginia Tech
9	Buford, Maury	P	6-1	195	8	Texas Tech
5	Burrow, Curtis	K	5-11	185	1	Central Arkansas
51	Bush, Blair	C	6-3	272	12	Washington
63	Campen, James	C	6-3	270	3	Tulane
58	Cannon, Mark	C	6-3	258	6	Texas-Arlington
30	Carruth, Paul Ott	RB	6-1	220	4	Alabama
26	Cecil, Chuck	S	6-0	202	2	Arizona
95	Crain, Kurt	LB	6-2	228	1	Auburn
60	Croston, Dave	T	6-5	280	2	Iowa
56	Dent, Burnell	LB	6-1	236	4	Tulane
80	Didier, Clint	TE	6-5	240	8	Portland State
99	Dorsey, John	LB	6-3	243	6	Connecticut
85	Epps, Phillip	WR	5-10	155	8	Texas Christian
27	Fontenot, Herman	RB	6-0	206	5	Louisiana State
21	Fullwood, Brent	RB-KR	5-11	209	3	Auburn
23	Greene, Tiger	S	6-0	194	5	Western Carolina
35	Haddix, Michael	RB	6-2	227	7	Mississippi State
74	Haley, Darryl	T	6-5	265	7	Utah
65	Hallstrom, Ron	G	6-6	290	8	Iowa
41	Harris, Darryl	RB	5-10	173	2	Arizona State
97	Harris, Tim	LB	6-5	235	4	Memphis State
50	Holland, Johnny	LB	6-2	221	3	Texas A&M
25	Howard, Bobby	RB	6-0	220	4	Indiana
53	Howard, Todd	LB	6-2	244	3	Texas A&M
24	Jakes, Van	CB	6-0	190	6	Kent State
38	Jefferson, Norman	CB	5-10	183	2	Louisiana State
81	Kemp, Perry	WR	5-11	170	2	California, Pa.
10	Kiel, Blair	QB-P	6-0	214	5	Notre Dame
22	Lee, Mark	CB	5-11	189	10	Washington
7	Majkowski, Don	QB	6-2	197	3	Virginia
34	Mason, Larry	RB	5-11	205	3	Troy State
88	Matthews, Aubrey	WR	5-7	165	4	Delta State
98	Moore, Brent	LB	6-5	242	2	Southern California
57	Moran, Rich	G	6-2	275	5	San Diego State
37	Murphy, Mark	S	6-2	201	6	West Liberty, W.Va.
79	Nelson, Bob	NT	6-4	275	2	Miami
91	Noble, Brian	LB	6-3	252	5	Arizona State
	Novoselsky, Brent	TE	6-3	232	2	Pennsylvania
96	Patterson, Shawn	DT-DE	6-5	261	2	Arizona State
28	Pitts, Ron	CB-S	5-10	175	4	UCLA
4	Roach, Kirk	K	6-1	217	1	Western Carolina
75	Ruettgers, Ken	T	6-5	280	5	Southern California
83	Scott, Patrick	WR	5-10	170	3	Grambling
84	Sharpe, Sterling	WR-KR	5-11	202	2	South Carolina
	Smith, Jeff	RB	5-9	204	5	Nebraska
89	Spagnola, John	TE	6-4	242	10	Yale
87	Stanley, Walter	WR-PR	5-9	179	5	Mesa, Colorado
54	Stephen, Scott	LB	6-2	232	3	Arizona State
29	Stills, Ken	S	5-10	186	5	Wisconsin
49	Sutton, Mickey	CB	5-8	172	4	Montana
45	Thomas, Lavale	RB	6-0	205	1	Fresno State
70	Uecker, Keith	G-T	6-5	284	7	Auburn
73	Veingrad, Alan	T	6-5	277	3	East Texas State
52	Weddington, Mike	LB	6-4	245	4	Oklahoma
86	West, Ed	TE	6-1	243	6	Auburn
	Wilkins, Gary	TE	6-2	235	2	Georgia Tech
90	Williams, Toby	NT	6-4	270	7	Nebraska
68	Winter, Blaise	NT-DE	6-3	275	5	Syracuse
33	Woodside, Keith	RB	5-11	203	2	Texas A&M
16	Wright, Randy	QB	6-2	203	6	Wisconsin

MINNESOTA VIKINGS

Address 9520 Viking Drive, Eden Prairie, Minnesota 55344.
Stadium Hubert H. Humphrey Metrodome, Minneapolis.
   Capacity 63,000 *Playing Surface* AstroTurf.
Team Colours Purple, Gold, and White.
0ead Coach Jerry Burns – 4th year.
Championships Division 1970,'71,'73,'74,'75,'76,'77,'78,'80;
   Conference 1973,'74,'76; NFL 1969.
History NFL 1961-69, NFC 1970-

Offense

Minnesota now is in the position of making fine adjustments to the squad in preparation for what everyone feels is a serious bid for a title. No other NFC team sent as many as nine players to the Pro Bowl and, of those, four were on offense. They were wide receiver Anthony Carter, quarterback Wade Wilson, tight end Steve Jordan and left tackle Gary Zimmerman. Wilson came through unexpectedly well to lead the NFC in passing with a rating of 91.5, and, at last, he must surely have established his seniority over Tommy Kramer. Having said that, Kramer could still run things and third-stringer Rich Gannon has the kind of swagger which suggests that he could cause a few problems for some team. The Vikings' strength on offense lies in the passing game, with Carter the jewel in the crown. With 72 receptions for 1,225 yards and six touchdowns, he had his most productive campaign by some way. On the other sideline, Hassan Jones had an even better average as he scorched the opposition for 19.5 yards per reception. Leo Lewis is an excellent third receiver and the club's use of Jordan is perfect for a pass-receiving tight end. By comparison the rushing game looks modest, with not one player ever dominating the opposition. Darrin Nelson was the club leader with a total which Eric Dickerson might get in two games. In truth, the system does not require a franchise runner, though there were hopes that D.J. Dozier could fit that description when he was drafted in 1987. In the event, rather than a shock-trooper, Dozier has been a reliable infantryman. The player whom the Vikings seem to like is Rick Fenney, who has come through to start at fullback and gives his all on every play, whether blocking or struggling for extra yards with a great second effort. The offensive line is the rock on which everything is based. Again, the Vikings seem to have struck gold with rookie Randall McDaniel, who came through to start at left guard. Another 1988 rookie, Todd Kalis, also impressed and settled in as a versatile backup. Former starter Dave Huffman returns to battle Kalis for the right guard spot vacated by Terry Tausch. The giants on the line are tackles Gary Zimmerman and Tim Irwin, while Kirk Lowdermilk's value at center really came home when he was injured. Two high draftees will ensure against complacency.

Defense

Minnesota's mix of brawl and guile produced the NFL's best defense, and their commitment to maintaining that status was clear on draft day when they gave up their first-round option in exchange for the former Pittsburgh Pro Bowl outside linebacker, Mike Merriweather. They followed up by taking another linebacker, David Braxton, in the second round. In all common sense, that area did have a slight priority, especially with Jesse Solomon needing to recuperate from injury and Pro Bowler Scott Studwell entering his 13th NFL campaign. Again, backup Walker Lee Ashley has departed. Studwell should continue to start at middle linebacker but the names of Solomon, David Howard, Merriweather, Ray Berry and Braxton go into the hat from which will emerge the starting outside pair. The strength of an awesome defensive line lies on the right side, which sent both tackle Keith Millard and end Chris Doleman to the Pro Bowl after they'd shared the team lead with eight sacks each. At times Millard runs riot while Doleman's pressure is unrelenting. Henry Thomas has made outstanding progress at right tackle. There is a slight worry at defensive left end, where the departure of Al Baker has left a gap to be filled. Former starter Doug Martin returns from injury, but he'll have to win back his spot in the face of competition from Al Noga and former Cardinals starter Curtis Greer. The secondary can boast all-pros in strong safety Joey Browner and left cornerback Carl Lee. The elegant Brad Edwards has established himself as the starting free safety. Issiac Holt is anything but elegant - he's often more like a loose cannon on the deck - but every team would love to have a player of his commitment. Reggie Rutland is a more controlled type and probably will share time with Holt at right cornerback. It is difficult not to understate the quality of this defense which still has room for improvement.

Defensive end Chris Doleman returned to the AFC-NFC Pro Bowl.

Special Teams

Placekicker Chuck Nelson does not have long range but, inside 40 yards, he is very accurate. And with the kind of field position the Vikings are likely to carve out, his consistency is what they need. Bucky Scribner's punts could use a little more hang time. Leo Lewis is a fine punt returner - he ranked fifth in the NFC - and Darrin Nelson, who is a respectable kickoff returner, may see greater action following the departure of Darryl Harris.

1989 DRAFT

Round	Name	Pos.	Ht.	Wt.	College
2.	Braxton, David	LB	6-1	227	Wake Forest
3.	Hunter, John	T	6-7	294	Brigham Young
4.	Ingram, Darryl	TE	6-3	221	California
6.	Mickel, Jeff	T	6-5	282	Eastern Washington
7.	Roland, Benji	DT	6-2	270	Auburn
8.	Stewart, Alex	DE	6-3	270	Cal State-Fullerton
11.	Baxter, Brad	RB	6-1	235	Alabama State
12.	Woodson, Shawn	LB	6-2	226	James Madison
12.	Ross, Everett	WR	5-11	184	Ohio State

VETERAN ROSTER

No.	Name	Pos.	Ht.	Wt.	NFL Year	College
	Allen, Anthony	WR	5-11	182	5	Washington
46	Anderson, Alfred	RB	6-1	217	6	Baylor
50	Berry, Ray	LB	6-2	230	3	Baylor
85	Bethea, Ryan	WR	6-3	210	1	South Carolina
47	Browner, Joey	S	6-2	210	7	Southern California
81	Carter, Anthony	WR	5-11	174	5	Michigan
	Curtis, Travis	S	5-10	180	2	West Virginia
56	Doleman, Chris	DE	6-5	262	5	Pittsburgh
42	Dozier, D.J.	RB-KR	6-0	208	3	Penn State
	Dusbabek, Mark	LB	6-3	235	1	Minnesota
27	Edwards, Brad	S	6-1	198	2	South Carolina
31	Fenney, Rick	RB	6-1	240	3	Washington
62	Foote, Chris	C	6-4	265	7	Southern California

No.	Name	Pos.	Ht.	Wt.	Year	College
29	Fullington, Darrell	S	6-1	183	2	Miami
	Galvin, John	LB	6-3	226	2	Boston College
16	Gannon, Rich	QB	6-3	197	3	Delaware
	Greer, Curtis	DE	6-4	258	8	Michigan
80	Gustafson, Jim	WR	6-1	178	4	St. Thomas, Minnesota
91	Habib, Brian	DT	6-6	271	1	Washington
82	Hilton, Carl	TE	6-3	230	4	Houston
30	Holt, Issiac	CB	6-2	199	5	Alcorn State
51	Howard, David	LB	6-2	234	5	Long Beach State
72	Huffman, David	T	6-6	283	10	Notre Dame
76	Irwin, Tim	T	6-6	290	9	Tennessee
84	Jones, Hassan	WR	6-0	198	4	Florida State
83	Jordan, Steve	TE	6-4	235	8	Brown
69	Kalis, Todd	G-T	6-5	269	2	Arizona State
9	Kramer, Tommy	QB	6-2	192	13	Rice
39	Lee, Carl	CB	5-11	188	7	Marshall
87	Lewis, Leo	WR-PR	5-8	167	9	Missouri
63	Lowdermilk, Kirk	C	6-3	264	5	Ohio State
79	Martin, Doug	DE	6-3	270	10	Washington
64	McDaniel, Randall	G	6-3	268	2	Arizona State
	McMillian, Audrey	CB	6-0	190	5	Houston
	Merriweather, Mike	LB	6-2	221	7	Pacific
75	Millard, Keith	DT	6-6	264	5	Washington State
1	Nelson, Chuck	K	6-0	175	6	Washington
20	Nelson, Darrin	RB	5-9	185	8	Stanford
96	Newton, Tim	DT	6-0	297	5	Florida
99	Noga, Al	DE	6-1	245	2	Hawaii
52	Rasmussen, Randy	G	6-2	254	6	Minnesota
36	Rice, Allen	RB	5-10	206	6	Baylor
48	Rutland, Reggie	CB	6-1	195	3	Georgia Tech
13	Scribner, Bucky	P	6-0	205	5	Kansas
	Smith, Daryl	CB	5-9	185	3	North Alabama
54	Solomon, Jesse	LB	6-0	236	4	Florida State
	Strauthers, Thomas	DE	6-4	264	6	Jackson State
55	Studwell, Scott	LB	6-2	229	13	Illinois
97	Thomas, Henry	DT	6-2	268	3	Louisiana State
11	Wilson, Wade	QB	6-3	206	9	East Texas State
65	Zimmerman, Gary	T	6-6	284	4	Oregon

TAMPA BAY BUCCANEERS

Address One Buccaneer Place, Tampa, Florida 33607.
Stadium Tampa Stadium, Tampa.
   Capacity 74,315 *Playing Surface* Grass.
Team Colours Florida Orange, White, and Red.
Head Coach Ray Perkins – 3rd year.
Championships Division 1979,'81.
History AFC 1976, NFC 1977-

Offense

The results may not show it but there is widespread feeling that the offense is making steady progress. In retrospect, it was a good move when the Bucs traded away Steve DeBerg, who had been their insurance for young quarterback Vinny Testaverde. Testaverde would have to continue his learning on the job and he was better for it. Only his inexperience in reading defenses, and immature judgement which can be corrected with patience, let him down. Nothing has diminished the original belief that he was a player who could come good in the NFL. Joe Ferguson, who has thrown more passes than any other active quarterback, is the reserve. The other pieces to the puzzle are not yet assembled but one very large piece, left tackle Paul Gruber, is well and truly in place. Gruber did nothing to hurt his reputation coming into the pros and he was considered unlucky not to go to the Pro Bowl. Gruber and center Randy Grimes form the strength of the line which was not seriously affected by injuries and was showing some cohesion by late December. The other unchallenged starters are left guard Rick Mallory and right tackle Rob Taylor, with John Bruhin expected to make a strong bid to oust right guard Dan Turk. With respectable pass protection and Testaverde's mobility, only 34 sacks were conceded. The passing targets are many and very speedy. There is little to choose between Bruce Hill and Mark Carrier, whose combined efforts produced 115 receptions for 2,010 yards and 14 touchdowns. Furthermore, the receptions came at a healthy average. They are joined by yet another burner, Danny Peebles, whom the Bucs saw as being too good to overlook, and former Oilers free agent Willie Drewrey. Ron Hall may just be the best young blocking tight end in the NFC and he's a highly competent receiver, so much so that the Bucs did not protect veteran Calvin Magee who has gone to Houston. At running back, an injury to James Wilder meant that two rookies, Lars Tate and William Howard, had opportunity thrust upon them. And the manner of their response suggests that, as a pair, they may be given the chance to start the season. With a little less burden to shoulder, the veteran Wilder could be productive, certainly as a receiver, for several more years.

Defense

The defense had real trouble against the pass but was very stingy against the run. That may be head coach Perkins' way of concentrating his efforts. Having given stature to the rush defense, he went all out to find a pass rusher, who came in the form of Broderick Thomas, who was considered the best outside linebacker available behind Derrick Thomas. The nephew of Chicago's Mike Singletary, Thomas is huge for the outside slot but has exceptional speed and, in addition to the pressure that he will surely exert, his very presence must help to release the likes of defensive end Ron Holmes, who was the Bucs' sack leader with the modest total of four. Holmes, defensive end Reuben Davis and nose tackle Curt Jarvis will form the three-man line against the run. John Cannon, a former starting defensive end, has a role to play as specialist pass rusher. At outside linebacker, one of last year's starters, Kevin Murphy and Winston Moss, will have to step down in favour of Thomas and, by the smallest margin, Murphy could be the one to keep his place. Without question, though, Moss will see lots of action and would serve as an excellent backup with Henry Rolling. The inside spots are in the secure ownership of Eugene Marve and Ervin Randle. The acquisition of Marve, who led the team with 121 tackles, was a master stroke. When Randle was out with injury, rookie free agent Sidney Coleman came in and was unexpectedly effective tackling with all the vigour of a man determined to confound the pro scouts who had overlooked him in the draft. With Harry Hamilton settling in at free safety and Mark Robinson as steady as needed when healthy, the defensive secondary has a firm base. Hamilton, a former Jets player, led the team with six interceptions and came second in tackles with 107. Left cornerback Ricky Reynolds stole four passes and defensed a team-best 22 more as he consolidated after his splendid rookie debut. At right cornerback, Bobby Futrell has moved ahead of former first-round pick Rod Jones. Draftee Anthony Florence was selected for his blazing speed, which is said to take him 40 yards in 4.4 seconds.

1989 SCHEDULE OF GAMES		
September		
10	at Green Bay	12:00
17	SAN FRANCISCO	4:00
24	NEW ORLEANS	1:00
October		
1	at Minnesota	12:00
8	CHICAGO	1:00
15	DETROIT	1:00
22	at Washington	1:00
29	at Cincinnati	1:00
November		
5	CLEVELAND	1:00
12	MINNESOTA	1:00
19	at Chicago	12:00
26	at Phoenix	2:00
December		
3	GREEN BAY	1:00
10	at Houston	12:00
17	at Detroit	1:00
24	PITTSBURGH	1:00

Special Teams

Donald Igwebuike, a last-minute pressure kicker, now ranks among the class of the NFL. In the continuing search for a punter, draftee Chris Mohr, whom Perkins coached at Alabama, came in the sixth round. This season, kick returns could be a major attraction. With Futrell returning punts and Donnie Elder handling the kickoffs, Tampa Bay was in good shape anyway, but free-agent signing Sylvester Stamps is a threat to break one every time he touches the ball.

1989 DRAFT

Round	Name	Pos.	Ht.	Wt.	College
1.	Thomas, Broderick	LB	6-2	252	Nebraska
2.	Peebles, Danny	WR	5-11	169	North Carolina State
4.	Florence, Anthony	DB	5-11	185	Bethune-Cookman
5.	Lawson, Jamie	RB	5-10	250	Nicholls State
6.	Mohr, Chris	P	6-4	212	Alabama
6.	Little, Derrick	LB	6-4	234	South Carolina
8.	Bax, Carl	G	6-4	273	Missouri
9.	Egu, Patrick	RB	5-10	200	Nevada-Reno
10.	Granger, Ty	T	6-5	272	Clemson
11.	Mounts, Rod	G	6-4	290	Texas A&I
11.	Griffin, Willie	DT-DE	6-2	289	Nebraska
11.	Duncan, Herb	WR	6-0	180	Northern Arizona
12.	Young, Terry	CB	5-10	178	Georgia Southern

VETERAN ROSTER

No.	Name	Pos.	Ht.	Wt.	NFL Year	College
	Anno, Sam	LB	6-2	230	3	Southern California
	Bell, Kerwin	QB	6-2	205	2	Florida
69	Bruhin, John	G	6-3	280	2	Tennessee
78	Cannon, John	DE	6-5	260	8	William & Mary
4	Carney, John	K	5-11	160	2	Notre Dame
88	Carrier, Mark	WR	6-0	185	3	Nicholls State
66	Clapp, Tommy	DE-NT	6-4	280	1	Louisiana State
	Cocroft, Sherman	S	6-1	190	5	San Jose State
53	Coleman, Sidney	LB	6-2	250	2	Southern Mississippi
71	Cooper, Mark	T-G	6-5	280	7	Miami
79	Davis, Reuben	DE-DT	6-4	290	2	North Carolina
	Drewrey, Willie	WR	5-7	164	5	West Virginia
40	Elder, Donnie	CB	5-9	175	4	Memphis State
12	Ferguson, Joe	QB	6-1	190	17	Arkansas
36	Futrell, Bobby	CB-PR	5-11	190	4	Elizabeth City State
94	Goff, Robert	DE-NT	6-3	270	2	Auburn
64	Graham, Dan	C	6-2	270	1	Northern Illinois
60	Grimes, Randy	C	6-4	275	7	Baylor
74	Gruber, Paul	T	6-5	290	2	Wisconsin
82	Hall, Ron	TE	6-4	245	3	Hawaii
39	Hamilton, Harry	S	6-0	195	6	Penn State
20	Harris, Odie	S	6-0	190	2	Sam Houston State
84	Hill, Bruce	WR	6-0	180	3	Arizona State
90	Holmes, Ron	DE	6-4	265	5	Washington
43	Howard, William	RB	6-0	240	2	Tennessee
1	Igwebuike, Donald	K	5-9	185	5	Clemson
95	Jarvis, Curt	NT	6-2	265	2	Alabama
	Johnson, Sidney	CB	5-9	170	2	California
22	Jones, Rod	CB	6-0	185	4	Southern Methodist
75	Kellin, Kevin	DE	6-5	270	4	Minnesota
97	Lee, Shawn	NT	6-2	290	2	North Alabama
68	Mallory, Rick	G	6-2	265	5	Washington
99	Marve, Eugene	LB	6-2	240	8	Saginaw Valley
73	McHale, Tom	T-G	6-4	275	3	Cornell
57	Moss, Winston	LB	6-3	235	3	Miami
59	Murphy, Kevin	LB	6-2	235	4	Oklahoma
58	Najarian, Peter	LB	6-2	230	2	Minnesota
85	Parks, Jeff	TE	6-4	240	4	Auburn
80	Pillow, Frank	WR	5-10	170	2	Tennessee State
54	Randle, Ervin	LB	6-1	250	5	Baylor
29	Reynolds, Ricky	CB	5-11	190	3	Washington State
89	Richardson, Greg	WR	5-7	170	3	Alabama
30	Robinson, Mark	S	5-11	200	6	Penn State
55	Rolling, Henry	LB	6-2	225	2	Nevada-Reno
98	Seals, Ray	DE	6-3	260	1	None
62	Simmonds, Mike	G	6-4	290	1	Indiana State
47	Smith, Don	RB-WR	5-11	195	2	Mississippi State
61	Sowell, Brent	T	6-5	275	1	Alabama
	Stamps, Sylvester	RB-KR	5-7	171	5	Jackson State
70	Swayne, Harry	DE	6-5	270	3	Rutgers
34	Tate, Lars	RB	6-2	215	2	Georgia
72	Taylor, Rob	T	6-6	295	4	Northwestern
14	Testaverde, Vinny	QB	6-5	215	3	Miami
50	Turk, Dan	G-C	6-4	260	4	Wisconsin
32	Wilder, James	RB	6-3	225	9	Missouri

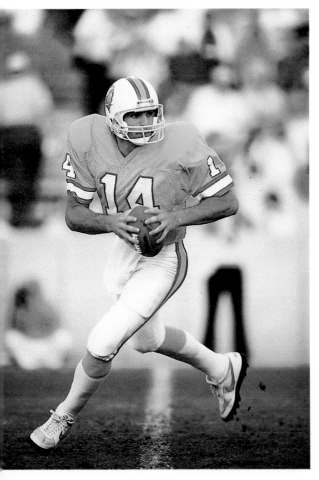

Vinny Testaverde continues to progress.

ATLANTA FALCONS

Address Suwanee Road at I-85, Suwanee, Georgia 30174.
Stadium Atlanta-Fulton County Stadium.
   Capacity 59,643 *Playing Surface* Grass (PAT).
Team Colours Red, Black, White, and Silver.
Head Coach Marion Campbell – 3rd year.
Championships Division 1980.
History NFL 1966-69, NFC 1970-

Offense

A whole series of injuries restricted the Falcons' progress to just the hint of a revival, which included a famous victory over San Francisco and, later, four wins in a five-week period. Guard Bill Fralic was one player they couldn't afford to lose. A Pro Bowler for the last three years, Fralic will return on the right side, displacing 1988 rookie Stan Clayton. Another rookie, Houston Hoover, did well after taking over as the starter at right tackle on Week Five. '. . . he makes their teeth rattle,' said CBS commentator John Madden. It is just possible, however, that the drafting of tackle Ralph Norwood signals an intention to use Hoover at guard, a position for which he may be more suited. In the short term, though, Hoover is unlikely to displace veteran left guard John Scully. At left tackle the reliable Mike Kenn is a veteran of five Pro Bowls. Wayne Radloff holds down the center position with the versatile Jamie Dukes on hand for relief. The departure of Gerald Riggs leaves John Settle with a heavy responsibility, but the style of his first 1,000-yard season in the pros suggests that he can carry the load. He'll be helped if Kenny Flowers, who was a 1987 second-round pick, can come back after missing the whole of last year with a knee injury. Gene Lang could move up to start at fullback but he would not be expected to set any records. Three draftees, led by Keith Jones, join James Primus and Keith Griffin in reserve. The quarterback position appears to have settled down, with Chris Miller the unquestioned starter. His passer rating was modest and he threw more interceptions than touchdown passes, but, in him, the Falcons see a steady guy who needs time and patience. Hugh Millen could come through as the senior backup. The wide receivers are led by Stacey Bailey and Floyd Dixon, two featherweight, but speedy operators. With both players having injuries in 1988, rookie Michael Haynes and former Raiders first-round pick Jessie Hester saw action. Bailey, who caught 67 passes for 1,138 yards in 1984, is a player of true class and must contribute if the Falcons are to become competitive. The serious knee ligament damage suffered by rookie tight end Alex Higdon sent the Falcons scurrying off to the free agent market, where, in Ron Heller, they found a jewel which the 49ers did not protect. A little later, the draft brought Shawn Collins, who has the speed to play at wide receiver and the size to handle himself at H-back.

Defense

Atlanta's period of rebuilding has assembled an exciting group, with a distinct weighting towards youth. Tony Casillas may never reach the heights expected of a player who was overpowering in college, but his strength against the run is put to good use at nose tackle. The starting defensive ends are Mike Gann and Rick Bryan, and there is excellent depth in the aggressive Charles Martin and former Eagles starter Greg Brown. At outside linebacker, the Falcons struck gold in last year's premier draftee, Aundray Bruce, and second-rounder Marcus Cotton. In the early going, some experts rated Cotton a little higher than Bruce, but an ankle injury suffered by Cotton brought an end to that intriguing little duel. Bruce led the team with six sacks and left inside linebacker John Rade was the top tackler with 137 collisions, five more than the other inside linebacker, Joel Williams. The quality is such that Jessie Tuggle, who started eight games in 1989, and former first-round pick Tim Green, who had a useful four sacks, probably will have to settle for joining Michael Reid on the substitutes' bench. The collegiate draft produced an expressive young man who has been described as the best cornerback to enter the league in the last ten years. 'The next Mike Haynes' and 'a bigger, faster Darrell Green' are phrases which have been used to describe Deion Sanders, who certainly is exceptionally talented. He'll start right away, probably at the expense of left cornerback Bobby Butler. On the other corner, Scott Case had a tremendous year, grabbing an NFL-leading ten interceptions. Robert Moore, who had five interceptions, has blossomed at strong safety and, with the possible return of free safety Bret Clark, the Falcons could have a secondary to match most in the NFL.

Special Teams

Rick Donnelly had plenty of practice, sharing the NFL lead with 98 punts. Though with a modest average, he didn't have any blocked and put 27 inside the opposing 20-yard line. In the competition for the vacant job of place-kicker, free agent signing Paul McFadden has an edge if only for his experience as a veteran with both the Eagles and the Giants. The loss of both Sylvester Stamps and Lew Barnes opens the way for draftee Deion Sanders to make his initial impact in the NFL.

1989 DRAFT

Round	Name	Pos.	Ht.	Wt.	College
1.	Sanders, Deion	CB	5-11	187	Florida State
1.	Collins, Shawn	WR-TE	6-3	217	Northern Arizona
2.	Norwood, Ralph	T	6-6	273	Louisiana State
3.	Jones, Keith	RB	6-1	205	Illinois
6.	Sadowski, Troy	TE	6-5	243	Georgia
7.	Johnson, Undra	RB	5-9	199	West Virginia
8.	Singer, Paul	QB	6-3	193	Western Illinois
9.	Dunn, Chris	LB	6-3	230	Cal Poly-SLO
11.	Paterra, Greg	RB	6-1	220	Slippery Rock
12.	Bowick, Tony	NT	6-2	260	Tennessee-Chattanooga

VETERAN ROSTER

No.	Name	Pos.	Ht.	Wt.	NFL Year	College
82	Bailey, Stacey	WR	6-1	157	8	San Jose State
	Baldinger, Gary	NT-DE	6-2	268	4	Wake Forest
	Beckman, Brad	TE	6-2	236	2	Nebraska-Omaha
	Brotzki, Bob	T	6-5	280	4	Syracuse
98	Brown, Greg	DE-NT	6-5	265	9	Kansas State
93	Bruce, Aundray	LB	6-5	245	2	Auburn
77	Bryan, Rick	DE	6-4	265	6	Oklahoma
23	Butler, Bobby	CB	5-11	175	9	Florida State
10	Campbell, Scott	QB	6-0	195	5	Purdue
25	Case, Scott	CB	6-0	178	6	Oklahoma
75	Casillas, Tony	NT	6-3	280	4	Oklahoma
74	Clayton, Stan	T-G	6-3	265	1	Penn State
20	Cooper, Evan	DB	5-11	194	6	Michigan
51	Cotton, Marcus	LB	6-3	225	2	Southern California
22	Dimry, Charles	DB	6-0	175	2	Nevada-Las Vegas
86	Dixon, Floyd	WR	5-9	170	4	Stephen F. Austin
3	Donnelly, Rick	P	6-0	190	5	Wyoming
64	Dukes, Jamie	G-C	6-1	278	4	Florida State
48	Flowers, Kenny	RB	6-0	210	2	Clemson
	Floyd, Norman	S	5-11	198	1	South Carolina
79	Fralic, Bill	G	6-5	280	5	Pittsburgh
65	Frank, Garry	G-C	6-2	280	1	Mississippi State
76	Gann, Mike	DE	6-5	275	5	Notre Dame
41	Gordon, Tim	S	6-0	188	3	Tulsa
99	Green, Tim	LB	6-2	245	4	Syracuse
26	Griffin, Keith	RB	5-8	185	5	Miami
81	Haynes, Michael	WR	6-0	180	2	Northern Arizona
	Heller, Ron	TE	6-3	235	3	Oregon State
89	Hester, Jessie	WR	5-11	170	5	Florida State
88	Higdon, Alex	TE	6-5	247	2	Ohio State
69	Hoover, Houston	T	6-2	285	2	Jackson State
78	Kenn, Mike	T	6-7	277	12	Michigan
33	Lang, Gene	RB	5-10	206	6	Louisiana State
87	Lee, Danzell	TE	6-2	237	3	Lamar
94	Martin, Charles	NT	6-4	280	6	Livingston
	McFadden, Paul	K	5-11	166	6	Youngstown State
7	Millen, Hugh	QB	6-5	216	2	Washington
12	Miller, Chris	QB	6-2	195	3	Oregon
84	Milling, James	WR	5-9	156	2	Maryland
	Modesitt, Jeff	TE	6-5	246	1	Delaware
34	Moore, Robert	S	5-11	190	4	Northwestern State, La.
67	Oswald, Paul	G	6-4	275	3	Kansas
49	Primus, James	RB	5-11	196	2	UCLA
59	Rade, John	LB	6-1	240	7	Boise State
55	Radloff, Wayne	C	6-5	277	5	Georgia
95	Reid, Michael	LB	6-2	226	3	Wisconsin
	Robison, Tom	G	6-4	290	2	Texas A&M
61	Scully, John	G	6-6	270	9	Notre Dame
44	Settle, John	RB	5-9	207	3	Appalachian State
37	Shelley, Elbert	S	5-11	180	3	Arkansas State
	Small, Fred	LB	6-0	231	1	Washington
	Taylor, Kitrick	WR	5-10	183	2	Washington State
35	Thomas, George	WR	5-9	169	1	Nevada-Las Vegas
58	Tuggle, Jessie	LB	5-11	225	3	Valdosta State
	Whitaker, Danta	TE	6-3	240	1	Mississippi Valley State
54	Williams, Joel	LB	6-1	227	11	Wisconsin-LaCrosse
	Young, Mitchell	DE	6-4	260	1	Arkansas State

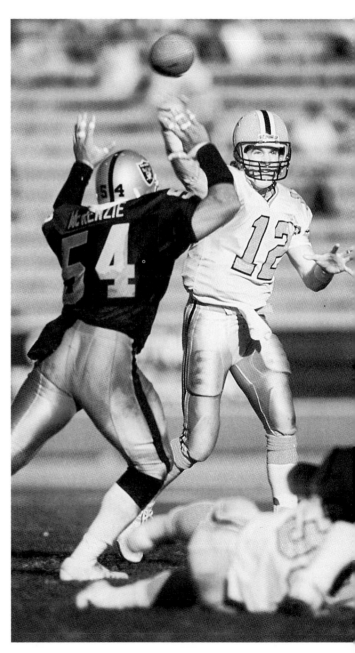

Quarterback Chris Miller has made solid progress.

LOS ANGELES RAMS

Address 2327 West Lincoln Avenue, Anaheim, California 92801.

Stadium Anaheim Stadium, Anaheim.
   Capacity 69,007 *Playing Surface* Grass.

Team Colours Royal Blue, Gold, and White.

Head Coach John Robinson – 7th year.

Championships Division 1973,'74,'75,'76,'77,'78,'79,'85;
   Conference 1979; NFL 1945,'51.

History NFL 1937-69, NFC 1970-
   (Until 1946, they were known as the Cleveland Rams.)

Offense

After a season in the wilderness, the Rams came bounding back and earned their fifth playoff appearance in the last six years. With another excellent crop of draftees in the bank, they expect to be no less effective in 1989. Their great offensive line rolls on, one minute moving earth by the megaton and the next finessing pass rushers aside. Reading from left to right, Irv Pankey, Tom Newberry, Doug Smith, Duval Love and Jackie Slater gave up just 28 sacks and opened up enough holes for a respectable rushing offense. Duval Love was inducted into the setup with no loss of strength and another building block for the next generation arrived in the form of third-round draftee tackle Kevin Robbins. He joins the multi-purpose player, Tony Slaton, and tackle Robert Cox in reserve. 1988 saw quarterback Jim Everett come of age as he produced the kind of goods which suggest long years of productivity ahead. Playing with a free rein, he attempted more passes than all but Miami's Dan Marino and Philadelphia's Randall Cunningham. And almost 60 per cent found their target. With that kind of service, wide receiver Henry Ellard opened up with an NFC-best 86 receptions for the league's best yardage total of 1,414. It is the kind of performance which he has threatened for some time. How glad the parties must be to have sorted out their contractual difficulties of a couple of years ago. Almost uniquely in the NFL, immediately following the leading receiver came two tight ends, Pete Holohan and Damone Johnson. The other wide receivers, Aaron Cox and Willie Anderson, have slipped into the role of deep targets. Their catches averaged 21.1 and 29 yards respectively. With any one of the backfield players likely to be open, the package presents a picture of ever-changing complexity. Looking at the running backs, the Rams used a blend of orthodoxy and imagination, with Greg Bell supplying the former, measured by 1,212 yards at an average of 4.2 and 16 touchdowns, and Robert Delpino slipping into the open for 30 catches. Delpino's role looks tailor-made for first-round draftee Cleveland Gary, whose dual-purpose character emerged in his senior season. Currently, Buford McGee is the blocking fullback but Gary will have to be found playing time and the same is true of last year's first-rounder, Gaston Green.

Defense

The Rams lost Gary Jeter, Greg Meisner, Jim Collins, Mickey Sutton and Johnnie Johnson in the free agent market, and they used the draft to obtain immediate replacements. Draftee defensive end Bill Hawkins is just a solid player, equally comfortable against both the run and the pass, though he will probably begin his career as a pass-rushing specialist on third downs. The Rams look just a little thin behind the starting trio of defensive ends Doug Reed and Shawn Miller, and nose tackle Alvin Wright. But this may be offset by a strengthening at linebacker with the arrival of draftees Frank Stams, Brian Smith, Mark Messner and George Bethune. The fast-improving Fred Strickland should challenge Mark Jerue to start at right inside linebacker in place of Collins, as the only change in a unit in which the other starters are Kevin Greene, Carl Ekern, and Mike Wilcher. Greene, who explodes off his mark, led the Rams with a personal-best 16.5 sacks, ahead of Jeter (11.5) and Wilcher's 7.5. The hardworking Ekern dominated the tackle list with 93. Three of the four rookies are outside specialists, Messner having played at defensive tackle in college. One of the pleasing features of watching the Rams in recent years has been the certainty with which Jerry Gray has become one of the NFL's top cornerbacks. A Pro Bowler for the past three years, Gray came second in the club with 63 tackles, defensed 13 passes and had three interceptions. His starting partner, LeRoy Irvin, is a former Pro Bowler with great speed and acceleration off the blocks as his trademark. With very limited opportunities, Anthony Newman grabbed two interceptions to serve notice that he intends being a part of the Rams' future. He could step up in place of Johnson at free safety, though Vince Newsome might have something to say about who starts in the safety positions. Michael Stewart, an uncompromising tackler, is the current starter at strong safety. Joining backup Clifford Hicks is the talented draftee, Darryl Henley.

1989 SCHEDULE OF GAMES		
September		
10 at Atlanta		1:00
17 INDIANAPOLIS		1:00
24 GREEN BAY		1:00
October		
1 at San Francisco		1:00
8 ATLANTA		1:00
16 at Buffalo (Mon.)		9:00
22 NEW ORLEANS		1:00
29 at Chicago		12:00
November		
5 at Minnesota		12:00
12 NEW YORK GIANTS		1:00
19 PHOENIX		1:00
26 at New Orleans (night)		7:00
December		
3 at Dallas		12:00
11 SAN FRANCISCO (Mon.)		6:00
17 NEW YORK JETS		1:00
24 at New England		1:00

Special Teams

'Steady' would be the word to describe both placekicker Mike Lansford and punter Dale Hatcher, though the latter is coming off a sub-par campaign. Returning kicks, the Rams usually are a danger, but the best they could offer last year was Ron Brown's 73-yard effort. However, it would be unwise to overlook the potential of a club which can field both Brown and Ellard, the latter who always is a danger to break open on a punt return.

1989 DRAFT

Round	Name	Pos.	Ht.	Wt.	College
1.	Hawkins, Bill	DE	6-5	261	Miami
1.	Gary, Cleveland	RB	6-2	226	Miami
2.	Stams, Frank	LB	6-4	237	Notre Dame
2.	Smith, Brian	LB	6-6	244	Auburn
2.	Henley, Darryl	CB	5-8	165	UCLA
3.	Robbins, Kevin	T	6-4	293	Michigan State
4.	Carlson, Jeff	QB	6-3	215	Weber State
5.	Jackson, Alfred	WR	6-0	177	San Diego State
6.	Kaumeyer, Thom	S	5-11	187	Oregon
6.	Messner, Mark	LB	6-3	244	Michigan
7.	Bethune, George	LB	6-4	220	Alabama
8.	Wheat, Warren	T-G	6-5	277	Brigham Young
9.	Kirk, Vernon	TE	6-2	250	Pittsburgh
10.	Williams, Mike	WR	5-11	180	Northeastern

VETERAN ROSTER

No.	Name	Pos.	Ht.	Wt.	NFL Year	College
83	Anderson, Willie	WR	6-0	169	2	UCLA
42	Bell, Greg	RB	5-10	210	6	Notre Dame
	Brown, Henry	DT	6-3	265	1	Florida
89	Brown, Ron	WR	5-11	181	6	Arizona State
84	Cox, Aaron	WR	5-9	174	2	Arizona State
72	Cox, Robert	T	6-5	270	3	UCLA
	Darby, Byron	DE	6-4	260	7	Southern California
	Davis, Wayne	LB	6-1	213	3	Alabama
39	Delpino, Robert	RB	6-0	205	2	Missouri
55	Ekern, Carl	LB	6-3	222	13	San Jose State
80	Ellard, Henry	WR-PR	5-11	175	7	Fresno State
11	Everett, Jim	QB	6-5	212	4	Purdue
51	Faryniarz, Brett	LB	6-3	225	2	San Diego State
25	Gray, Jerry	CB	6-0	185	5	Texas
30	Green, Gaston	RB	5-10	189	2	UCLA
91	Greene, Kevin	LB	6-3	238	5	Auburn
5	Hatcher, Dale	P	6-2	211	5	Clemson
9	Herrmann, Mark	QB	6-4	186	9	Purdue
28	Hicks, Clifford	CB-PR	5-10	188	3	Oregon
81	Holohan, Pete	TE	6-4	232	9	Notre Dame
47	Irvin, LeRoy	CB	5-11	184	10	Kansas
59	Jerue, Mark	LB	6-3	234	7	Washington
86	Johnson, Damone	TE	6-4	230	4	Cal Poly-SLO
52	Kelm, Larry	LB	6-4	226	3	Texas A&M
1	Lansford, Mike	K	6-0	183	8	Washington
67	Love, Duval	G	6-3	280	5	UCLA
90	McDonald, Mike	LB	6-1	235	5	Southern California
24	McGee, Buford	RB	6-0	206	6	Mississippi
98	Miller, Shawn	DE	6-4	255	6	Utah State
79	Mullin, R.C.	T	6-6	300	1	Southwestern Louisiana
66	Newberry, Tom	G	6-2	279	4	Wisconsin-LaCrosse
26	Newman, Anthony	CB	6-0	199	2	Oregon
22	Newsome, Vince	S	6-1	183	7	Washington
58	Owens, Mel	LB	6-2	224	9	Michigan
75	Pankey, Irv	T	6-5	267	10	Penn State
95	Piel, Mike	DE	6-4	263	1	Illinois
93	Reed, Doug	DE	6-3	250	6	San Diego State
78	Slater, Jackie	T	6-4	275	14	Jackson State
61	Slaton, Tony	C-G	6-3	265	5	Southern California
56	Smith, Doug	C	6-3	260	12	Bowling Green
23	Stewart, Michael	S	5-11	195	3	Fresno State
53	Strickland, Fred	LB	6-2	224	2	Purdue
37	Washington, James	S	6-1	191	2	UCLA
54	Wilcher, Mike	LB	6-3	240	7	North Carolina
99	Wright, Alvin	NT	6-2	265	4	Jacksonville State

Quarterback Jim Everett has true class.

NEW ORLEANS SAINTS

NFC WESTERN DIVISION

Address 1500 Poydras Street, New Orleans, Louisiana 70112.
Stadium Louisiana Superdome, New Orleans. *Capacity* 69,548 *Playing Surface* AstroTurf.
Team Colours Old Gold, Black, and White.
Head Coach Jim Mora – 4th year.
Championships None.
History NFL 1967-69, NFC 1970-

Offense

'A day late and a dollar short.' Cruel though it may sound, that reflection might just be the most accurate after a season which saw the Saints regroup to no avail. Had they been playing in the AFC West they'd probably have gone 12-4. Two one-point losses, a two-pointer and one by three points meant that they watched the postseason on TV. But the Saints are as close as that and they could so easily reach the playoffs, even in the tough NFC West. Quarterback Bobby Hebert may not represent the state of the art but he has worked hard to fit into the Saints' system, and that head coach Jim Mora likes his style is the only thing that matters. With Hebert at the controls, gradually, the offense has been able to ease away from what was a survival kit, focusing on power rushing, to include a mix of passes. It has meant that wide receiver Eric Martin could enjoy his first 1,000-yard season as a pro. Equally, Martin's starting partner, Lonzell Hill, was able to make a significant contribution. Rookie Brett Perriman did enough to earn his status as the third-ranking receiver. Both Derrick Shepard and Darrell Colbert, who were signed as free agents, could find roster spots. Hoby Brenner has been the unchallenged starter at tight end since the beginning of the 1982 season, but, increasingly, his status has come under threat from John Tice, who is another who can shove people around and adjust to catch passes. Looking at the men who throw their weight around for a living, the offensive linemen, the Saints are comfortable. And that may be an understatement about a line which gave up only 24 quarterback sacks in 1988. The strength lies on the left side in guard Brad Edelman and tackle Jim Dombrowski, but that is no disrespect to center Steve Korte, right guard Steve Trapilo and right tackle Daren Gilbert. The chances are that Stan Brock will regain his former starting spot from Gilbert, who would join a pool of reserves which includes Joel Hilgenberg and Chuck Commiskey. At running back, three years of careful selection have produced a fine group out of which Dalton Hilliard and Buford Jordan have emerged as the starters. Backups Rueben Mayes and Craig (Ironhead) Heyward just as easily could carry the fight to the opposition. Overall it is a unit with strength in every area and no real weaknesses.

Defense

Defense was given priority in the first four rounds of the draft, with the line receiving the plum selection in defensive end Wayne Martin. Martin could bring effervescence to a defensive line which, collectively, logged only ten sacks last year. Starting nose tackle Tony Elliott has been released, making way for Bruce Clark, who will have to make the conversion from his more familiar role of defensive end. Last year's starting defensive ends were Frank Warren and Jim Wilks. With James Geathers, whose forte is pass rushing, also in the mix, the final formula will emerge only during the preseason when Martin's strengths have been identified. Following the departure of last year's starter, Van Jakes, and backup Michael Adams, reinforcement for the cornerback position was a necessity. And they went all-out with selections in rounds two, three and four and a fourth in round 11. One of the draftees seems certain to start on the right corner, and it is possible that veteran Reggie Sutton could displace Dave Waymer on the other. Brett Maxie and Antonio Gibson form a good pair at safety. Maxie, who was a free agent discovery in 1985, still has not reached his potential. Substituting when Gibson was on NFL suspension, Gene Atkins led the team with four interceptions and provides instant cover in the case of injury. The Saints' real strength lies at linebacker, an area which produced the joint sack leaders in Rickey Jackson and Pat Swilling, and the top tacklers, inside specialists Vaughan Johnson and Sam Mills. Johnson was considered unlucky not to accompany Mills to the Pro Bowl. Jackson had a brilliant season and he too must have been desperately close to adding to his sequence of four Pro Bowl selections. It is difficult to overstate the importance of this quartet, which, in all common sense, runs the show. The problem is that none of the backups is up to the class of the starters, on whose continued fitness may rest the Saints' fortunes in 1989.

1989 SCHEDULE OF GAMES		
September		
10	DALLAS	12:00
17	at Green Bay	12:00
24	at Tampa Bay	1:00
October		
1	WASHINGTON	12:00
8	at San Francisco	1:00
15	NEW YORK JETS	3:00
22	at Los Angeles Rams	12:00
29	ATLANTA	12:00
November		
6	SAN FRANCISCO (Mon.)	8:00
12	at New England	1:00
19	at Atlanta	1:00
26	LOS ANGELES RAMS (night)	7:00
December		
3	at Detroit	1:00
10	at Buffalo	1:00
18	PHILADELPHIA (Mon.)	8:00
24	INDIANAPOLIS	12:00

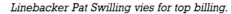

Linebacker Pat Swilling vies for top billing.

Special Teams

The departure of dual-purpose kick returner Mel Gray left a gap which may be filled by Derrick Shepard, in support of Atkins, fielding kickoffs while 12th-round draftee Mike Cadore might come through to assist Hill returning the punts. The kicking game is one of the league's best. Despite a couple of lapses, placekicker Morten Andersen earned his fourth consecutive trip to the Pro Bowl. The steady Brian Hansen was the NFC punter in the 1985 game.

1989 DRAFT

Round	Name	Pos.	Ht.	Wt.	College
1.	Martin, Wayne	DE	6-4	260	Arkansas
2.	Massey, Robert	CB	5-10	182	North Carolina Central
3.	Phillips, Kim	CB	5-9	188	North Texas
4.	Mayes, Mike	CB	5-10	180	Louisiana State
5.	Haverdink, Kevin	T	6-5	284	Western Michigan
6.	Turner, Floyd	WR	5-11	188	Northwestern State, La.
7.	Griggs, David	LB	6-3	239	Virginia
8.	Hadley, Fred	WR	6-0	176	Mississippi State
9.	Leggett, Jerry	DE-LB	6-4	260	Cal State-Fullerton
10.	Henderson, Joe	RB	6-0	205	Iowa State
11.	Nicholson, Calvin	CB	5-10	180	Oregon State
12.	Cadore, Mike	WR	5-8	172	Eastern Kentucky

VETERAN ROSTER

No.	Name	Pos.	Ht.	Wt.	NFL Year	College
7	Andersen, Morten	K	6-2	221	8	Michigan State
28	Atkins, Gene	S	6-1	200	3	Florida A&M
76	Board, Dwaine	DE	6-5	248	10	North Carolina A&T
85	Brenner, Hoby	TE	6-4	240	9	Southern California
67	Brock, Stan	T	6-6	292	10	Colorado
75	Clark, Bruce	DE	6-3	275	8	Penn State
	Colbert, Darrell	WR	5-10	174	3	Texas Southern
66	Commiskey, Chuck	G-T	6-5	290	4	Mississippi
41	Cook, Toi	S	5-11	188	3	Stanford
79	Derby, Glenn	T	6-6	290	1	Wisconsin
72	Dombrowski, Jim	T	6-5	298	4	Virginia
95	Dumbauld, Jon	DE	6-4	259	2	Kentucky
63	Edelman, Brad	G	6-6	270	8	Missouri
91	Fizer, Vincent	LB	6-4	250	1	Southern
52	Forde, Brian	LB	6-2	225	2	Washington State
11	Fourcade, John	QB	6-1	208	3	Mississippi
97	Geathers, James	DE	6-7	290	5	Wichita State
27	Gibson, Antonio	S	6-3	204	4	Cincinnati
77	Gilbert, Daren	T	6-5	280	5	Cal State-Fullerton
74	Gregory, Ted	NT	6-1	265	2	Syracuse
10	Hansen, Brian	P	6-3	209	6	Sioux Falls, S.D.
92	Haynes, James	LB	6-2	233	6	Mississippi Valley State
3	Hebert, Bobby	QB	6-4	215	6	Northwestern State, La.
34	Heyward, Craig	RB	5-11	251	2	Pittsburgh
61	Hilgenberg, Joel	C-G	6-2	252	6	Iowa
87	Hill, Lonzell	WR	6-0	189	3	Washington
21	Hilliard, Dalton	RB	5-8	204	4	Louisiana State
57	Jackson, Rickey	LB	6-2	243	9	Pittsburgh
53	Johnson, Vaughan	LB	6-3	235	4	North Carolina State
23	Johnson, Walter	LB	6-0	240	3	Louisiana Tech
20	Jordan, Buford	RB	6-0	223	4	McNeese State
55	Kohlbrand, Joe	LB	6-4	242	5	Miami
60	Korte, Steve	C	6-2	260	7	Arkansas
24	Mack, Milton	CB	5-11	182	3	Alcorn State
84	Martin, Eric	WR	6-1	207	6	Louisiana State
39	Maxie, Brett	S	6-2	194	5	Texas Southern
36	Mayes, Rueben	RB	5-11	200	4	Washington State
51	Mills, Sam	LB	5-9	225	4	Montclair State
80	Perriman, Brett	WR	5-9	175	2	Miami
83	Scales, Greg	TE	6-4	253	2	Wake Forest
	Shepard, Derrick	WR-KR	5-10	187	3	Oklahoma
29	Sutton, Reggie	CB	5-10	180	3	Miami
56	Swilling, Pat	LB	6-3	242	4	Georgia Tech
82	Tice, John	TE	6-5	249	7	Maryland
54	Toles, Alvin	LB	6-1	227	5	Tennessee
65	Trapilo, Steve	G	6-5	295	3	Boston College
68	Walker, Jeff	T	6-4	295	2	Memphis State
73	Warren, Frank	DE	6-4	290	9	Auburn
33	Waters, Mike	TE	6-2	230	3	San Diego State
44	Waymer, Dave	CB	6-1	188	10	Notre Dame
94	Wilks, Jim	DE	6-5	266	9	San Diego State
18	Wilson, Dave	QB	6-3	206	8	Illinois

SAN FRANCISCO 49ers

Address 4949 Centennial Boulevard, Santa Clara, California 95054.
Stadium Candlestick Park, San Francisco.
  Capacity 64,252 *Playing Surface* Grass.
Team Colours Forty Niners Gold and Scarlet.
Head Coach George Seifert – 1st year.
Championships Division 1970,'71,'72,'81,'83,'84,'86,'87,'88; Conference 1981,'84,'88; Super Bowl 1981,'84,'88.
History AAFC 1946-49, NFL 1950-69, NFC 1970-

Offense

The reigning Super Bowl Champion usually carries over its apparent invincibility and this year is no different. Center Randy Cross has retired and the loss of both John Frank, whose retirement was premature, and Ron Heller left them with Brent Jones as the sole remaining tight end. But there are replacements in abundance. The chances are that Jesse Sapolu will step in for Cross. It could lead to some shuffling around with, perhaps, Guy McIntyre moving to left guard to make way for free agent signing Terry Tausch. Bruce Collie and Jeff Bregel will be involved in the competition. Two solid starting tackles, Steve Wallace and Harris Barton, are backed up by former starter Bubba Paris. Unlike last season, Joe Montana enters the campaign as the unchallenged starting quarterback. He is coming off one of the great performances of his storied career and would appear to be set for several more years. Should Montana go down with injury, backup Steve Young could take over with not much loss of effectiveness. It is interesting to compare the styles of a cool, slender Montana, all class and finesse, and the chunky, challenging, Young. The rapier and the cutlass. At wide receiver, the peerless Jerry Rice didn't win the NFL receiving title but he did most of the other things that matter. After just four years Rice already has secured his place in NFL history. The other starter, John Taylor, took his first steps along the road to greatness. Taylor's last reception won the Super Bowl. With a fine pair of hands and smooth moves, he is a touch faster than Rice. There is yet more speed in the shape of Terry Greer, a former CFL player, and Mike Sherrard, the Cowboys' first-round pick in 1986, whose career was threatened by two leg fractures. The 49ers can afford to give Sherrard all the time he needs to recover full fitness and confidence. Former Houston starter Jamie Williams and draftee Wesley Walls have joined veteran Brent Jones in the competition for playing time at tight end. Running back Roger Craig would be a popular selection for the NFC's best, both as a pure rusher and for his dual-purpose threat. Together with fullback Tom Rathman, he forms a formidable backfield pair. The backups include Terrence Flagler, Harry Sydney and former Houston player, Spencer Tillman.

Defense

On defense the 49ers were equally impressive, ranking third overall in the NFL. Making the initial collision in the middle of the action, nose tackle Michael Carter is an established Pro Bowler who demands double-teaming on every play. Remarkably, he was able to penetrate the middle for 6.5 sacks in 1988. Larry Roberts and Kevin Fagan are the named starting defensive ends but the 49ers show such a great variety of defensive patterns that, in many cases, the notion of starters doesn't mean much at all. Essentially, Roberts and Fagan are run defenders, with Daniel Stubbs, Jeff Stover, Pete Kugler and another nose tackle, Pierce Holt, seeing action as the circumstances change. Stubbs, who had six sacks, is now becoming the kind of player the 49ers saw in college. The leading sacker was Charles Haley, who plays a role which is not that much different from that of stand-up defensive end. With 11.5 sacks last year to follow his club-leading 6.5 of 1987, he confirmed his class. The leading tackler was Michael Walter, who teams up with Riki Ellison to give San Francisco an unbreakable heart at inside linebacker. Ellison is constantly pressed by Jim Fahnhorst while the top pick in the draft produced another human missile, Keith DeLong. 1988 rookie Bill Romanowski slipped in and out of the system with ease. The secondary parades the threat of Ronnie Lott and the momentum of Jeff Fuller in the safety positions. Lott, whose style has evolved from one of violent contact to almost psychological dominance, may be bound for the Hall of Fame. Not by much over the reserves do Tim McKyer and Don Griffin start at cornerback. And that conclusion is more a compliment to the likes of Tory Nixon and former Pro Bowler Eric Wright than an implication of weakness in McKyer and Griffin. Tom Holmoe is the senior backup at safety. McKyer led the team with seven interceptions ahead of Lott, who had five.

1989 SCHEDULE OF GAMES		
September		
10 at Indianapolis	12:00	
17 at Tampa Bay	4:00	
24 at Philadelphia	1:00	
October		
1 LOS ANGELES RAMS	1:00	
8 NEW ORLEANS	1:00	
15 at Dallas	12:00	
22 NEW ENGLAND	1:00	
29 at New York Jets	4:00	
November		
6 at New Orleans (Mon.)	8:00	
12 ATLANTA	1:00	
19 GREEN BAY	1:00	
27 NEW YORK GIANTS (Mon.)	6:00	
December		
3 at Atlanta	1:00	
11 at Los Angeles Rams (Mon.)	6:00	
17 BUFFALO	1:00	
24 CHICAGO	1:00	

Special Teams

First-year placekicker Mike Cofer is a scrappy operator, but he has a strong leg and will improve his consistency with time. Rookie punter Barry Helton, on the other hand, was inconsistent and may have to compete for his job in camp. John Taylor's fluid style produced touchdowns covering 77 and 95 yards, raising his punt return average to an NFL-best 12.6 yards. Surprisingly, kickoff returning was a problem and, entering camp, there is no obvious man for the job.

1989 DRAFT

Round	Name	Pos.	Ht.	Wt.	College
1.	DeLong, Keith	LB	6-2	220	Tennessee
2.	Walls, Wesley	TE	6-5	248	Mississippi
3.	Henderson, Keith	RB	6-2	202	Georgia
4.	Barber, Mike	WR	5-10	172	Marshall
5.	Jackson, Johnny	CB-S	6-1	201	Houston
6.	Hendrickson, Steve	LB	6-0	244	California
9.	Harmon, Rudy	LB	6-1	230	Louisiana State
10.	Sinclair, Andy	C	6-2	272	Stanford
11.	Bell, Jim	RB	6-0	204	Boston College
11.	McGee, Norm	WR	6-0	170	North Dakota
12.	Goss, Antonio	LB	6-3	228	North Carolina

VETERAN ROSTER

No.	Name	Pos.	Ht.	Wt.	NFL Year	College
79	Barton, Harris	T	6-4	280	3	North Carolina
65	Bregel, Jeff	G	6-4	280	3	Southern California
31	Brooks, Chet	CB	5-11	191	2	Texas A&M
95	Carter, Michael	NT	6-2	285	6	Southern Methodist
66	Cochran, Mark	T	6-5	285	2	Baylor
6	Cofer, Mike	K	6-1	190	2	North Carolina State
69	Collie, Bruce	G	6-6	275	5	Texas-Arlington
33	Craig, Roger	RB	6-0	224	7	Nebraska
50	Ellison, Riki	LB	6-2	225	7	Southern California
75	Fagan, Kevin	DE	6-4	265	3	Miami
55	Fahnhorst, Jim	LB	6-4	230	6	Minnesota
32	Flagler, Terrence	RB	6-0	200	3	Clemson
49	Fuller, Jeff	S	6-2	216	6	Texas A&M
83	Greer, Terry	WR	6-1	192	4	Alabama State
29	Griffin, Don	CB	6-0	176	4	Middle Tennessee State
54	Hadley, Ron	LB	6-2	240	4	Washington
94	Haley, Charles	LB	6-5	230	4	James Madison
9	Helton, Barry	P	6-3	205	2	Colorado
46	Holmoe, Tom	S	6-2	195	6	Brigham Young
78	Holt, Pierce	NT	6-4	280	2	Angelo State
84	Jones, Brent	TE	6-4	230	3	Santa Clara
57	Kennedy, Sam	LB	6-3	235	2	San Jose State
67	Kugler, Pete	DE	6-4	255	7	Penn State
42	Lott, Ronnie	S	6-0	200	9	Southern California
62	McIntyre, Guy	G	6-3	265	6	Georgia
22	McKyer, Tim	CB	6-0	174	4	Texas-Arlington
16	Montana, Joe	QB	6-2	195	11	Notre Dame
20	Nixon, Tory	CB	5-11	186	5	San Diego State
64	O'Connor, Paul	G	6-3	258	1	Miami
77	Paris, Bubba	T	6-6	306	7	Michigan
15	Paye, John	QB	6-3	205	1	Stanford
26	Pollard, Darryl	CB	5-11	187	3	Weber State
44	Rathman, Tom	RB	6-1	232	4	Nebraska
80	Rice, Jerry	WR	6-2	200	5	Mississippi Valley State
91	Roberts, Larry	DE	6-3	275	4	Alabama
35	Rodgers, Del	RB-KR	5-10	203	5	Utah
53	Romanowski, Bill	LB	6-4	231	2	Boston College
61	Sapolu, Jesse	G	6-4	260	4	Hawaii
90	Shell, Todd	LB	6-4	225	4	Brigham Young
	Sherrard, Mike	WR	6-2	194	2	UCLA
72	Stover, Jeff	DE	6-5	275	8	Oregon
96	Stubbs, Daniel	DE	6-4	260	2	Miami
	Sweeney, Kevin	QB	6-0	190	3	Fresno State
24	Sydney, Harry	RB	6-0	217	3	Kansas
	Tausch, Terry	G	6-5	276	8	Texas
82	Taylor, John	WR-PR	6-1	185	3	Delaware State
60	Thomas, Chuck	C	6-3	280	4	Oklahoma
	Tillman, Spencer	RB	5-11	208	3	Oklahoma
58	Turner, Keena	LB	6-2	222	10	Purdue
74	Wallace, Steve	T	6-5	276	4	Auburn
99	Walter, Michael	LB	6-3	238	7	Oregon
	Washington, Chris	LB	6-4	240	6	Iowa State
	Williams, Jamie	TE	6-4	255	7	Nebraska
85	Wilson, Mike	WR	6-3	215	9	Washington State
21	Wright, Eric	CB	6-1	185	8	Missouri
8	Young, Steve	QB	6-2	200	5	Brigham Young

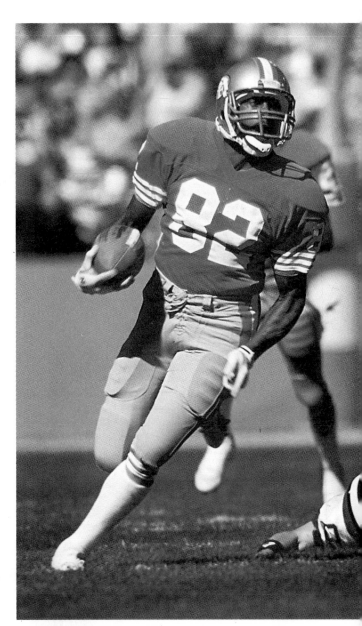

John Taylor was the NFL's leading punt returner and scored touchdowns on returns of 77 and 95 yards.

CHAPTER EIGHT

1989 NATIONAL FOOTBALL LEAGUE SCHEDULE

(All times local)

FIRST WEEK
Sunday, September 10   Kickoff
Buffalo at Miami 4:00
Cincinnati at Chicago 12:00
Cleveland at Pittsburgh 4:00
Dallas at New Orleans 12:00
Houston at Minnesota 3:00
Kansas City at Denver 2:00
Los Angeles Rams at Atlanta 1:00
New England at New York Jets 4:00
Phoenix at Detroit 1:00
San Diego at Los Angeles Raiders 1:00
San Francisco at Indianapolis 12:00
Seattle at Philadelphia 4:00
Tampa Bay at Green Bay 12:00

Monday, September 11
New York Giants at Washington 9:00

SECOND WEEK
Sunday, September 17
Dallas at Atlanta 1:00
Detroit at New York Giants 4:00
Houston at San Diego 1:00
Indianapolis at Los Angeles Rams 1:00
Los Angeles Raiders at Kansas City 12:00
Miami at New England 1:00
Minnesota at Chicago 3:00
New Orleans at Green Bay 12:00
New York Jets at Cleveland 1:00
Philadelphia at Washington 1:00
Phoenix at Seattle 1:00
Pittsburgh at Cincinnati 1:00
San Francisco at Tampa Bay 4:00

Monday, September 18
Denver at Buffalo 9:00

THIRD WEEK
Sunday, September 24
Atlanta at Indianapolis 12:00
Buffalo at Houston 12:00
Chicago at Detroit 1:00
Green Bay at Los Angeles Rams 1:00
Kansas City at San Diego 1:00
Los Angeles Raiders at Denver 2:00
Minnesota at Pittsburgh 1:00
New Orleans at Tampa Bay 1:00
New York Jets at Miami 4:00
Phoenix at New York Giants 1:00
San Francisco at Philadelphia 1:00
Seattle at New England 1:00
Washington at Dallas 12:00

Monday, September 25
Cleveland at Cincinnati 9:00

FOURTH WEEK
Sunday, October 1
Atlanta vs. Green Bay at Milwaukee 12:00
Cincinnati at Kansas City 12:00
Denver at Cleveland 1:00
Indianapolis at New York Jets 1:00
Los Angeles Rams at San Francisco 1:00
Miami at Houston 12:00
New England at Buffalo 1:00
New York Giants at Dallas 3:00
Pittsburgh at Detroit 1:00
San Diego at Phoenix 1:00
Seattle at Los Angeles Raiders 1:00
Tampa Bay at Minnesota 12:00
Washington at New Orleans 12:00

Monday, October 2
Philadelphia at Chicago 8:00

FIFTH WEEK
Sunday, October 8
Atlanta at Los Angeles Rams 1:00
Buffalo at Indianapolis 12:00

Chicago at Tampa Bay 1:00
Cincinnati at Pittsburgh 1:00
Cleveland at Miami 1:00
Dallas at Green Bay 12:00
Detroit at Minnesota 12:00
Houston at New England 1:00
Kansas City at Seattle 1:00
New Orleans at San Francisco 1:00
New York Giants at Philadelphia 1:00
Phoenix at Washington 4:00
San Diego at Denver 2:00

Monday, October 9
Los Angeles Raiders at New York Jets 9:00

SIXTH WEEK
Sunday, October 15
Detroit at Tampa Bay 1:00
Green Bay at Minnesota 12:00
Houston at Chicago 12:00
Indianapolis at Denver 2:00
Kansas City at Los Angeles Raiders 1:00
Miami at Cincinnati 1:00
New England at Atlanta 1:00
New York Jets at New Orleans 3:00
Philadelphia at Phoenix 1:00
Pittsburgh at Cleveland 4:00
San Francisco at Dallas 12:00
Seattle at San Diego 1:00
Washington at New York Giants 1:00

Monday, October 160
Los Angeles Rams at Buffalo 9:00

SEVENTH WEEK
Sunday, October 22
Atlanta at Phoenix 1:00
Dallas at Kansas City 12:00
Denver at Seattle 1:00
Green Bay at Miami 1:00
Indianapolis at Cincinnati 1:00
Los Angeles Raiders at Philadelphia 1:00
Minnesota at Detroit 1:00
New England at San Francisco 1:00
New Orleans at Los Angeles Rams 1:00
New York Giants at San Diego 1:00
New York Jets at Buffalo 1:00
Pittsburgh at Houston 12:00
Tampa Bay at Washington 1:00

Monday, October 23
Chicago at Cleveland 9:00

EIGHTH WEEK
Sunday, October 29
Atlanta at New Orleans 12:00
Detroit vs. Green Bay at Milwaukee 12:00
Houston at Cleveland 1:00
Kansas City at Pittsburgh 1:00
Los Angeles Rams at Chicago 12:00
Miami at Buffalo 1:00

New England at Indianapolis 1:00
Philadelphia at Denver 2:00
Phoenix at Dallas 12:00
San Diego at Seattle 1:00
San Francisco at New York Jets 4:00
Tampa Bay at Cincinnati 1:00
Washington at Los Angeles Raiders 1:00

Monday, October 30
Minnesota at New York Giants 9:00

NINTH WEEK
Sunday, November 5
Buffalo at Atlanta 1:00
Chicago at Green Bay 12:00
Cincinnati at Los Angeles Raiders 1:00
Cleveland at Tampa Bay 1:00
Dallas at Washington 8:00
Detroit at Houston 12:00
Indianapolis at Miami 1:00
Los Angeles Rams at Minnesota 12:00
New York Giants at Phoenix 2:00
New York Jets at New England 1:00
Philadelphia at San Diego 1:00
Pittsburgh at Denver 2:00
Seattle at Kansas City 12:00

Monday, November 6
San Francisco at New Orleans 8:00

TENTH WEEK
Sunday, November 12
Atlanta at San Francisco 1:00
Chicago at Pittsburgh 1:00
Cleveland at Seattle 1:00
Dallas at Phoenix 2:00
Denver at Kansas City 12:00
Green Bay at Detroit 1:00
Indianapolis at Buffalo 1:00
Los Angeles Raiders at San Diego 5:00
Miami at New York Jets 1:00
Minnesota at Tampa Bay 1:00
New Orleans at New England 1:00
New York Giants at Los Angeles Rams 1:00
Washington at Philadelphia 1:00

Monday, November 13
Cincinnati at Houston 8:00

ELEVENTH WEEK
Sunday, November 19
Buffalo at New England 1:00
Detroit at Cincinnati 1:00
Green Bay at San Francisco 1:00
Kansas City at Cleveland 1:00
Los Angeles Raiders at Houston 3:00
Miami at Dallas 12:00
Minnesota at Philadelphia 1:00
New Orleans at Atlanta 1:00
New York Jets at Indianapolis 8:00
Phoenix at Los Angeles Rams 1:00

San Diego at Pittsburgh 1:00
Seattle at New York Giants 4:00
Tampa Bay at Chicago 12:00

Monday, November 20
Denver at Washington 9:00

TWELFTH WEEK
Thursday, November 23(Thanksgiving Day)
Cleveland at Detroit 12:30
Philadelphia at Dallas 3:00

Sunday, November 26
Atlanta at New York Jets 1:00
Chicago at Washington 4:00
Cincinnati at Buffalo 1:00
Houston at Kansas City 12:00
Los Angeles Rams at New Orleans 7:00
Minnesota vs. Green Bay at Milwaukee 12:00
New England at Los Angeles Raiders 1:00
Pittsburgh at Miami 1:00
San Diego at Indianapolis 1:00
Seattle at Denver 2:00
Tampa Bay at Phoenix 2:00

Monday, November 27
New York Giants at San Francisco 6:00

THIRTEENTH WEEK
Sunday, December 3
Chicago at Minnesota 7:00
Cincinnati at Cleveland 1:00
Denver at Los Angeles Raiders 1:00
Green Bay at Tampa Bay 1:00
Houston at Pittsburgh 1:00
Indianapolis at New England 1:00
Los Angeles Rams at Dallas 12:00
Miami at Kansas City 12:00
New Orleans at Detroit 1:00
New York Jets at San Diego 1:00
Philadelphia at New York Giants 1:00
San Francisco at Atlanta 1:00
Washington at Phoenix 2:00

Monday, December 4
Buffalo at Seattle 6:00

FOURTEENTH WEEK
Sunday, December 10
Atlanta at Minnesota 12:00
Cleveland at Indianapolis 4:00
Dallas at Philadelphia 1:00
Detroit at Chicago 12:00
Kansas City at Green Bay 12:00
New England at Miami 8:00
New Orleans at Buffalo 1:00
New York Giants at Denver 2:00
Phoenix at Los Angeles Raiders 1:00
Pittsburgh at New York Jets 1:00
San Diego at Washington 1:00
Seattle at Cincinnati 1:00

Tampa Bay at Houston 12:00

Monday, December 11
San Francisco at Los Angeles Rams 6:00

FIFTEENTH WEEK
Saturday, December 16
Dallas at New York Giants 12:30
Denver at Phoenix 2:00

Sunday, December 17
Buffalo at San Francisco 1:00
Green Bay at Chicago 12:00
Houston at Cincinnati 1:00
Los Angeles Raiders at Seattle 5:00
Miami at Indianapolis 1:00
Minnesota at Cleveland 1:00
New England at Pittsburgh 1:00
New York Jets at Los Angeles Rams 1:00
San Diego at Kansas City 12:00
Tampa Bay at Detroit 1:00
Washington at Atlanta 4:00

Monday, December 18
Philadelphia at New Orleans 8:00

SIXTEENTH WEEK
Saturday, December 23
Buffalo at New York Jets 12:30
Cleveland at Houston 7:00
Washington at Seattle 1:00

Sunday, December 24
Chicago at San Francisco 1:00
Denver at San Diego 1:00
Detroit at Atlanta 1:00
Green Bay at Dallas 12:00
Indianapolis at New Orleans 12:00
Kansas City at Miami 1:00
Los Angeles Raiders at New York Giants 1:00
Los Angeles Rams at New England 1:00
Phoenix at Philadelphia 1:00
Pittsburgh at Tampa Bay 1:00

Monday, December 25
Cincinnati at Minnesota 8:00

Postseason

Sunday, Dec. 31   AFC and NFC First Round Playoffs
Saturday, Jan. 6   AFC and NFC Divisional Playoffs
Sunday, Jan. 7   AFC and NFC Divisional Playoffs
Sunday, Jan. 14   AFC and NFC Championship Games
Sunday, Jan. 28   Super Bowl XXIV at the Louisiana Superdome, New Orleans, Louisiana
Sunday, Feb. 4   AFC-NFC Pro Bowl at Honolulu, Hawaii

ALL-TIME HEAD-TO-HEAD RESULTS

	Buffalo	Indianapolis	Miami	New England	N.Y. Jets	Cincinnati	Cleveland	Houston	Pittsburgh	Denver	Kansas City	L.A. Raiders	San Diego	Seattle
Buffalo	—	18-18-1	11-34-1	25-32-1	29-28-0	5-11-0	2-7-0	11-18-0	5-6-0	14-9-1	15-12-1	12-13-0	9-17-2	1-2-0
Indianapolis	18-18-1	—	12-27-0	17-20-0	19-19-0	5-5-0	6-13-0	6-5-0	4-10-0	2-6-0	3-6-0	3-4-0	4-6-0	2-0-0
Miami	34-11-1	27-12-0	—	25-21-0	24-22-1	8-3-0	4-4-0	10-10-0	8-4-0	5-2-1	7-7-0	4-15-1	6-9-0	3-2-0
New England	32-25-1	20-17-0	21-25-0	—	26-31-1	7-4-0	2-7-0	15-14-1	3-5-0	12-15-0	7-11-3	13-12-1	13-12-2	6-2-0
N.Y. Jets	28-29-0	19-19-0	22-24-1	31-26-1	—	8-5-0	4-8-0	11-15-1	1-9-0	11-10-1	13-14-1	11-12-2	7-14-1	3-7-0
Cincinnati	11-5-0	5-5-0	3-8-0	4-7-0	5-8-0	—	18-19-0	22-17-1	17-20-0	6-9-0	8-10-0	5-12-0	8-11-0	6-2-0
Cleveland	7-2-0	13-6-0	4-4-0	7-2-0	8-4-0	19-18-0	—	24-14-0	47-31-0	3-11-0	6-5-1	2-10-0	5-6-1	2-8-0
Houston	18-11-0	5-6-0	10-10-0	14-15-1	15-11-1	17-22-1	14-24-0	—	12-27-0	19-11-1	13-21-0	11-22-0	13-17-1	4-3-0
Pittsburgh	6-5-0	10-4-0	4-8-0	5-3-0	9-1-0	20-17-0	31-47-0	27-12-0	—	6-8-1	11-5-0	6-9-0	9-5-0	4-3-0
Denver	9-14-1	6-2-0	2-5-1	15-12-0	10-11-1	9-6-0	11-3-0	11-19-1	8-6-1	—	22-35-0	18-38-2	29-28-1	13-11-0
Kansas City	12-15-1	6-3-0	7-7-0	11-7-3	14-13-1	10-8-0	5-6-1	21-13-0	5-11-0	35-22-0	—	23-34-2	27-29-1	11-10-0
L.A. Raiders	13-12-0	4-3-0	15-4-1	12-13-1	12-11-2	12-5-0	10-2-0	22-11-0	9-6-0	38-18-2	34-23-2	—	37-20-2	11-13-0
San Diego	17-9-2	6-4-0	9-6-0	12-13-2	14-7-1	11-8-0	6-5-1	17-13-1	5-9-0	28-29-1	29-27-1	20-37-2	—	10-10-0
Seattle	2-1-0	0-2-0	2-3-0	2-6-0	7-3-0	2-6-0	8-2-0	3-4-0	3-4-0	11-13-0	10-11-0	13-11-0	10-10-0	—
Dallas	3-1-0	6-3-0	2-4-0	6-0-0	4-0-0	2-2-0	9-16-0	4-2-0	11-13-0	3-2-0	2-1-0	1-3-0	3-1-0	3-1-0
N.Y. Giants	2-2-0	3-7-0	0-1-0	2-1-0	3-3-0	0-3-0	16-26-2	3-0-0	41-26-3	3-2-0	5-1-0	1-3-0	3-2-0	3-2-0
Philadelphia	4-1-0	5-5-0	2-4-0	4-2-0	4-0-0	0-5-0	11-30-1	4-0-0	43-25-3	3-2-0	1-0-0	2-3-0	2-2-0	2-1-0
Phoenix	3-2-0	5-4-0	0-5-0	4-1-0	2-1-0	1-3-0	10-31-3	3-2-0	21-29-3	0-1-1	1-3-1	1-1-0	1-3-0	2-0-0
Washington	3-2-0	6-15-0	2-5-0	3-1-0	4-0-0	3-2-0	8-32-1	2-3-0	41-27-3	3-2-0	1-2-0	2-4-0	4-0-0	3-1-0
Chicago	3-1-0	15-21-0	1-4-0	3-3-0	2-1-0	1-2-0	3-6-0	2-2-0	14-4-1	4-4-0	3-1-0	3-3-0	1-4-0	1-4-0
Detroit	1-1-1	16-17-2	1-2-0	2-2-0	2-3-0	2-2-0	12-4-0	2-2-0	13-9-1	2-4-0	3-3-0	2-4-0	3-2-0	1-3-0
Green Bay	1-3-0	18-18-1	0-5-0	2-2-0	1-4-0	2-4-0	8-5-0	2-3-0	16-11-0	1-3-1	2-1-1	1-5-0	3-1-0	3-2-0
Minnesota	4-2-0	6-12-1	1-5-0	2-2-0	1-3-0	2-3-0	7-2-0	2-2-0	6-4-0	3-2-0	2-2-0	2-5-0	3-3-0	1-3-0
Tampa Bay	4-1-0	1-4-0	1-3-0	0-3-0	1-3-0	1-2-0	0-3-0	1-2-0	0-3-0	0-2-0	2-4-0	0-2-0	0-3-0	0-2-0
Atlanta	2-2-0	0-9-0	1-4-0	2-3-0	2-2-0	1-5-0	1-7-0	4-2-0	1-7-0	3-4-0	0-2-0	2-4-0	2-1-0	0-4-0
L.A. Rams	3-1-0	15-20-2	1-4-0	1-3-0	3-2-0	2-3-0	7-9-0	3-2-0	13-4-2	3-3-0	3-0-0	2-4-0	2-2-0	4-0-0
New Orleans	1-2-0	1-3-0	1-4-0	0-5-0	1-4-0	3-3-0	2-8-0	3-2-1	5-4-0	1-4-0	2-2-0	1-3-1	1-3-0	2-2-0
San Francisco	1-2-0	15-21-0	2-4-0	4-1-0	4-1-0	6-1-0	5-8-0	4-2-0	6-7-0	2-4-0	3-1-0	2-4-0	2-3-0	3-1-0